Sport, Leisure and Social Just

Social inequalities are often reproduced in sport and leisure contexts. However, sport and leisure can be sites of resistance as well as oppression; they can be repressive or promote positive social change. This challenging and important book brings together contemporary cases examining different dimensions of inequality in sport and leisure, ranging from race and ethnicity to gender, sexual orientation, disability, religion and class.

Presenting research-based strategies in support of social justice, this book places the experiences of disadvantaged communities centre stage. It addresses issues affecting participation, inclusion and engagement in sport, while discussing the challenges faced by specific groups such as Muslim women and LGBT young people. Including original theoretical and methodological insights, it argues that the experiences of these marginalised groups can shed a light on the political struggles taking place over the significance of sport and leisure in society today.

Sport, Leisure and Social Justice is fascinating reading for students and academics with an interest in sport and politics, sport and social problems, gender studies, race and ethnicity studies, or the sociology of sport.

Jonathan Long is a Professor in the Institute for Sport, Physical Activity and Leisure at Leeds Beckett University, UK. His research on social change has a strong focus on 'race' and ethnicity.

Thomas Fletcher is a Senior Lecturer at Leeds Beckett University, UK. He specialises in the social and cultural aspects of sport, leisure and sports events.

Beccy Watson is a Reader at Leeds Beckett University, UK. She researches interrelationships between gender, race and class to inform understandings of identities, leisure, changing cities and intersectional approaches.

Routledge Critical Perspectives on Equality and Social Justice in Sport and Leisure

Series editors:

Kevin Hylton
Leeds Beckett University, UK
Jonathan Long
Leeds Beckett University, UK

This series presents important new critical studies that explore and explain issues relating to social justice and equality in sport and leisure. Addressing current debates and examining key concepts such as inclusion and exclusion, (anti)oppression, neo-liberalism, resistance, merit(ocracy), and sport for all, the series aims to be a key location for scholars, students and policy makers interested in these topics.

Innovative and interrogative, the series will explore central themes and issues in critical sport and leisure studies, including: theory development, methodologies and intersectionality; policy and politics; 'race', ethnicity, gender, class, sexuality, disability; communities and migration; ethics and morals; and media and new technologies. Inclusive and transdisciplinary, it aims to showcase high quality work from leading and emerging scholars working in sport and leisure studies, sport development, sport coaching and PE, policy, events and health studies, and areas of sport science that consider the same concerns.

Available in this series:

Sport, Leisure and Social Justice
Edited by Jonathan Long, Thomas Fletcher and Beccy Watson

Sport, Leisure and Social Justice

Edited by Jonathan Long,
Thomas Fletcher and
Beccy Watson

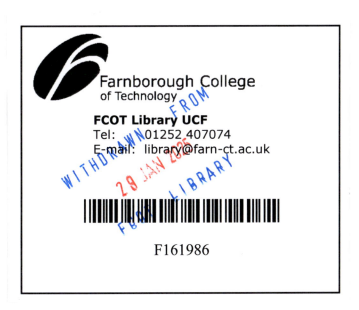

Routledge
Taylor & Francis Group

LONDON AND NEW YORK

First published 2017 by Routledge

2 Park Square, Milton Park, Abingdon, Oxfordshire OX14 4RN
52 Vanderbilt Avenue, New York, NY 10017

Routledge is an imprint of the Taylor & Francis Group, an informa business

First issued in paperback 2019

British Library Cataloguing in Publication Data
A catalogue record for this book is available from the British Library

Library of Congress Cataloging in Publication Data
A catalog record for this book has been requested

ISBN: 978-1-138-96045-9 (hbk)
ISBN: 978-0-367-23294-8 (pbk)

Typeset in Sabon
by Wearset Ltd, Boldon, Tyne and Wear

Contents

Notes on contributors   viii
Foreword   xi
Acknowledgements   xvii

1 Introducing sport, leisure and social justice   1
JONATHAN LONG, THOMAS FLETCHER AND
BECCY WATSON

2 Principles of social justice for sport and leisure   15
PAUL WETHERLY, BECCY WATSON AND
JONATHAN LONG

3 The British Labour Party, social justice and the politics of
leisure 1945–2015   28
PETER BRAMHAM AND STEPHEN WAGG

4 Gender justice and leisure and sport feminisms   43
BECCY WATSON AND SHEILA SCRATON

5 Feminist leisure research: shifts and developments   58
SAMANTHA HOLLAND

6 Gender justice? Muslim women's experiences of sport and
physical activity in the UK   70
ROZAITUL MATZANI, KATHERINE DASHPER AND
THOMAS FLETCHER

7 Lesbian, gay, bisexual and transgender young people's
experiences of PE and the implications for youth sport
participation and engagement   84
SCARLETT DRURY, ANNETTE STRIDE, ANNE FLINTOFF
AND SARAH WILLIAMS

8 Working towards social justice through participatory
research with young people in sport and leisure   98
ANNETTE STRIDE AND HAYLEY FITZGERALD

9 Cypher Wild: leisure, hip-hop and battles for social justice   111
BRETT D. LASHUA AND MATTHEW WOOD

10 Integration or special provision? Positioning disabled
people in sport and leisure   126
HAYLEY FITZGERALD AND JONATHAN LONG

11 'Knowing me, knowing you': biographies and subjectivities
in the study of 'race'   139
KEVIN HYLTON AND JONATHAN LONG

12 Black women, Black voices: The contribution of a
Spivakian and Black feminist analysis to studies of sport
and leisure   153
AARTI RATNA

13 Researching the wrong in sport and leisure: ethical
reflections on mapping whiteness, racism and the far-right   168
KARL SPRACKLEN

14 'Problems at the boundary'? South Asians, coaching and
cricket   180
THOMAS FLETCHER, DAVE PIGGOTT AND
JULIAN NORTH

15 The policy and provision landscape for racial and gender
equality in sport coaching   194
ALEXANDRA J. RANKIN-WRIGHT, KEVIN HYLTON AND
LEANNE NORMAN

16 Moving forward: critical reflections on doing social justice
    research   209
    GABBY RICHES, ALEXANDRA J. RANKIN-WRIGHT,
    SPENCER SWAIN AND VIJI KUPPAN

    Index   222

Contributors

All the contributors to this collection are involved with the Centre for Diversity, Equity and Inclusion at Leeds Beckett University. The Centre's web pages can be found here: www.leedsbeckett.ac.uk/research/research-areas/research-centres/centre-for-diversity-equity-and-inclusion.

Peter Bramham is now officially retired, but is still making contributions to the work of the Centre around policy and politics.

Katherine Dashper is a Senior Lecturer who specializes in the social and cultural aspects of sport, leisure and events.

Scarlett Drury is a Senior Lecturer in Physical Education and Sport Pedagogy.

Hayley Fitzgerald is a Reader who is internationally known for her work on disability sport, especially among young people.

Thomas Fletcher is a Senior Lecturer at Leeds Beckett University, UK. He specialises in the social and cultural aspects of sport, leisure and sports events.

Anne Flintoff is Professor of Physical Education and Sport whose teaching, research and consultancy centres on issues of equity and social inclusion, particularly around gender, in physical education and sport.

Samantha Holland is a Senior Research Fellow with an interest in gender, embodiment, ageing, subcultures, and leisure.

Kevin Hylton is Head of the Research Centre for Diversity, Equity and Inclusion and Professor of Equality and Diversity in Sport, Leisure and Education.

Viji Kuppan is currently doing his PhD research bringing together Critical Race Studies and Critical Disability Studies to examine the experience of football fans.

Brett D. Lashua is a member of the Centre for Diversity, Equity and Inclusion interested in socio-cultural dimensions of leisure, particularly popular music and urban change.

Jonathan Long is a Professor in the Institute for Sport, Physical Activity and Leisure at Leeds Beckett University, UK. His research on social change has a strong focus on 'race' and ethnicity.

Rozaitul Matzani conducted her Master's research at Leeds (Metropolitan) Beckett University and sis now at the University of Brunei Darussalam.

Leanne Norman is a Senior Research Fellow using a critical feminist sociological lens to examine the culture of coaching to address gender equality.

Julian North is a Senior Research Fellow undertaking commissioned research in participant and player development and coaching.

Dave Piggott is a Principal Lecturer in sports coaching.

Alexandra J. Rankin-Wright is a Research Officer in the School of Sport and recently completed her PhD on racial and gender equality and diversity in sport coaching in the UK context.

Aarti Ratna is a Senior Lecturer in the sociology of sport and leisure. Her research centres on the connections between sport, 'race' and gender, with particular focus upon the agencies of women of the South Asian diaspora.

Gabby Riches was recently awarded her PhD from Leeds Beckett University for her research on female metal fans in the moshpits.

Sheila Scraton is Professor Emerita having previously been Director of University Research and Professor of Leisure and Feminist Studies.

Karl Spracklen was until recently the Head of the Centre for Diversity, Equity and Inclusion and is now Professor of Music, Leisure and Culture at Leeds Beckett University.

Annette Stride is a Senior Lecturer in sport business management and physical education and has a particular research interest in the PE and physical activity experiences of Muslim girls.

Spencer Swain was recently awarded his PhD for an ethnography of the liminal spaces of khat chewing as a form of dark leisure.

Stephen Wagg is Professor of Sport and Society, currently researching the relationship between sport and protest, the history of cricket and the politics of amateurism in sport.

Beccy Watson is a Reader at Leeds Beckett University, UK. She researches interrelationships between gender, race and class to inform understandings of identities, leisure, changing cities and intersectional approaches.

Paul Wetherly is a Reader in Politics with research interests in multi-culturalism, theories of the state and political ideology.

Sarah Williams (MBE) has worked as the Equality and Diversity Manager at the Rugby Football League and Lawn Tennis Association and as an independent consultant.

Matthew Wood is an independent performer, working as a hip-hop scholar-activist in Edmonton (Canada).

Foreword

As CEO of Kick It Out and a magistrate I routinely encounter matters of social justice in sport and leisure and have to remind myself that they are part of wider social processes. This foreword is a reflection of personal perspectives and experiences.

It is often said that sport can be a source for good. The notion that anyone can participate in some sort of sport and receive recreational and personal benefits, is hard to argue against. But there are limitations to such participation: age, infirmity, disability, affordability, access to facilities or religious or cultural affiliations. Sport can also be divisive. Some educational experts regard competitive sport for younger children as harmful, creating attitudes of both arrogance and dominance among those regarded as 'winners' while creating labels of 'losers' and 'failures' among the rest.

When assessed, the divisiveness in sport runs deeper than it might at first appear, and is evident along the lines of race, sex and social class. Discrimination and bias affects not only sports participants but also the followers of amateur sports and the paying spectators or television viewers of professional and elite sports. It is quite evident that participants and dedicated supporters of sports such as skiing, golf, lawn tennis, rowing, sailing and equestrian events require a considerable amount of money merely to be in those arenas, and much more in any quest to achieve elite status. Others rely on charitable and family sacrifices to overcome their economic disadvantage if they are to hold on to aspirations of being competitively successful. It is one of the curiosities of everyday life that it is often the poorest people who do the most to subsidise elite sport through their disproportionate weekly cash splash on the National Lottery, which distributes sponsorship to elite sports people through its 'good causes' funds.

Without his parents' support and long-term dedication, it is unlikely Andy Murray would have become the World Number One tennis player and similarly his brother Jamie would not be the World Number One doubles player. This was often the story shared by athletes and their families throughout the Olympics and Paralympics. Although UK Sport and Sport England funding has undoubtedly made a difference to athletes' performances, without the practical day-to-day support from parents and family members many would not have made it to the top of their sport.

Inequalities abound. Consider the contrast between some of the highest paid women tennis players, not just in terms of rewards, but the way they are regarded. Maria Sharapova, for example, is white, blond and before her ban had significant sponsors and backers even though in terms of performance she had not been as successful as some others. The world's best and most successful tennis player is Serena Williams, a black woman whose demeanour, body size and attitudes are often the subject of critical media comment. Her father was the driving force behind her success. He began teaching her without any real experience and has been derided for not putting her through the white-run professional academies which he clearly could not afford.

Golf is another sport that necessitates money. My fellow countryman Rory McIlroy was able to afford to train from a very early age only because of the sacrifices of his parents. Despite the best efforts of some in the sport golf carries an association with exclusion on other grounds too. The fact that certain golf clubs continue to insist on membership rules which exclude on grounds of gender and class is unacceptable to someone working for an equality organisation.

Sport is often deemed to be about 'them and us'. The stereotypes are legendary. White men can't sprint; black people can't swim; women don't really understand football; disability means separation. Even if not publicly shared, scratch the surface or evoke a locker room mentality and it is not surprising how quickly 'banter' degenerates into abuse. The recent example of the Harvard Men's football team, who through a publication known as 'the scouting report' rated their equivalent female players on their attractiveness and discussed them in lewd terms, is sadly not exceptional. Harvard president Drew Faust said:

> I was deeply distressed to learn that the appalling actions of the 2012 men's soccer team were not isolated to one year or the actions of a few individuals, but appear to have been more widespread across the team and have continued beyond 2012, including in the current season.

Efforts to laugh off or dismiss such behaviour as 'banter' make an appeal to the belief that such views are the norm, ignoring their consequences. Six of the female players, through an article entitled *Stronger Together*,[1] stated they were 'beyond hurt to realise these individuals could encourage, silently observe, or participate in this kind of behaviour, and for more than four years have neglected to apologise until this week'.

The abuse extends to those who seek to educate and challenge such divisiveness. The phrase 'political correctness gone mad' is a common refrain levelled at organisations such as Kick It Out, as if we have become incapable of contextualisation, uncomprehending of ignorance and even defunct of humour.

Challenging social injustice

Tommie Smith, John Carlos and Peter Norman on the podium of the 1968 Olympics in Mexico represented a breakthrough for protest against injustice at the highest level of international sport. Smith and Carlos, both African Americans, stood atop the medals podium and gave a Black Power salute, protesting about their unequal treatment as US athletes and as citizens denied equal rights. Peter Norman was the third and less well known athlete on that podium. A white Australian, while he did not participate in the salute, he wore a badge expressing his support and was a known opponent of white Australian social policies. All three were ostracised from the Olympic movement and their national sporting authorities. Similarly, for his refusal to be drafted to fight in the Vietnam War, Muhammad Ali was branded a traitor and was vilified by the white establishment for using his Islamic religious beliefs to highlight the oppression and racism of the USA. Although Ali is accepted as a hero now, it would be interesting to see how his very strong public views would be seen by many Americans if reiterated by one of today's sport stars.

I say that in the context of the backlash against Barack Obama and his 'right' to be President, the vitriol of the recent presidential campaign and the controversy around Colin Kaepernick and the national anthem protests in the NBA. This last has been associated with the Black Lives Matter campaign against police killings of black males in the USA and has extended to other leading African American sporting icons also boycotting the national anthem when played at competitions. These protests too have drawn criticism and ostracism amidst accusations that they are disloyal and traitors. It shows that solidarity and nationalism are wrapped together (often literally in the flag) and flourish most when winning, but the moment that injustice and unequal treatment are challenged the approval and praise very quickly evaporate to be replaced by criticism and abuse. Former heroes become villains and often suffer detrimental consequences.

Sporting separation

Separation in sport through forms of nationalism and religion is still often seen most clearly in Northern Ireland where I come from. Although for many the 'Troubles' are in the past, sport remains a much segregated part of society there. Catholics play GAA (Gaelic Athletic Association) football, camogie and hurling. Middle-class Protestants play rugby and hockey. Football and boxing remain the two sports that are accepted in both communities but are also seen mainly as working-class sports. The boxer Barry McGuigan is still regarded as one of the few Northern Ireland sporting heroes who bridged both communities, even though he is originally from the South of Ireland. Certainly, if you were to ask the different sides of the community who they supported in the recent European Championships (football/soccer), you would find that the majority will have split along religious lines with many Catholics supporting the Republic's team (Ireland) and many Protestants supporting the Northern Ireland team. Although the IFA (Irish Football Association) has done much to address the sectarianism that existed within the National Football Stadium at Windsor Park in Belfast, the Catholic community remains uneasy about visiting the home of Northern Ireland football.

Power to change

What is clear, is that power rests with the same people who make the decisions, who can influence attitudes through media coverage, funding and access to sports resources. Even now many BAME people, women, LGBT and disabled participants in sports keep their heads down and do not criticise the injustices they see around them for fear of losing out on funding, sponsorship, support and selection.

The same can be seen when token appointments are made to the boards of governing bodies. There are constraints on speaking up publicly against inequalities and discriminatory processes for fear of losing coveted places on such boards. The recent publication of the Code of Sports Governance mandates UK Sport and Sport England to strip any governing bodies of public money unless they ensure that at least 30 per cent of their boards are female. However, this fails to address other diverse groups and seems to indicate a scale of diversity importance. Surely this was a great opportunity to make all those in receipt of public money actually consider all aspects of diversity in their boards and elsewhere in their organisations.

It seems ironic that the diversity of football teams with regard to their players is clear to see and yet the same can still not be said of either managers or coaches. The paucity of black managers is a much talked about point both within and outside football. However, even the most cursory look at other sports' governing bodies, sports directors and coaches, suggests that football is certainly not unique in this lack of diversity.

Of course sport can bring people together positively. For instance, football has brought together refugees who have previously been fighting each other in warring factions to play football with each other. This is not just about football, as evidenced by the Street Football Association which brings together homeless people for sporting tournaments but with the long-term aim of building confidence to support them into accommodation and long-term engagement with other support organisations. The opportunity to use sport for tackling prejudice, bigotry and hatred, enabling individuals from different backgrounds and circumstances to learn with each other about each other, is significant. Often sport brings together fans from disparate areas who may never engage with each other in any other way that has that level of parity. However even here, how safe does a young Muslim woman wearing a hijab feel going to watch her team play? Moreover, the chants at some clubs towards Leicester City fans of 'You are just a town full of bombers' suggests that racism is targeting not only the Muslim community but indeed any Asian communities. Kick It Out has also observed the rise of anti-Semitism around football, often reflected most clearly on social media with phrases such as 'Gas the Jews', underscoring the view that anti-Semitism is a 'lightly sleeping giant'.

Given the scale of the task involved in campaigning for all forms of equality, Kick It Out, with its limited resources, works with the football authorities, professional clubs, players, fans and communities helping them to take their equality responsibilities seriously and tackle discrimination at all levels of the game. Our goal is for football to be an environment in which people flourish in a supportive community, where fairness is practiced for the good of all participants. Apart from exposing and challenging discrimination we promote awareness of the benefits of equality, inclusion and diversity, run a mentoring and leadership programme with a view to diversifying the workforce, share information about good practice and support others in tackling discrimination: for example, we recently developed an app to make it easy for fans to report abuse. In line with one of the themes of this book, we like to think of ourselves as a voice for ethical football, but although our focus is very much on football we also work with those in other sports who share common cause.

For many, sport is a reflection of a power struggle; a competition against self and others, whoever you are, wherever you are. On the one hand it is about doing something for fun and enjoyment and also about keeping the body and mind healthy, but on the other hand it is also about proving yourself better than the next person or making a statement, pushing yourself, doing your personal best. At the same time sport reflects life chances; much depends on where you are born, your social and economic circumstances, access to facilities and equipment and your family's background and predilection for sport. If there is to be true social justice within sport these factors need to be considered and honestly addressed with some innovative solutions.

Roisin Wood
Kick It Out[2]

Notes

1 Published in *The Harvard Crimson*, 29 October 2016, www.thecrimson.com/article/2016/10/29/oped-soccer-report.
2 Kick It Out is football's equality and inclusion organisation in England and Wales.

Acknowledgements

As with all our research enterprises we wish to acknowledge the contribution of colleagues in the Centre for Diversity, Equity and Inclusion who are not listed as authors here. In particular we are grateful for the contribution, guidance, help and support of our former colleague, Professor Margaret Talbot, who died while we were writing our various inputs for the book. The research culture we work in shapes our own research endeavours and outputs.

Special thanks to M. Selim Yavuz for assistance in preparing the manuscript.

We would also like to extend our thanks to the editorial and production staff at Routledge.

We have decided to donate the royalties for this book to Kick It Out and local charities.

Chapter 1

Introducing sport, leisure and social justice

Jonathan Long, Thomas Fletcher and Beccy Watson

The concern for social justice

We write at a time when the Sutton Trust has just produced its most recent report on the ability of the British elite to reproduce itself (Kirby, 2016). The work that underpinned *The spirit level* (Wilkinson and Pickett, 2009) and Dorling's (2015) research on the 1 per cent emphasises the extent of inequality in our society. Although particularly marked in the United Kingdom (UK), the Organisation for Economic Co-operation and Development (OECD) report on *Trends in income inequality and its impact on economic growth* (Cingano, 2014) demonstrates its presence around the world. We do not take income/wealth inequality as the sole focus of social justice, but as a marker for other concerns to do with fairness, equality, exclusion, discrimination, power differentials and privilege. There may well be legislation in place (for example, the Equality Act in the UK) designed to redress certain 'imbalances', but there are persistent inequalities on the basis of sociocultural and economic difference. Faced with this panoply of injustice, the challenge for academic researchers, practitioners and policy makers is how best to reduce the oppression and marginalisation of some of society's most vulnerable people (Stewart, 2014). Research in pursuit of social justice reflects an ideological orientation about fairness and power differentials between groups of people.

Social justice research is more than simply assessing the existence of disadvantage, it is about embedding and assessing research influence and impact. There is a large body of sport and leisure research in the UK and elsewhere that claims a social justice lens. Our work is informed to varying degrees by much of this. We find useful Stewart's (2014) metaphor that research to enhance social justice is like a stick that pokes and nudges for social change. Stewart asserts that for a social justice agenda, the influence of research ranges from weak to strong depending on its ability to shift social relations in the direction of a more just world. As Parry *et al.* (2013) point out, the most useful research goes beyond describing the oppression of different groups to focusing on the advocacy necessary to address power differences in society. Raising awareness is a necessary first step, but it is not sufficient in itself. Stewart also notes how *explanations* of the reasons why a group is oppressed or marginalised not only describe the existence of injustice, but identify culpability and suggest solutions for working towards social change. Explanatory research acknowledges a need for researchers to gain a deeper understanding of the meanings of injustice applied to sport and leisure and to address what future research and actions are needed if social change is to be realised. Despite its potential Stewart warns that explanatory research has historically under-delivered because 'political action and academic theory, although compatible, are traditionally treated as two distinct end states' (2014: 331).

When dealing with a normative concept like social justice it is easy to presume that our own norms (and indeed, the contexts in which we live) prevail. Those who occupy a position of relative power and influence (e.g. white, middle-class, able-bodied, heterosexual men) need to be wary of blindness towards their privileges. It is vital that these privileges are subject to critique, especially when a strong thrust of critical research is to promote social change with the aim of improving lives and reducing barriers to opportunities (Fletcher and Hylton, 2016). As reflected by the contributions here, we do not want to argue that social justice is an area of study that demands a singular 'right' approach, but like other critical researchers, endeavour to conduct research that, through its transformative potential (Parry, 2014; Stewart, 2014; Watson *et al.*, 2013) will encourage social change.

Social justice, sport and leisure

An obvious aspect of social justice in the context of sport and leisure is access and participation: all people having the right to participate regardless of their 'race'/ethnicity, gender, sexuality, class, (dis)ability or other identity markers (Henderson, 2014). Yet the view is often advanced that inequality is inevitable in sport because people have different 'abilities' and, from a meritocratic viewpoint, 'get out what they put in'. The extension to the argument that the 'success' of some will help maximise the position of those who are worst off is reflected in assumptions that the trickle-down effects of consumption by the wealthy lead to benefits for others. This enables elite sports clubs/institutions, for example, to argue for the lion's share of resources on the basis that their excellence will promote wider participation (in the arts the parallel is that it will 'raise standards') and the laissez-faire idea of rewarding individual resourcefulness and 'the devil take the hindmost' is commonplace.

Data from the *Taking Part Survey* and the *Active People Survey* demonstrate how social inequalities are reproduced in different forms of leisure and sport. For example, the *Active People Survey 8* suggests that South

Asian participation in sport (particularly among Pakistani and Bangladeshi women) falls consistently below other social groups (Hylton *et al.*, 2015). A number of factors have been identified as contributing to this under-representation (Long *et al.*, 2009), including: low incomes; long working hours; religious observance; shortage of facilities in areas with large minority ethnic populations; language barriers; and racism(s) (Hylton *et al.*, 2015). It has also been suggested that there are barriers associated with cultural value systems (Fletcher *et al.*, 2014; Long *et al.*, 2015).

Despite the potential of sport and leisure practices to respond to a social justice agenda they may be overlooked as somehow apolitical. Carrington (2012: 4), for example, argues that it is sport's

> assumed innocence as a space ... and a place ... removed from everyday concerns of power, inequality, struggle and ideology, that has, paradoxically, allowed it to be filled with a range of contradictory assumptions that have inevitably spilled back over and into wider society.

He suggests that taking this contradiction seriously – that is the political nature of the apparently apolitical – helps us towards a deeper and richer understanding of politics. In various guises the theme of social justice has recurred through the forty years of the history of the Leisure Studies Association (Carnicelli *et al.*, 2016), partly as a result of the promptings of this group of contributors, and tends to have wider currency in policy debates at times when inequality and hardship are recognised. Of the eight criteria Harvey (2009: 100) identifies for determining social justice, at least four have been frequently addressed by leisure scholars: inherent equality whereby all have an equal claim in matters of distribution; need; merit; and contribution to the common good. Leisure and sport remain thus influential fields in our pursuit of social justice.

Rather than passive mechanisms that merely reflect inequality, sport and leisure are also sources of conflict and resistance, acting as sites for the negotiation of individual and collective power struggles. Indeed, they are actively involved in producing, reproducing, sustaining and sometimes resisting various manifestations of, and discourses around, oppression and inequality (Dashper and Fletcher, 2013). There is a dialogic in which sport and leisure practices are a product of the society in which we live and, at the same time, can both be repressive and effect positive social change. One of the challenges for critical social researchers, therefore, is to encourage sports organisations and government agencies to subject their claims of fairness, merit, entitlement and inclusion to scrutiny (Long and Spracklen, 2011). The onus on sport in particular, but also the arts and other dimensions of leisure, to contribute to health initiatives, crime reduction or community development, stems from presumed virtuous characteristics.

However, overlooking their less fortunate characteristics, for example elitism, corruption, partisanship and exclusion, may compromise the ability to deliver equality, inclusion and social justice. As claims appear about the contribution or challenge to personal wellbeing, social capital, community cohesion, integration or quality of life, we need to recognise the processes involved and arbitrate on them. As with any process of negotiation it is important to acknowledge the voices of multiple parties.

The Centre for Diversity, Equity and Inclusion developing research in sport and leisure

Whether examining sport, PE, recreation, leisure, culture, the arts or tourism we use 'social justice' as the motivation shaping much of the research at the Centre for Diversity, Equity and Inclusion through a desire for social change. Our concern is to use research to redress inequality within civic society and promote social justice, demonstrating that sport and leisure can make a real difference, and allowing people to be active citizens. It is founded on the proposition that a more equal society would mean individual and collective potential could be more easily realised. Since the 1980s there has been a succession of academics at Leeds Polytechnic/ Metropolitan University/Beckett University who have had a strong interest in the socio-political dimensions of sport and leisure. Our work, and the very name of the research centre, *Diversity, Equity and Inclusion* (DEI), stems from a sense of the importance of natural justice. The membership of the Centre is diverse: some are interested in sport, physical education, health and wellbeing, some in music, alcohol, events, tourism or the arts. It is not that we are uninterested in the development of elite sport or arts activity; rather, we acknowledge that oppression and inequality are most overtly experienced at the level of the everyday. 'Sport' is seen as a feature of wider social and cultural practices and processes associated with 'leisure' and we view leisure as a practice and context that is socially and culturally negotiated (not taken as given) within which sport is a matter of constrained choice or preference. Some researchers within the Centre focus on gender, some on 'race' and ethnicity, on disability, on sexual preference, and some assert the primacy of class. At no stage have we sought to impose a single paradigm, theoretical perspective or methodological framework and therefore there are a range of issues and questions in circulation. However, what binds us as researchers is a commitment to social justice, equality and fairness. There is a collective frustration regarding the unfulfilled potential of sport and leisure in tackling social injustices and some take the opportunity to project the significance of leisure and sport contexts onto social science analysis and debate more broadly.

The goal of the Centre is to produce research that will help to counter marginalisation and oppression and we argue that if sport and leisure institutions are to realise their potential for improving people's quality of life and promoting positive social change, they have to remain open to alternative voices and avoid the temptation to 'speak for' those who are 'othered'. The experiences of marginalised groups offer insights to explain contemporary political struggles over what sport and leisure mean, who has access to sport and leisure spaces, and their place within wider society. We benefit from the contributions of different disciplinary backgrounds and experiences of members as they help to ensure that our work is subjected to continual internal scrutiny, allowing nothing to be taken for granted. It requires a measure of reflexivity and an intersectional appreciation of the situatedness of what we study, adapting approaches from critical theory in problematising issues and concepts.

As several members of the Centre had been involved with the Leisure Studies Association since the mid-1970s it was perhaps not surprising that we took a lead from the critical theory (Marxism and feminism) that was conspicuous there in the 1980s. This was subsequently developed into a more general approach using critical thinking to dissect and analyse contemporary and emergent issues and concepts. In addition to the early focus on class and gender the Centre now boasts a critical mass of scholars interested in 'race'/ethnicity, dis(ability), sexuality and embodiment. Much of the work within the Centre examines the interrelationships between social identities and power. Ironically sport and leisure is an area that was all too easily overlooked by critical theorists in mainstream disciplines and came more into its own with the emergence of post-modernist theories which drew attention to cultural formulations, lifestyles and the construction of personal identities (Scraton and Watson, 2015).

Just as we have witnessed shifts in the academic environment so there have been shifts in the political environment and consequent policies for sport and leisure. Within such shifting contexts we identify some common features of the work of the Centre:

a   We share a common concern to make sure that the views and lives of those involved in our research are not trivialised. It is not unusual for policy research to cast disadvantaged groups as a problem, whether through their lack of resources or demand for services, as people who refuse to integrate or as a persecuted minority (Hylton and Long, 2015). There are undoubtedly issues that need to be addressed among those, but we also need more fundamental research that will introduce to the policy arena a nuanced understanding of the lives of disadvantaged people, problematising disadvantage without using a deficit model that makes them the problem.

b   We try to avoid the temptation to 'speak for' others. Spivak (1988) asked, 'Can the subaltern speak?', taking issue with Western researchers who purport to 'speak for' (or even who listen to) those who have been already constructed in discourse, but who have had limited opportunity to define their own identities. Spivak (1988: 295) advocates 'speaking to' those who have been marginalised or silenced in this way, arguing that, otherwise, we will merely reproduce the 'Other' as our own 'self's shadow' (ibid.: 280).

c   Just as the contribution of different disciplinary perspectives is appreciated, so too there is a growing appreciation of the intersectionality of different facets of people's lives/identities, and a willingness to critique the concept (Watson and Scraton, 2013).

d   We subscribe to the view that our interest in the lifeworlds of individuals and their embodied experiences should not be at the expense of ignoring the wider body politic.

e   Without prescribing particular methods and techniques we recognise that these are not neutral.

f   We link theory to practice with a strong interest in praxis, the complexity of the enactment of theory.

The goal of creating a socially inclusive world of sport and leisure cannot be simply a response to a particular problem at a particular time (Carrington *et al.*, 2016), yet sensitivity to context is crucial. Indeed, as Hylton and Long (2015: 2) argue in relation to ethnicity, 'In an equal society policies should be devised and administered without recourse to considerations of ethnicity, but that condition will not be achieved without corrective action to remedy the current disadvantage of certain segments of society'. If inequalities are to cease to be of significance, and if promises such as 'sport for all' are to be realised, then the analysis of policy needs to be related to broader relations of power in the culture of both sport and society. Equal opportunities will remain unobtainable if the central tenets of the reproduction of privilege are allowed to remain uncontested (Channon *et al.*, 2016).

This collection

Representing as it does the work of the Centre for Diversity, Equity and Inclusion (DEI), rather than being 'international' this collection addresses worldwide concerns. We see similar, though by no means as substantial, attempts elsewhere. For example, recent issues of the two leading North American leisure journals have addressed social justice: *Leisure Sciences* in 2014 (Volume 36, Issue 4) and *Journal of Leisure Research* in 2013 (Volume 46, Issue 1). We are guided by Cohen (1985: 15) who likened justice to other categories that are:

almost impossible to spell out with precision. The attempt to do so invariably generates argument, sometimes worse. But their range of meanings can be glossed over in a commonly accepted symbol – precisely because it allows its adherents to attach their own meanings to it. They share the symbol, but do not necessarily share its meanings.

Within a particular debate it is important to share both definitions and meanings, but in a collection like this we are content with having social justice as a shared symbol and do not seek to impose a singular definition, but rather allow contributors to explore social justice in their own terms. Over the years some commentators have implied that leisure and sport scholars have been rather loose in their theorisation and implementation of concepts like social justice and equality (e.g. Blackshaw, 2014; Coalter, 1997). Following this Introduction, therefore, the book continues with a chapter devoted to unpacking the concept of social justice, and then different authors articulate how social justice features in their own work. Generally, the book presents research-based strategies in support of social justice by placing disadvantaged segments of the population centre stage. The collection advocates the view that social justice is enhanced when the research process integrates a commitment to breaking down and challenging aspects of social structures. As Stewart (2014) argues, a significant appeal of social justice research is the possibility of an outcome-oriented emancipatory focus.

Contributions reflect a commitment to academic research that is purposeful in providing not only theoretical suppositions, but information and data to address the need to guide policy makers and social and political commentators towards evidence-based considerations. According to Ouseley (2016: 219):

> Research material must ... be easy to use by community and voluntary led organisations and activists so that they can challenge any collective failure of institutions and service providers in meeting their equality and fair-treatment responsibilities.

We look here to speak to others who are interested in examining the social role of processes that commonly go unnoticed/unremarked because they are taken for the everyday. These are subject areas to which everyone can lay a claim to some measure of expertise. Leisure, sport, the arts, cultural pastimes, physical activity are just what we do as human agents on an everyday basis, but as such, they are central to who we are.

We are certainly not the only ones to argue that social justice is a crucial concept if sport and leisure are to play a part in reducing marginalisation and promoting inclusion (see, for example, Allison, 2000; Parry et al., 2013), though there are few books in the field that speak to a similar range of characteristics of potential disadvantage. A major strength of this collection is its diversity of sport and leisure case studies examining different dimensions of inequality. In the past we have had a strong emphasis on class, but here most notably 'race' and ethnicity, gender, sexual orientation, disability and youth are more evident, and their juxtaposition facilitates considerations of intersectionality. It does this through a collection of theoretical, methodological and empirical chapters that address:

a   How different theoretical positions assist our understanding of social justice and what reformulations might be necessary in response to empirical evidence;
b   How different methods can better capture the nature of people's sport and leisure experiences as they seek recognition;
c   How sport and leisure lives can, in practice, contribute to the political change necessary to secure social justice.

The contributions do not separate these three dimensions; nor, indeed, do we separate contributions into individual 'protected characteristics'. Rather than imposing a monolithic theoretical or methodological approach we celebrate the different perspectives of the contributors in pursuing a social justice agenda across disciplinary boundaries and demonstrate how our research is located at these intersections. The values of the contributors clearly differ, but what they share is a recognition of inequality and a desire to promote social justice; they believe that inequality fundamentally does matter and is not commensurate with a socially just society. Part of our argument is that we may live in a post-modern, post-feminist, post-Marxist, post-colonial world, but there is no less need for radical critique to disrupt the status quo wherever social injustice is encountered. Arguments about whether complete equality is possible or desirable are arcane, so far are we from that state, either in society as a whole or in the dimensions written about here. We are content to try to move toward a more just society.

Just as social justice agendas cross disciplinary boundaries so we make no effort here to categorise contributions by discipline. At the same time we have avoided imposing a contrived distinction between theory, methods and empirical work in organising the contributions. Equally, given the nature of social justice and current debates about intersectionality, we did not want to promote artificial divisions between gender, 'race'/ethnicity, age, (dis)ability or any other social marker. The goal of our book is to: embrace a range of markers of disadvantage; combine theoretical, methodological and empirical contributions; draw on a diversity of approaches while being committed to the principle of social justice and devising research in support of change; and examine substantive ideas that speak to audiences beyond the UK.

Recurring themes of the book

In pursuit of social justice one of the main concerns of the Centre has been the persistence and reinforcement of *inequality* and inequity. This lies at the root of all of the contributions here, concerned as they are with disadvantaged elements of society (see Chapter 2 by Wetherly, Watson and Long). These are people who have fewer economic resources and social and cultural capital, so it is unsurprising that they are less likely to participate in the kinds of activity recorded in the *Active People* or *Taking Part* surveys or be represented at higher levels of sports organisations. Researchers from our Centre have joined many others in trying to persuade the world of sport and leisure that formal equal opportunity (it is here and you can have/buy some of it if you want to) is insufficient and that 'fair' equal opportunity requires changes to the surrounding context to ensure proper access.

For example, the analysis of attitudes to sport and physical activity among women who are Muslim conducted by Matzani, Dashper and Fletcher (Chapter 6) identifies a series of mechanisms (e.g. sex-segregated spaces) for making sport and physical activity more inclusive and welcoming. And as a result of their examination of LGBT young people Drury, Stride, Flintoff and Williams (Chapter 7) advocate the need for more critical questioning of the pervasiveness or normative discourses of gender and sexuality in formal PE settings and consider how such discourses can be challenged. Among other things, they cite the importance of teacher education and equipping teachers with suitable resources for tackling homophobic and transphobic bullying. To identify appropriate resources, Stride and Fitzgerald (Chapter 8) discuss the importance of devising inclusive methodologies for examining social injustice. In this case, they discuss the potential contribution of participatory approaches for working with young people and people with disabilities. In a similar vein, Fitzgerald and Long (Chapter 10) consider how responses to the challenge of providing equal opportunity might vary depending upon different conceptions of disability. It is our contention that as inequalities increase we have a growing responsibility to ensure an informed platform for debate in a climate in which, Bramham and Wagg (Chapter 3) argue, even the British Labour Party has followed the shift from social democratic welfarism to neo-liberalism. In the face of so much inequity it can be hard to make sure the spotlight plays on the potential for sport and leisure to redress the balance rather than re-emphasise it.

Sport and leisure are heavily implicated in the (re)production of inequalities, but as already identified they may also offer opportunities for challenge, and possibly transformation. To that end the roles of leisure and sport have to be considered in the context of wider social structures and discourses: they are representations of these social relations and thus are entangled in issues of *identity* and *difference*. For example, through a case study of one hip-hop social gathering (a 'cypher') in Edmonton, Canada, Lashua and Wood (Chapter 9) evaluate the potential of leisure as a site in broader conversations and struggles for identity and social justice. Drury, Stride, Flintoff and Williams (Chapter 7) demonstrate how identities may be performed differently in different spaces and may be severely constrained in the face of (in their case) heteronormative pedagogies and behaviours. Adopting an inter-generational perspective for examining leisure lives, Holland (Chapter 5) examines how women negotiate the multiple demands on their identities as mothers and workers. She identifies how, within the gendered context of the home, for these women at least, very little has changed between generations, and notes how efforts to find moments of time to themselves commonly require some measure of subterfuge to realise them.

We have deliberately avoided bracketing the contributions into sections on gender/ethnicity/class/sexual orientation/age or any of the other commonly researched dimensions of our selves. While some contributions might readily fit such categories, others explore their *intersections*. For example, Watson and Scraton (Chapter 4) advocate some of the potential of intersectionality for a feminist analysis of leisure and sport though they do not suggest that is the only means of addressing inequalities. While alert to the many exhortations to engage in intersectional research for its transformative potential, we are also mindful of Bilge's (2014) warning that it may become frustrated as a knowledge project oriented towards social justice by getting mired in the cultural politics of neoliberalism. Having emphasised the diversity to be found within any intersection, Matzani, Dashper and Fletcher (Chapter 6) demonstrate how women who are Muslim may find sports participation particularly problematic, as they face challenges to their involvement based on gender, religious, cultural and sometimes ethnic grounds. Consequently, they cannot be said to receive social justice because they have neither parity of provision nor cultural recognition.

The categorisation/classification of people by presumed significant characteristics is part of their *representation*: the way they are understood by others. For example, Ratna (Chapter 12) emphasises that the way the lives of Black women are represented through sporting debates and narratives matters fundamentally because they can either reproduce stereotypical assumptions or facilitate other ways of knowing their lived subjectivities. Meanwhile Hylton and Long (Chapter 11) argue that from the privileged position of the academic we should argue for the importance of including people from minoritised communities at decision-making tables rather than simply protesting that through our research we represent their views. This is all the more significant in light of the argument of Bramham and Wagg (Chapter 3) that UK political parties have turned their backs on a responsibility to represent the most disadvantaged in society. Ideally we look to a shift from people being represented by researchers, policy makers or politicians to people being instrumental in representing their (own) interests politically or re-presenting themselves through alternative imaginings. Lashua and Wood (Chapter 9) for example, tell of the liberating effect of young First Nation people re-presenting themselves through their musical expression.

Central to the challenge of securing social justice in sport and leisure are a range of *institutions*, sometimes serving to promote change, sometimes frustrating and depressing it. Even when participation by minoritised groups does increase, as with other forms of leisure, playing sport alone is not sufficient to demonstrate fully equal participation. Indeed, it is inappropriate to protest full equality if people are excluded from the roles that run sport (from coaching to committees to paid employment). For example, Fletcher, Piggott and North (Chapter 14) examine the efforts of South Asian males to be involved in cricket coaching. They outline some of the nuanced mechanisms and processes that contribute to the marginalisation of South Asian communities from cricket coaching (especially higher coaching) roles, including white privilege. They make the point that even if participation profiles match national demographics formal equality of opportunity will be inadequate and 'positive action' will be required if sports organisations are to recruit a workforce that reflects participation demographics. Similarly, Rankin-Wright, Hylton and Norman (Chapter 15) explore racial and gender equality and diversity in sport coaching, focusing specifically on organisational perspectives and bringing into question institutional accountability. They uncover a frequent and almost unquestioned prioritising of sporting excellence over inclusive working practices. Thus, while there is now greater recognition of the importance of equality within sports organisations, such policies are not given a high priority and are actively resisted by those reluctant to acknowledge the presence of inequality. As a consequence they often lose out when faced with competing demands from more 'important' projects.

It may be that we as researchers working towards social justice need not just to look to our conceptual tools, but to our *methodological approaches* too. As we move towards working with historically under-represented groups we recognise the need to adopt innovative research techniques that better capture the lived experiences of different groups and communities. Such methodological innovations are justified by emphasising the 'failures' of conventional methods such as interviews, though we sympathise with Merriman's (2014: 168) view that 'the push to promote innovative [methods] is in danger of encouraging researchers to abandon methods labelled 'conventional' … rather than rethinking and reworking these methods, or expanding and diversifying their repertoire of approaches'. Nonetheless, the epistemological challenges in knowing the world of the other may require novel research approaches that might make for more productive outcomes with a better chance of securing social change. For example Stride and Fitzgerald (Chapter 8) reflect on their experiences of using participatory approaches with young people and people with disabilities. Their contribution emerges from the premise that researchers working on social justice projects are not necessarily researching in socially just ways so they use participatory approaches to research more fairly and equitably.

In addressing this agenda for justice and change some contributors consider the *role of the researcher* trying to break through the binary of 'other'/'self'. Hylton and Long (Chapter 11) stress the importance of understanding our own narratives if we are to be effective interpreters/analysts of our research encounters with 'othered' segments of society. They also offer a cautionary reminder that to use biographies successfully to analyse (in their case) 'race' and ethnicity we need to move beyond purely individualised experiences and use critical theory to give due consideration to the contextual forces of power and ideology (see also Ratna (Chapter 12)).

However, Spracklen (Chapter 13) argues that in exploring the worlds of the marginalised and excluded we need to be wary of becoming apologists for positions that seek to deny social justice. Spracklen's contribution offers a reflection on his experiences of engaging with members of the Far Right. He cautions that our political commitment to social justice can take us to methodological spaces and ethical choices that focus on the politics of exclusion rather than the politics of resistance. He suggests that to understand the mechanics of exclusion and hegemony it is sometimes necessary to explore the voices and spaces of the hegemons in sport and leisure. For all its promises and pitfalls, for Spracklen, the social justice agenda must remain paramount even if that compromises future access to the field.

Keen as we are to promote social *change*, it behoves us not to make exaggerated claims on the basis of our research. Academic research is a contributory step, but change will only occur if this research is translated into practice. The very nature of our work on the leisure lives and leisure spaces of those marginalised by intersectional inequalities, those whose choices remain constrained, means that we are embroiled in a kaleidoscope of competing policy agendas where the speed of change is often painfully slow. We have to be realistic about what our research can achieve. For example, despite more than thirty years of feminist leisure research Holland's contribution (Chapter 5) still portrays women as having to 'snatch' leisure time amidst their family and work responsibilities. Social institutions like patriarchy are very resilient and behavioural patterns ingrained. Nonetheless we can play a part in changing not just academic discourses but also the language and agendas of policy makers and practitioners. We can of course also do our best to live the change ourselves in our dealings with others. This approach resonates with David Gillborn's response to questions when he delivered the 2016 annual race lecture at Leeds Beckett University.[1] He invoked the words of the late cultural theorist, Stuart Hall, who advised that 'you struggle where you are'. What he meant by this is that there is no silver bullet that will tackle social injustice. Change is gradual; we fight the battles that we can fight.

The final Chapter 16 in this collection is left to the community of postgraduate researchers in DEI to identify the significance of the Centre's research for their own innovative research and for future studies of sport and leisure.

Note

1 David Gillborn's lecture can be found at: www.youtube.com/watch?v=6ipIli C0QHM; and the ensuing question and answer session at: www.youtube.com/watch?v=4Ma7oM46b2g.

References

Allison, M. (2000) 'Leisure, diversity, and social justice', *Journal of Leisure Research* 32(2): 2–6.

Bilge, S. (2014) 'Whitening intersectionality: evanescence of race in intersectionality scholarship', in: Hund, W. and Lentin, A. (eds) *Racism and sociology*. Berlin: Lit Verlag, 175–205.

Blackshaw, T. (2014) 'The crisis in sociological leisure studies and what to do about it', *Annals of Leisure Research* 17(2): 127–144.

Carnicelli, S., Fletcher, T. and Snape, R. (2016) 'Leisure Studies Association: past, present and future', *Brazilian Journal of Leisure Studies* 2(2): 34–45.

Carrington, B. (2012) *Race, sport and politics: the sporting black diaspora*. London: Sage.

Carrington, B., Fletcher, T. and McDonald, I. (2016) 'The politics of "race" and sports policy in the United Kingdom', in: Houlihan, B. (ed.) *Sport in society*, 3rd edn. London: Sage, 222–249.

Channon, A., Dashper, K., Fletcher, T. and Lake, R. (2016) 'The promises and pitfalls of sex integration in sport and physical culture', *Sport in Society* 19 (8–9): 1111–1124.

Cingano, F. (2014) *Trends in Income Inequality and its Impact on Economic Growth*, OECD Social, Employment and Migration Working Papers, No. 163. Paris: OECD Publishing.

Coalter, F. (1997) 'Leisure sciences and leisure studies: different concept, same crisis?', *Leisure Sciences* 19(4): 255–268.

Cohen, A. (1985) *The symbolic construction of community*. London: Tavistock.

Dashper, K. and Fletcher, T. (2013) 'Introduction: diversity, equity and inclusion in sport and leisure', *Sport in Society* 16(10): 1227–1233.

Dorling, D. (2015) *Inequality and the 1%*. 2nd edn. London: Verso.

Fletcher, T. and Hylton, K. (2016) 'Whiteness and race in sport', in: Nauright, J. and Wiggins, D. (eds) *Routledge handbook of sport, race and ethnicity*. Abingdon: Routledge, 87–106.

Fletcher, T., Piggott, D., North, J., Hylton, K., Gilbert, S. and Norman, L. (2014) *Exploring the barriers to South Asian cricket players' entry and progression in coaching*. London: England and Wales Cricket Board.

Harvey, D. (2009) *Social justice and the city*. 2nd edn. Athens: University of Georgia.

Henderson, K. (2014) 'The imperative of leisure justice research', *Leisure Sciences* 36(4): 340–348.

Hylton, K. and Long, J. (2015) 'Confronting "race" and policy: "How can you research something you say does not exist?"', *Journal of Policy Research in Tourism, Leisure and Events* 8(2): 202–208.

Hylton, K., Long, J., Fletcher, T. and Ormerod, N. (2015) *Cricket and South Asian communities*. Leeds: Yorkshire Cricket Board.

Kirby, P. (2016) *Leading People 2016: the educational backgrounds of the UK professional elite*. London: Sutton Trust.

Long, J. and Spracklen, K. (2011) 'Positioning anti-racism in sport and sport in anti-racism', in: Long, J. and Spracklen, K. (eds) *Sport and challenges to racism*. Basingstoke: Palgrave Macmillan, 3–19.

Long, J., Dashper, K., Fletcher, T. and Ormerod, N. (2015) *Understanding participation and non-participation among BME communities in Wales*. Leeds: Institute for Sport, Physical Activity and Leisure. Available from: http://sport.wales/media/1647168/bme_sport_in_wales_-_final.pdf (accessed 8 September 2016).

Long, J., Hylton, K., Spracklen, K., Ratna, A. and Bailey, S. (2009) *Systematic review of the literature on black and minority ethnic communities in sport and physical recreation*. Available from: http://eprints.leedsbeckett.ac.uk/596/1/BME%20Final%20Full%20%20Report.pdf (accessed 11 March 2016).

Merriman, P. (2014) 'Rethinking mobile methods', *Mobilities* 9(2): 167–187.

Ouseley, H. (2016) 'Confronting "race" and policy: identities, rights and responsibilities', *Journal of Policy Research in Tourism, Leisure and Events* 8(2): 218–220.

Parry, D. (2014) 'My transformative desires: enacting feminist social justice leisure research', *Leisure Sciences* 36(4): 349–364.

Parry, D., Johnson, C. and Stewart, W. (2013) 'Leisure research for social justice: a response to Henderson', *Leisure Sciences* 35(1): 81–87.

Scraton, S. and Watson, B. (2015) 'Leisure and consumption: a critical analysis of free time', in: Holborn, M. (ed.) *Contemporary Sociology*. London, Polity Press, 388–414.

Spivak, G. C. (1988) 'Can the subaltern speak?', in: Nelson, C. and Grossberg, L. (eds) *Marxism and the interpretation of culture*. Basingstoke: Macmillan, 271–313.

Stewart, W. (2014) 'Leisure research to enhance social justice', *Leisure Sciences* 36(4): 325–339.

Watson, B. and Scraton, S. (2013) 'Leisure studies and intersectionality', *Leisure Studies* 32(1): 35–47.

Watson, B., Tucker, L. and Drury, S. (2013) 'Can we make a difference? Examining the transformative potential of sport and active recreation', *Sport in Society* 16(10): 1233–1247.

Wilkinson, R. and Pickett, K. (2009) *The spirit level: why more equal societies almost always do better*. London: Allen Lane.

Chapter 2

Principles of social justice for sport and leisure

Paul Wetherly, Beccy Watson and Jonathan Long

Introduction

As identified in the opening chapter, leisure and sport scholars have sometimes played fast and loose with notions of social justice, using it, and
similar terms, to justify positions without proper consideration of what is
entailed. The purposes of this chapter are therefore, first, to set out some
of the key currents in political thought on social justice as a contested
concept and, second, to relate those to sport and leisure contexts. Having
established some of the basic principles we shall consider issues that
require choices like those arising from alternative conceptions of fairness.
We make no claims for an exhaustive consideration, but one shaped by the
interests of the authors: a political theorist collaborating with critical social
science researchers working in the field.

What is social justice?

According to Swift (2014: 13), 'The basic concept of justice is that it is
about giving people what is due to them, and not giving them what is not
due to them'. More specifically, social justice is about ensuring that:

> each person gets a fair share of the benefits, and carries a fair share of
> the responsibilities, of living together in a community.... Social justice
> tells us how different types of goods and bads should be distributed
> across a society.
>
> (Miller, 2005: 3&5)

Hence social justice may also be referred to as distributive justice.

From this position, giving people *what is due* to them involves giving
them a *fair share*, and what they are due a fair share of is not just the benefits (or 'goods') of living together in society such as income or material
resources, but also the burdens (or 'bads') of responsibilities such as work
and taxation. Clearly, an individual's wellbeing or enjoyment of life is the

result of both the benefits s/he enjoys and the burdens s/he has to carry. For example, we might think of goods and bads partly in terms of the nexus of work, income and leisure. The amount of time people have for leisure and the leisure activities they can engage in, such as sport, are conditioned by the number of hours worked and the income earned. Social justice also has to do with the security of work, working conditions and the intrinsic rewards of work, including job satisfaction and opportunities for in-work leisure. Giving people what is due to them is a matter of giving them what they are entitled to; in the round, social justice concerns the duties that the members of society owe to each other. The mechanism for securing the rights entailed by social justice is the state, which 'is justified in making sure that people carry out their duties to one another' (Swift, 2014: 15).

However, this abstract concept of social justice raises two hard questions, the answers to which differentiate available theories. First, the reference to benefits and burdens makes the scope of social justice potentially very wide since benefits and burdens can be defined very broadly. Thus the question concerns what kinds of things matter in terms of their distribution from the point of view of social justice. Clearly, people have different preferences, ideas of 'goods' and 'bads', and conceptions of the kinds of lives they want to lead. For example, it is obvious that people have different preferences regarding leisure, both in terms of time and how they use it; participation in sport does not loom large in everyone's idea of a 'good life'. However, social justice is not confounded by subjective preferences since 'goods' and 'bads' are conceptualised in universalist terms; that is, things that are benefits or burdens for people everywhere. For the same reason social justice is not confounded by cultural norms. What matters for social justice is the distribution of 'general purpose' resources that enable people to have a good life *as they see it*.

In practice a main focus in debates about social justice is how well-off people are in terms of the distribution of income and wealth. This emphasis may be justified on the assumption that how much income people have conditions their level of wellbeing or happiness because money is a 'general purpose' resource. Money expands the range of options open to people in deciding the kind of life they want to lead whereas, conversely, poverty entails lack of freedom (Cohen, 1994). More expansively, Barry (2005: 17) defines social justice in terms of 'life chances' as a question of 'the distribution of rights, opportunities and resources'. For Sandel (2009: 19), 'to ask whether a society is just is to ask how it distributes the things we prize – income and wealth, duties and rights, powers and opportunities, offices and honours'. Rawls (2009) claims we all have a rational interest in 'primary goods' (liberties, opportunities, wealth, income, self-respect) since these are the basis for individuals to participate in society and pursue any conception of the good life.

The second question, therefore, whatever the currency of social justice, is what does giving each person his or her due require? What constitutes a fair share? More specifically, does social justice require equality where 'the principle of equality says that the amount of amenity and burden in one person's life should be roughly comparable to that in any other's' (Cohen, 1994: 11)? Or is inequality compatible with social justice? Answering this type of question requires the elucidation of reasons or principles that either mandate equality or, alternatively, permit inequality. For example, one such reason that has loomed large in debates on social justice is the extent to which inequalities can be attributed to choices and actions for which individuals are responsible. Thus the first question boils down to 'distribution of what?', and the second question is 'how much inequality?'.

Conceptions of social justice

Different conceptions of social justice are sustained by competing principles such that it is difficult, and might not be possible, to resolve the debates 'once and for all' (Sandel, 2009: 19). Sen (2010: 13) illustrates 'the possible sustainability of plural and competing reasons for justice' with the example of deciding which of three people should be given a flute. The three competing reasons are: the distribution that would lead to the greatest overall welfare (utility); the distribution that would prioritise the interests of the poorest (equality); and the distribution that would respect people's choices and efforts (merit) (Sen, 2010: 12–15).

Sandel (2009) also offers three approaches to justice: welfare (utility), freedom and virtue. Within the approach based on freedom, he identifies two rival camps, laissez-faire and fairness. In the former 'justice consists in respecting and upholding the voluntary choices made by consenting adults' (his version of Sen's 'merit'), while for the latter 'justice requires policies that remedy social and economic disadvantages and give everyone a fair chance at success' ('equality' for Sen) (Sandel, 2009: 20). The discussion that follows will concentrate on the 'fairness camp' and thus conceive social justice in terms of remedying social and economic disadvantages, at the expense of the 'laissez-faire' camp or neoliberalism. This selectivity is justified by the constraints of space and because it is debateable whether neoliberalism should be considered as an approach to social justice; indeed, the concept of social justice is rejected by Hayek (Plant, 2004). We will see that the egalitarian thrust is combined with other principles, notably merit and need.

Rawls (1971, cited in Wolff, 2006: 157–158) identified two propositions that incorporate three principles of justice:

1   Each person is to have an equal right to the most extensive total system of equal basic liberties compatible with a similar system of liberty for all.

2   Social and economic inequalities are to be arranged so that they are both: (a) to the greatest benefit of the least advantaged ... and (b) attached to offices and positions open to all under conditions of fair equality of opportunity.

(See also Rawls, 1993. For discussion, see Arneson, 2006; Sen, 2010.) In short, the three principles are the liberty principle (1), the equal opportunity principle (2b) and the 'difference' principle (2a) which mandates that the worst-off in society (the least advantaged) should be as well-off as possible. The difference principle balances equity and efficiency insofar as inequality is justified only to the extent that higher rewards for those at the top provide incentives for greater efficiency that makes the poorest better off. We can see that the three principles encompass Rawls' conception of primary goods which everyone has a rational interest in having more of – liberties, opportunities, wealth and income – such that the difference principle is essentially concerned with wealth and income. According to Rawls the three principles are to be conceived hierarchically such that liberty has priority over fair equal opportunity, and equal opportunity has priority over improving the condition of the poorest.

Rawls' approach has dominated subsequent discussion of social justice. For example, Miller (2005: 5) proposes four principles of social justice that partly echo Rawls:

i   Equal citizenship: every citizen is entitled to an equal set of civil, political and social rights, including the means to exercise these rights effectively.
ii   The social minimum: all citizens must have access to resources that adequately meet their essential needs, and allow them to live a secure and dignified life.
iii   Equality of opportunity: a person's life chances, and especially their access to jobs and educational opportunities, should depend only on their own motivation and aptitudes, and not on irrelevant features such as gender, class or ethnicity.
iv   Fair distribution: resources that do not form part of equal citizenship or the social minimum may be distributed unequally, but the distribution must reflect relevant factors such as personal desert and personal choice.

Miller combines a floor (ii) defined in terms of meeting 'essential' or 'basic' needs with the idea that above this floor some inequalities are just (iv), on the assumption of equal opportunities so that differences in life-chances result from differences in 'motivation and aptitudes' (iii). Above the minimum inequalities are just to the extent that they are attributable to 'personal desert and personal choice' (iv). Principles (iii) and (iv) are closely related – together they say that differences in individuals' life-chances are just when they reflect differences in 'personal desert' based on their choices in regard to effort (motivation) and the use of their talents or skills (aptitudes) in a context of equal opportunity. Equal opportunity is understood as the removal of discrimination on grounds 'such as gender, class or ethnicity'.

The similarities between Rawls and Miller are apparent in the principles of liberty (i and 1), equal opportunity or procedural justice (iii and 2b) and fair distribution (iv and 2a). In both of these conceptions a just society is one in which: people are free to live as they choose; people have equal opportunities to compete for advantage, through attaining positions that confer unequal rewards; and unequal rewards are permitted only to the extent that they comply with a principle of fair distribution.

Liberty and equal citizenship

The priority accorded by Rawls to 'equal basic liberties' (i.e. civil rights) exemplifies the liberal character of his conception of justice. Civil rights are sometimes characterised in terms of 'negative' rights or 'negative freedom' because they require the removal of (and 'freedom from') interferences or hindrances that might come from other individuals or the law. Miller's characterisation of 'equal citizenship' is on the same lines as Rawls' liberty principle, though Miller also includes 'social rights'. Such rights are often characterised in terms of 'positive freedom' as they involve claims on resources in the form of state welfare. Understood as 'freedom to' make meaningful choices and participate in society, social rights are better conceived as ingredients of the 'social minimum' which stipulates the resources that all citizens require to 'allow them to live a secure and dignified life' (ii). It is through this ability to participate in society that the policy link to social inclusion is established.

Equality of opportunity

The principle of equality of opportunity, particularly in its formal sense, prohibits discrimination on the basis of 'irrelevant' features such as gender, class or ethnicity so that selection is based only on 'merit', meaning the relevant criteria of candidates' motivation and aptitudes (or talents). However, formal equal opportunity can be criticised as insufficient in contrast with conceptions of 'substantive' and 'fair' equal opportunity. Substantive equal opportunity is concerned with the actual representation of 'major social groups' (e.g. defined by gender or ethnicity) in valued roles and positions. According to O'Neill (1977), substantive equal opportunity requires that the success rates of major social groups are the same, an outcome that may also be termed 'proportional equal opportunity' (Baker,

1987). The crucial assumption is that the major social groups do not differ, on average, in terms of their motivations and aptitudes, or would not differ in the absence of the effects of forms of constraint or manipulation. Thus the substantive conception of equal opportunity motivates efforts to identify and remove these constraints and manipulations, such as gender or racial stereotypes, norms and differences in socialisation or upbringing.

'Fair' (or what Cohen (2009) has termed 'left-liberal') equal opportunity is also concerned with social and family background. In this view formal equal opportunity is insufficient because it neglects the crucial influence of differences in social background on the development of motivation and talents. Thus,

> Left-liberal equality of opportunity ... sets itself against the constraining effect ... of those circumstances of birth and upbringing that constrain ... their victims ... by ... causing them to labour and live under substantial disadvantages (Cohen, 2009: 16). Policies attempting to rectify these disadvantages 'include head-start education for children from deprived backgrounds.
>
> (Cohen, 2009: 16–17)

Miller also endorses a left-liberal approach:

> To ensure equality of opportunity it is not enough that fair procedures are used at the point at which people are applying for jobs or educational places. It is also necessary that they should have had the same chance to acquire the relevant skills and abilities despite differences in family background and so forth.
>
> (Miller, 2005: 11)

If it were possible for left-liberal equality of opportunity to be fully realised, people's fates would be determined 'not at all by their social backgrounds' but only by 'their native [i.e. natural] talent and their choices' (Cohen, 2009: 17). Miller (2005: 15) similarly states that fair 'equality of opportunity does not aim to defeat biology'. These statements beg the question of whether there are natural differences in talents and, if there are, how significant they are compared to the effects of social background on the chances to acquire talents. According to Miller, such natural differences within the population are real and significant and there is correlation both between the natural talents (i.e. measured intelligence) of parents and their offspring, and between people's natural talents and their occupational status and income. This means that, even if fair equal opportunity is fully realised there will 'still [be] some overall correlation in occupational status and income across the generations' and this is, for Miller, justified (2005: 14–15). If, on the other hand, there are no natural differences, or they are small, left-liberal equality of opportunity can in principle go a long way to equalise chances to acquire skills, perhaps so far that 'we should regard the demands of social justice as being met to the extent that there are equal educational attainments at the age of 18' (Barry, 2005: 47).

However, the aim of evening up the chances to acquire skills 'despite' differences in family background is clearly very challenging. Miller's (2005: 11) view of what is possible is much less optimistic than Barry's as 'differences in family background will always matter'. For example, pre-school programmes cannot, to use Miller's example, enable children raised in families on welfare to catch up with those raised in professional families. This seems to be a somewhat defeatist acceptance that differences in public resources can never be sufficient to offset differences in private resources. But there is a broader point here, that differences in 'social background', which left-liberal equality of opportunity is intended to redress, refers to more than the single dimension of differences in the socio-economic status and resources of families, but to a range of deep social problems affecting people's fates in highly unequal societies and requiring a range of policy interventions.

Both Rawls and Miller conceive equality of opportunity in terms of competition for advantage in terms of income and wealth, and this gives it a narrow focus, concerned particularly with education and employment opportunities. However, as Wolff (2011: 156) notes, 'Opportunity need not ... be understood in competitive terms. Access to opportunity might be considered to be part of a flourishing life, rather than a mere means to another good'. Wolff refers specifically to 'a variety of cultural and social goods [such as] art, music, sport [and] outdoor pursuits'. This raises the question of how the provision of these goods should be organised, the role of markets and public provision, and whether they should be included in the social minimum.

Fair distribution

What is the relationship between equality of opportunity and 'fair distribution'? Equality of opportunity can be characterised in terms of a fair procedure for selecting between candidates for various social roles and positions (or procedural justice). However, equality of opportunity in this sense does not address fair distribution in terms of the rewards attached to these positions. Differentials in the labour market result from a number of factors for which individuals who hold different jobs cannot claim responsibility. Even if left-liberal equality of opportunity were fully achieved the question of fair distribution would still be open.

Determining a fair distribution involves choosing between rival principles: 'sufficiency', 'priority to the worst-off' and 'equality'. Miller's 'social minimum' exemplifies the principle of sufficiency and therefore can be seen as an aspect of fair distribution. The social minimum 'tells us what the minimum share of resources is that everyone must have ... given our circumstances, in order to be able to live a decent life' (Miller, 2005: 8). In Miller's view, the minimum goes beyond income to include welfare services such as healthcare and education (social rights), and other dimensions including the quality of the physical environment and access to leisure facilities. Securing the social minimum requires a correction of market outcomes through redistribution to improve the position of the least advantaged up to the minimum standard.

Rawls' 'difference principle' accords priority to the worst-off. In this view social justice requires going beyond a minimally decent life to ensuring that the worst-off are as well-off as possible. In the Rawlsian scheme, how well-off the poorest members of society are, and the gap between them and the well-off is an empirical question, and will depend on behavioural norms bearing on the operation of incentives. The social minimum and difference principle both focus on improving the position of the least well-off but neglect their relative position and the wider pattern of inequality. The redistributive requirements of the social minimum might not be very great, and so long as the minimum is secured there is nothing wrong with how resources above the minimum are distributed, however unequally. For the difference principle the 'right amount' of inequality is whatever makes the least advantaged as well-off as possible. In contrast the principle of equality states that inequality per se also matters and requires a narrowing of the gap between rich and poor.

Reducing inequality is justified in two ways. First, large inequalities have harmful consequences, including a range of social problems (Wilkinson and Pickett, 2009), in the shape of economic instability, corrosion of community and corrosion of equal citizenship. In addition, the greater the inequality in society the harder it is to achieve fair equality of opportunity. Second, even if left-liberal equality of opportunity were fully achieved, removing the effects of differences in social background, the remaining factors that explain why some end up better-off than others (differences in natural talents and the vagaries of the market) are essentially matters of luck for which individuals cannot claim responsibility.

This also invites the question about how far inequality can be reduced. Cohen advocates 'socialist equality of opportunity' which seeks to correct for inborn disadvantage (i.e. differences in natural talents) as well as social disadvantage. In other words socialist equality of opportunity does not permit inequalities stemming from differences in natural talents that left-liberal equality of opportunity allows (Cohen, 2009). In socialist equality of opportunity, in contrast to the Rawlsian scheme, differences in rewards are not necessary to motivate economic performance. Thus Cohen envisages 'a system where each gets the same income per hour, but can choose how many hours she works' (Cohen, 2009: 20) such that differences in income reflect only different choices that people make about the work/ income–leisure trade-off (i.e. she might have more income by virtue of making the choice to spend more time at work rather than leisure).

Why does it matter to leisure and sport?

It is our contention that social justice matters fundamentally to leisure and sport and, further, that sport and leisure can contribute to achieving greater social justice. At the same time they are the settings for difficult debates within these principles of social justice. As forms of leisure, sport and the arts are fields supposedly characterised by autonomy and choice; they are presumed to be exemplars of the primacy of talent, yet choice is constrained and talent is questioned and compromised. The rhetoric of 'fair play', 'level playing fields' and rewarding merit and dedication echoes around sport, yet stands against evidence of discrimination, cheating and corruption. Hence, Lumpkin *et al.* (1994) argue that this 'fair play' is dependent on justice, honesty, responsibility and beneficence. Consequently, whether in turn sport can engender concepts of fair play in society (even if they do exist in sport) remains unclear and poses challenges conceptually and in practice.

The concept of social justice informs questions about why certain inequalities persist and what impact these inequalities have on access and participation. The principle of 'liberty and equal citizenship' might require a social minimum in the form of a right to leisure and the 'freedom to', and establishing what is 'due' to people. However, these are not only historically (Sheridan, 2003) but also culturally relative; for example, the part of the earlier social contract that included the provision of parks, libraries, swimming pools and later 'leisure centres' is now being questioned as conceptions of 'equality of opportunity' and 'fair distribution' shift. It is easier to accept people's right to leisure as a primary good (Rawls, 2009) than to assess whether people's leisure is adequate, especially in the context of a scarcity of resources and the continuing rise of consumption driven societies (Rojek, 2010).

There is a long history of initiatives designed in the interest of social justice to demonstrate that leisure can help to redress social ills: for example, the Peckham Experiment (Pearse and Crocker, 1943) and the Quality of Life experiments (DoE, 1977).[1] Ideas of equal citizenship and a right to a minimum have underpinned government initiatives like the focus on social inclusion (DCMS, 1999), which both asserted citizens' right to enjoy sport and the arts, but also argued their contribution to social justice through promoting health, education, employment and the reduction of criminal/deviant behaviour. This positioning re-emerges in *Sporting Future: A New Strategy for an Active Nation* (HM Government, 2015) which positions sport ideologically as a social 'good', central to 'our' national identity and sport's functional contribution to commitment, discipline and healthy lifestyles.

The least active are exhorted to take part in sport to improve wellbeing, yet while provision is expected to be demand-led and cost-effective, inequalities are unlikely to be tackled effectively. And in relation to health and wellbeing in particular, there is an unwillingness to undermine the tenet of personal responsibility. Nonetheless, the various policy drives for participation by all reflect invocations of equal opportunities and some formal barriers to participation have been removed. Despite that, in sport in particular, organisations have felt impelled to campaign for equal opportunities. The highest profile campaigns have been against racism in sport, though *Kick It Out* now addresses a generic equalities agenda (www.kickitout.org) reflecting the state's intervention through national legislation that makes it illegal under the Equality Act (2010) to discriminate purely on the basis of a set of 'protected characteristics' to limit employment or consumption.

In working towards gender justice, sex equality legislation has arguably allowed greater opportunities for women to gain access and achieve success in sport, the arts and other leisure environments, yet nationally as well as globally women still have not achieved equality with men (Watson and Scraton, Chapter 4 in this volume). This begs further questions about whether women want the same opportunities as men and how achieving gender justice is greater than addressing the oppositions between men/women and masculinities/femininities to achieve 'fairness'. This requires an understanding of how women (and girls) perceive and experience the possibilities of being accepted within, as well as having access to, leisure/the arts/sport.

As the principle of social inclusion asserts people's right to a stake in society by benefiting from what it has to offer and at the same time recognising their responsibility to contribute, its relationship to sport and the arts (DCMS, 1999) might be seen as a means of promoting social justice. However, we might question why anyone would think to use football (particularly men's professional football), for example, to promote social inclusion given that, as some argue, in its current manifestation it is racist, sexist, homophobic, given to violence and dependent on cheating others (see, for example, Wagg, 2002; Spracklen *et al.*, 2006; Hughson *et al.*, 2017). Further, it exemplifies the disparity between the high pay of elite sporting professionals, like box office stars, and that of the majority of fans. Although some commentators see this as just reward for natural talent within a competitive market, others are outraged at this injustice. We might observe that if it were purely a question of merit then there would be a higher proportion of Black, Asian and minority ethnic (BAME) football managers. There might also be greater investment in women's football, in LGBT football and increased opportunities for access to and involvement in football by disabled people. While there are very large sums of money involved in segments of sport, the participation of many is jeopardised for want of financial support for involvement at the 'grassroots'. Some might claim that the worst-off are not further disadvantaged by this investment in the elite, though at the same time selling off playing fields, closing local authority leisure centres and cuts in public service provision (across youth, social care and health) indicates that 'worse off' is itself a relative term.

Beyond the financial, other matters of fair distribution are equally hard to arbitrate. As Cohen (2009) argued above, equality of opportunity does not equate with equality of outcome, certainly in terms of securing equal participation. We have to beware presuming that everyone wants to participate in sport (or any other form of leisure), never mind any individual sport, and they would not appreciate it being thrust upon them. However, it behoves those in sport and leisure to ensure that no one is denied entry. That denial may arise from factors operating across the population, but which are more salient among disadvantaged groups: income constraints, shortage of time through working long hours, no access to a private car, few suitable facilities nearby, lack of information or just feeling out of place for want of the appropriate cultural capital. The attitude that 'we're here and anyone can come and get involved' is unlikely to be sufficient to redress unequal levels of participation, never mind social injustice. In the arts there has been a long-standing appreciation of the distinction between democratisation of culture (the principle that quality experiences should be accessible to all), cultural democracy (the principle that everyone should have a say in what is produced and made available) and a democracy of cultures (where art forms from different cultures are given proper consideration). It is a debate that has not been resolved intellectually, but practical outcomes can be readily observed. In sport we can chart consideration of the first of those principles, but the other two are rarely addressed, though there is now some appreciation that, for example, women and people from minority ethnic communities may be more likely to participate if the 'sporting offer' is redefined away from the form approved by sports councils and governing bodies (Hylton et al., 2015; Long et al., 2015).

Conclusion

Not only must leisure and sport scholars grapple with the complexity of different forms of social justice, even beyond those considered here – compensatory, distributive, utilitarian, rights-based, equal opportunities based (Pankratz, 1993) – but also consider how we can effectively employ and embody principles of social justice without reproducing processes of 'othering' which speak of or about individuals and groups experiencing inequality, marginalisation and/or oppression. While campaigns and policy understandably address single characteristics, researchers are being exhorted to engage with the concept of intersectionality as a means of redressing inequalities whilst simultaneously accounting for multiple subject positions (Watson and Scraton, 2013). To aspire to social justice as an outcome requires continual engagement with difference as a political and politicised project, not merely an expression of diversity or plurality. As Harvey (2009: 15) points out, social justice is a concept contingent on processes operating in society to control resources and shape opinions ('constructions' of the world).

If sport and leisure are to play a part in reducing marginalisation and promoting social inclusion the principles of social justice need to be confronted. In evaluating the relationship between sport, leisure and social justice we need to attend to a series of questions: to what extent sport and leisure are 'virtuous' and therefore capable of promoting justice; what balance there might be between positive and negative aspects of sport and other elements of leisure; what transference there is between sport/leisure and 'society'; and what the distributional consequences might be. That will allow social justice to be part of a manifesto for change in leisure and sport, removing barriers and providing fair access (for all), and at the same time offer a paradigmatic lens through which the unfair distribution of resources can be acknowledged, accounted for and addressed.

Note

1 Opened in 1935 the Peckham Centre might be regarded as the forerunner of today's Active Living Centres where members of the community were able to mix with medical staff, social workers and nursery workers in a facility that provided consultation, advice and support amongst recreational facilities, a café and bar. The Quality of Life experiments were conducted in Stoke-on-Trent, Clwyd, Sunderland and Dumbarton to examine the impact that leisure interventions could have on individual and community wellbeing.

References

Arneson, R. J. (2006) 'Justice after Rawls', in: Dryzek, J. S., Hong, B. and Phillips, A. (eds) *The Oxford Handbook of Political Theory*. Oxford: Oxford University Press, 45–64.

Baker, J. (1987) *Arguing for Equality*. London: Verso.

Barry, B. (2005) *Why Social Justice Matters*. Cambridge: Polity.

Cohen, G. A. (1994) 'Back to socialist basics', *New Left Review* I(207): 3–16.

Cohen, G. A. (2009) *Why Not Socialism?* Cambridge, MA: Harvard University Press.

DCMS (Department for Culture, Media and Sport) (1999) *Policy Action Team 10: Report to the Social Exclusion Unit – Arts and Sport*. London: HMSO.

DoE (Department of the Environment) (1977) *Leisure and the Quality of Life: A Report on Four Local Experiments* (Volume 1). London: HMSO.

Harvey, D. (2009) *Social Justice and the City*, 2nd edn. Athens, GA: University of Georgia.

HM Government (2015) *Sporting Future: A New Strategy for an Active Nation.* London: Cabinet Office.

Hughson, J., Moore, K., Spaaij, R. and Maguire, J. (eds) (2017) *Routledge Handbook of Football Studies.* London: Routledge.

Hylton, K., Long, J., Fletcher, T. and Ormerod, N. (2015) *South Asian Communities and Cricket (Bradford and Leeds).* Report to the Yorkshire Cricket Partnership from the Institute for Sport, Physical Activity and Leisure: Leeds. http://eprints.leedsbeckett.ac.uk/1341.

Long, J., Dashper, K., Fletcher, T. and Ormerod, N. (2015) *Understanding Participation and Non-Participation in Sport amongst Black and Minority Ethnic Groups in Wales.* Cardiff: Sport Wales.

Lumpkin, A., Stoll, S. K. and Beller, J. M. (1994) *Sport Ethics: Applications for Fair Play.* 2nd edn. New York: WCB/McGraw-Hill.

Miller, D. (2005) 'What is social justice?' in: Pearce, N. and Paxton, W. (eds) *Social Justice: Building a Fairer Britain.* London: Politico's, 3–20.

O'Neill, O. (1977) 'How do we know when opportunities are equal?' in: Vetterling-Braggin, M., Elliston, F. A. and English, J. (eds) *Feminism and Philosophy.* Totowa, NJ: Rowman and Littlefield, 227–235.

Pankratz, D. (1993) *Multiculturalism and Public Arts Policy.* Westport, CT: Bergin and Garvey.

Pearse, I. and Crocker, L. (1943) *The Peckham Experiment.* London: George Allen and Unwin.

Plant, R. (2004) 'Neo-liberalism and the theory of the state', *The Political Quarterly* 75(1): 24–37.

Rawls, J. (1971) *A Theory of Justice.* Cambridge, MA: Harvard University Press.

Rawls, J. (2009) *A Theory of Justice*, 2nd edn. Cambridge, MA: Harvard University Press.

Rawls, J. (1993) *Political Liberalism.* New York, NY: Columbia University Press.

Rojek, C. (2010) *The Labour of Leisure.* London: Sage.

Sandel, M. (2009) *Justice: What's the Right Thing to Do?* London: Allen Lane.

Sen, A. (2010) *The Idea of Social Justice.* Harmondsworth: Penguin.

Sheridan, H. (2003) 'Conceptualizing "fair play": a review of the literature', *European Physical Education Review* 9(2): 163–184.

Spracklen, K., Hylton, K. and Long, J. (2006) 'Managing and monitoring equality and diversity in UK sport: an evaluation of the sporting equals racial equality standard and its impact on organizational change', *Journal of Sport and Social Issues* 30(3): 289–305.

Swift, A. (2014) *Political Philosophy: A Beginner's Guide for Students and Politicians.* Cambridge: Polity Press.

Wagg, S. (ed.) (2002) *British Football and Social Exclusion.* London: Frank Cass.

Watson, B. and Scraton, S. (2013) 'Leisure studies and intersectionality', *Leisure Studies* 32(1): 35–47.

Wilkinson, R. and Pickett, K. (2009) *The Spirit Level: Why More Equal Societies Almost Always Do Better.* London: Allen Lane.

Wolff, J. (2006) *An Introduction to Political Philosophy.* Oxford: Oxford University Press.

Wolff, J. (2011) 'Equality and social justice', in: McKinnon, C. (ed.) *Issues in Political Theory.* Oxford: Oxford University Press, 147–167.

Chapter 3

The British Labour Party, social justice and the politics of leisure 1945–2015

Peter Bramham and Stephen Wagg

Introduction

This chapter looks historically at the leisure policies and practices of the British Labour Party. It explores what has been the party's uneasy and ambivalent relationship with the concept of social justice over the seventy-year period between 1945 and 2015. The biblical measure of a lifetime, three-score years and ten, is conveniently and entirely appropriate because to think about time and space from a generational perspective is one important building block or foundation stone for historical sociology (Abrams, 1982). Leisure researchers need to understand historical change and continuity wherein the human agency of generational cohorts is disciplined by material and structural constraints. In his paraphrase of Marx's famous dictum, Philip Abrams (1982: xiv) once stated:

> People make their own history – but only under definite circumstances and conditions: we act through a world of rules which our action creates, breaks and renews – we are creatures of rules, the rules are our creations: we make our own world – the world confronts us as an implacable and autonomous system of social facts.

Leisure and leisure policies have long been recognised as sites for individuals, communities and institutions to exercise regulation and control as well as for the celebration of freedoms and resistance to oppression. In this regard our previous work on leisure has represented our attempts to understand and explain how different generations come to terms with institutional processes of class, gender and race in the diverse fields of comedy, sport, dance and postmodern culture (Bramham and Wagg, 2009, 2011, 2014).

This chapter is in a similar vein. It seeks to map out the trajectory of Labour Party policies as they affected leisure during that same period. As we shall argue there are changing rationales underlying leisure policy and these express unique historical contexts. Each version of 'the leisure project' (Bramham, 2006) tries to manage a coherent position on modernity, on leisure, policy research and policy evaluation.

A report by the United Nations (UN DSEA 2006: 11–12) commented that the concept of social justice

> emerged as an expression of protest against what was perceived as the capitalist exploitation of labour and as a focal point for the development of measures to improve the human condition. It was born as a revolutionary slogan embodying the ideals of progress and fraternity. Following the revolutions that shook Europe in the mid-1800s, social justice became a rallying cry for progressive thinkers and political activists. Proudhon, notably, identified justice with social justice, and social justice with respect for human dignity. By the mid-twentieth century, the concept of social justice had become central to the ideologies and programmes of virtually all the leftist and centrist political parties around the world.

The organisation in British politics most closely associated with the concept of social justice, therefore, has been the Labour Party, Clause Four of whose constitution between 1918 and 1995 undertook:

> To secure for the workers by hand or by brain the full fruits of their industry and the most equitable distribution thereof that may be possible upon the basis of the common ownership of the means of production, distribution, and exchange, and the best obtainable system of popular administration and control of each industry or service.[1]

In the history of the Labour Party, and of the wider labour movement, some have pursued what we have termed 'the leisure project' whereas others, inside or outside the labour movement, have valued leisure neither as an important policy area nor as material to the generic quest for social justice. The paradox remains that leisure, sport in particular, should be the ideal and most popular site in civil society to pursue broad democratic goals of securing social justice. Sporting narratives and egalitarian metaphors express the demands for social justice: how many times have we heard political pleas for 'a level playing field', cries of 'foul play' or for individuals and organisations to 'play by the rules'?

Labour, leisure and the social democratic tradition

The phrase 'the leisure project' can be usefully deployed to capture the politics of leisure, leisure policy and leisure research. In our political history, leisure policy sits comfortably within, and more importantly centres on, a social democratic tradition in politics. In the 1940s and 1950s the emerging politics of the post-war period was shaped by consensus: Conservative and Labour politicians agreed on the fundamental direction for the welfare state, created largely by the Labour governments of 1945–51. Keynesian economic policies and the collective provision of social justice in the conquest of Lord Beveridge's five giants of Want, Disease, Squalor, Idleness and Ignorance were broadly agreed upon. Re-distributive strategies were deemed necessary to secure and to maintain fair and efficient allocation of resources as symbolised and celebrated in the National Insurance Act of 1946, the nationalisation of key industries (the Bank of England in 1946, coal in 1947, the railways in 1948 and iron and steel in 1950) and, despite some initial and vitriolic resistance from health professionals to state employment, the establishment of the National Health Service (NHS) in 1948. Tucked well away in the archives are Labour Party memos from 1946 and 1947 on the need for a 'Socialist policy for leisure' which, as Kynaston (2007: 175) noted, nevertheless expressed a heartfelt distaste for the apparently passive leisure pursuits of the working classes, namely cinema-going and gambling. The thrust of this memo – that there was a higher culture to which a majority of their voters could, and should, be drawn – was to inform the Labour Party's policy on leisure matters for decades to come; it also went to the heart of the party's difficulties in framing a successful leisure policy.

Such was the bi-partisan political confidence in social reformism during these decades that, in the 1959 General Election, Harold MacMillan's Conservative Party manifesto was committed unequivocally to nationalisation and to the consolidation of welfare strategies introduced by the Attlee government of 1945–51. Moreover, prior to this General Election, in acknowledgement of the growth in free time and disposable income experienced by increased numbers of Britons, the Labour Party produced a policy document explicitly about leisure. Called *Leisure for Living*, it stressed the importance of the arts and in doing so almost certainly drew on the record of the wartime Council for the Encouragement of Music and the Arts (CEMA) in bringing the arts to the people: in factory canteens, tube stations and internment camps. Jennie Lee, a noted figure on the left of the party and later to become the UK's first minister for the arts, scribbled in the margin of her copy of *Leisure for Living*, 'People are free to accept and enjoy – or to reject through lack of interest – the best in all of the arts. Make more generally available' (Hollis, 1997: 246–248). At its annual conference the following year the Trades Union Congress passed Resolution 42, that 'Congress recognises the importance of the arts in the life of the community, especially now when many Unions are securing a shorter working week and greater leisure time for their members'. At this time, Britain was still a society based on mass production, with a large industrial workforce. The nature of government was essentially corporatist, with the state taken for granted as the provider of a range of services. This welfarism extended to the field of leisure, wherein the government would support the relevant professional bodies. In their manifesto of 1964 Labour undertook to:

i   End the present parsimony in the supply of public funds for out-door recreation: develop the national parks: preserve access to the coast and protect it from pollution and unplanned development: set up a sports council to supply in consultation with local authorities and voluntary bodies the physical equipment, coaching facilities and playing fields that are so badly needed.

ii The Youth Service will be developed with grants for youth centres, swimming pools, coffee bars and other facilities without which the present service cannot function.

iii Give much more generous support to the Arts Council, the theatre, orchestras, concert halls, museums and art galleries.

iv Encourage and support independent film makers both for the cinema and television.

(www.politicsresources.net/area/uk/man/lab64.htm,
accessed 18 February 2016)

When Labour won the General Election of 1964 and Lee was made Minister for the Arts the contradictions in this policy for leisure, culture and the arts soon became evident.

Labour leaders and their supporters in the academic world (notably the Leeds-born writer on culture Richard Hoggart) endorsed the notion of an elite culture. They saw social justice in this regard simply as making this culture more accessible to the less well-off and to those living in 'the regions', many of whom were Labour voters, while enhancing public appreciation of this high culture through education (Black, 2006: 326).[2] This in turn meant continued government support for the Arts Council of Great Britain, opera houses, symphony orchestras, art galleries, museums and the like. Lee aimed to make 'excellence' more diffuse, without 'diluting it' (Hollis, 1997: 251). But these traditional flagships generally attracted little working-class interest and, in any event, were largely concentrated in London. 'What has your ministry of arts done beyond the Thames and Millbank?' complained one correspondent. 'We in Wales have not bene-fited … don't patronise us by sending a company to play a Greek tragedy here at the Miners' Institute' (Black, 2006: 325). Indeed, it has been sug-gested that Lee drew more support from patrician, opera-loving and theatre-going Conservatives than she did from the Labour movement (Black, 2006: 325–326). Despite their claims of access for all, the Arts Council policies and the BBC's Third Programme (another key purveyor of elite culture) scarcely touched the majority of the UK's working popula-tion. Come to that nor, necessarily, did youth centres, national parks or stately homes maintained by the National Trust, all key items of Labour's favoured leisure provision at this time.

However, although Lee would remain wedded to the 'Few, But Roses' elitist policy of the Arts Council (supporting the 'Big Three' of the Royal Ballet, the Royal Shakespeare Company and the English National Opera; Hutchinson, 1982), she would still, via her White Paper of 1965, be sympathetic to local artistic activity. This torch was taken up during the 1970s and 1980s by the community arts movement that celebrated ideas of cultural democracy and local participation. The art generated here was invariably and deliberately non-elitist and non-Metropolitan, and was calculated to promote activism and participation. Examples included the Hull Truck Theatre and the socialist 7/84 theatre company, both begun in 1971, and the flourishing community arts programmes funded by the Greater London Council in the early 1980s.

Labour, leisure and the politics of identity

At the beginning of the 1970s leisure needs were identified as citizens' rights, and as the icing on the cake that was the welfare state. Policy debates, particularly within the Labour Party, concentrated on the coming leisure society and the 'leisure shock' likely to be experienced by people insufficiently prepared for this future (see Jenkins and Sherman, 1981). However, in the 1990s and 2000s, the leisure society paradigm began to disappear (see, for example, Gilchrist and Wheaton, 2008) and subsequent policy debates focused on higher needs defined through identity, respect and wellbeing, with these championed as the more holistic and emotional dimensions of humanity.

Through the decades that followed the Second World War the Labour Party had been buffeted by contradictions derived from the changing formations of modernity. In particular, it had struggled to come to terms with a growing neo-liberal ideology which had not only shaped the economy but had also permeated political, social and cultural formations. During the 1980s the strident voice of Thatcherism, what Stuart Hall (1979) termed 'authoritarian populism', had loudly taken centre stage and begun to be heard in most parts of civil society. Indeed, it had become a kind of non-negotiable common sense. During that same decade, local Labour parties were silenced as they tried to resist the neo-liberal project of central government with a form of local socialism, the best examples being South Yorkshire County Council and the Greater London Council (GLC) under the leadership of Ken Livingstone (1981–86). However, the Labour Party re-branded in 1996 with the manifesto *New Labour, New Life for Britain* and, in doing so, itself fully embraced neo-liberal policies.

Politically the leisure project, too, has gone through a number of mutations. In the first phase (1950s–70s) the leisure project rested on the concept of a 'leisure society' and the means to realise this vision were seen as new technologies in work, new strategies in leisure education and new local authority departments in recreation, urban planning and leisure management. Alongside new quangos,[3] such as the Countryside Commission, public sector professionals established fresh networks through which to deliver a range of inclusive leisure policies and management practices which together constituted what academics termed 'community recreation' (see Haywood, 1994). Many Labour-controlled local authorities guided these new policy communities and sought to challenge male, middle-class dominance in sport and leisure centres.

The next generation of leisure academics, led by Marxist cultural studies (see in particular Clarke and Critcher, 1985) and by feminist analysis (see Deem, 1986; Green *et al.*, 1990), questioned the expectation of a leisure society. This, they held, could never be realised because of the restructuring of the world economy and its global division of labour: leisure was now paradoxically recast as the 'enforced leisure' of unemployment. Flexible and 'reorganised' global capitalism (Burrell, 2013) shifted work from primary and secondary sectors of Western economies and relocated it to cheaper labour markets in Asia and the Far East. European nation states could now guarantee neither work nor welfare for their indigenous populations. Consequently, academics posited a legitimation crisis for the nation state with the collapse of Fordist regimes of accumulation (i.e. mass employment, mass consumption and generous welfare spending). There was, thus, a disjunction between the formations of modernity wherein politics could not cope with economic and cultural change. Leisure, the latest addition to the welfare state in the 1960s, had become fully established at the very moment that its economic foundation was decimated by the 'Oil Crisis' and global retrenchment. The idealised vision of a future society based on leisure fell victim to its own narrow definition of leisure, primarily as free time and rational recreation, while failing to grasp the inequalities in production and reproduction in capitalist society. Leisure times and spaces were inaccessible to some and in many cases no more than play centres for white bourgeois heterosexual, usually metropolitan, males. If first-phase theory cast leisure as public education and recreation management, the second wave demanded that leisure should be contextualised within media, class and popular culture. Marxists and feminists focused on the contested site of leisure and gendered negotiations about free time, resources and safe access to public spaces.

So, the original project of the 'leisure society' came to be seen as 'leisure as control' (Clarke and Critcher, 1985), although there was always scope for resistance. Much of the resistance to the narrow definition of leisure pursuits was inspired by the aforementioned Labour-controlled local authorities. During the 1980s and 1990s, Labour had, as we observed, developed leisure policies that challenged the neo-liberal policies of central government by attempting to introduce socialist alternatives. This development in leisure policy was theorised as constituting a dual state (national versus local government) arrangement (Henry and Bramham, 1986) and was later termed Left Post-Fordism (see Henry, 2001). A generational analysis helps us understand these shifts in Labour policies. During the 1970s and into the early 1980s, cities like Sheffield were controlled by 'traditional Labour', namely white working-class men with strong links to manual trade unions. By the mid-1980s and early 1990s, the Labour Party leadership was made up of younger middle-class university educated professionals which commentators referred to as the 'New Urban Left'.

This second wave of understanding leisure was typified by the work of the Centre for Contemporary Cultural Studies (CCCS) as it traced the 'rainbow coalition' of single issue groups within the GLC and elsewhere. Social scientists began to listen to and articulate what Spivak termed 'subaltern' voices of 'post-colonial' minorities (see, for example, Gilroy, 1987 and Spivak, 2006) and sexualities (Butler, 2006). The postmodern turn in social theory meant a comparative loss of interest in the collective public sphere as it sharpened its focus on the private sphere, concentrating instead on diverse and individualised lives in what were held to be 'New Times'. In the 1980s the Labour Party too turned away from its more traditional (and declining) base of urban male working-class supporters and paid more attention to the demands of single-issue movements, such as those relating to race and racism, women and sexism and the environment and sustainability. In the early 1990s, under the leadership of John Smith and his successor Tony Blair, the Labour Party was determined to loosen its ties to its trade union and socialist past, notably, by abandoning Clause Four of the party's constitution in 1995. Through careful media management, the Labour Party diluted its commitment to social justice by shifting to 'the centre ground' of UK politics, appealing to 'Middle England' and to the 'aspirational' voters, keen to see their children prosper through education: 'We must never concede the politics of aspiration for all' (Blair 2005). This aptly summarises the transition effected by 'New' Labour from collective public provision to a narrative of individual advancement.

'New' labour, leisure and postmodern society

Labour were elected to government with a 'landslide' 197 seat majority in the General Election of 1997. This enormous electoral mandate failed to translate into radical egalitarian socialist policies or very much that had previously resembled 'social justice'. Influential sociologist Stuart Hall (2003) wrote:

> It took only a few weeks for the basic direction to become clear: the fatal decision to follow Conservative spending commitments, the

sneering renunciation of redistribution ('tax and spend!'), the demoni-
sation of its critics ('Old Labour!'), the new ethos of managerial
authoritarianism, the quasi-religious air of righteous conviction, the
reversal of the historic commitment to equality, universality and collective social provision.

So it was with successive 'New Labour' administrations' approach to leisure.
Whereas in the late 1950s the Labour Party had been promising playing
fields, youth centres and funding for orchestras, its manifesto for the 1997
general election, the first under 'New' Labour stewardship, was noticeably
more vague about leisure. Beneath the heading 'We will help you get more
out of life', bullet points included 'Reform the Lottery', 'Back World Cup
bid' and a promise to 'develop a strategic vision that matches the real power
and energy of British arts, media and cultural industries' (www.politic
sresources.net/area/uk/man/lab97.htm, accessed 19 February 2016).

   In the field of leisure, citizens would now be seen primarily as *consumers* and, politically, priority would be given to the leisure industries as
means to generate jobs, trade and international prominence for Britain.
The incoming Blair government quickly nailed its colours to the mast in
this respect: they immediately endorsed the (then beleaguered) Millennium
Dome project as a national exhibit and tourist destination, inviting corporate capital to rescue it; they rescinded a previous undertaking not to allow
cigarette advertising on Formula One racing cars (thus prioritising spec-
tator sport over public health); and the Prime Minister invited a cluster of
'Cool Britannia' musicians and other show business figures to a party at
Downing Street. This set the pattern for 'New Labour' governance on
leisure. Jennie Lee's notion of the edifying effects of high culture seemed a
distant memory when in 2003 Kim Howells, the Labour minister for
tourism, film and broadcasting, called the entries for that year's Turner
Prize (for visual artists under fifty) 'cold, mechanical, conceptual bullshit'
and referred to British film-makers as 'a small, miserable bunch of chattering classes … ashamed to be associated with hugely profitable films'
(Morris, 2003). A similar populism informed Labour Health Minister John
Reid's declaration the following year that smoking, a taken-for-granted
health hazard in the welfarist years, should be sanctioned as a working-
class pleasure (http://news.bbc.co.uk/1/hi/uk_politics/3789591.stm, posted
9 January 2004, accessed 20 February 2016).

   With the emergence of the New Right in the UK in the 1980s, the social
democratic values which had sustained universalist welfare-state provision
had come under further scrutiny. If confidence in public policy had been
wounded by earlier criticisms from the Left, it was killed off by neo-
liberalism. Rather than developing an inclusive leisure society, Thatcherism
had been about market deregulation, national rediscovery of the work
ethic, longer, more flexible working hours and state funding through the

National Lottery – widely condemned as a tax on the poor (see, for example, Bickley, 2009). For socialists and welfarists alike, the original leisure project had been recast and fragmented in the corrosive light of consumer culture. At the local level, this had meant new regimes of Compulsory Competitive Tendering for leisure services, new quangos such as the Audit Commission, Standardised Spending Assessments, local state reorganisation and the emergence of new managerial and professional roles. Commentators have termed this collection of market-led leisure policies as Right Post-Fordism (see, for instance, Henry, 2001). For their part, Labour-controlled cities had begun to look towards leisure more narrowly as a means to urban regeneration and community development. Some writers felt this signified the death of more progressive community-based initiatives grounded in the public sector (see Lentell, 1994; McDonald, 1995). In this third postmodern phase policy became distanced from the leisure society project and refocused on 'working for leisure'. At the beginning of the new Millennium, this policy concern was re-energised by the Department of Trade and Industry as 'work-life balance', after some earlier excursions by governments into 'quality of life' evaluations.

During the 1990s leisure research correspondingly turned its gaze towards postmodern culture. Rojek (1993) now wrote of leisure as a time to escape from routine and the widely influential theorist Zygmunt Bauman (1996) re-conceived leisure as restlessness, expressed, for instance, in travel and tourist experiences (Rojek and Urry, 1997; Urry, 1990, 1995). By the late 1990s free time and 'quality time' were increasingly conceived as being about shopping around, exploring the seductive delights offered by media and consumer culture, the frisson of the tourist gaze. Leisure and culture now became central drivers behind projects of urban renaissance and regeneration that redefined 'leisure as tourism' and the night-time economy. The research of Manchester-based academics (see passim, Lovett and O'Connor, 1995; O'Connor and Wynne, 1996; Redhead, 1993) and Comedia, the consultancy founded in 1978 by Charles Landry (see www.comedia.org.uk, accessed 24 March 2016), became influential in shaping Labour-controlled postmodern cities. O'Connor and Lovett, for example, were advisors to the founders of Urbis, a museum in Manchester, dedicated to portrayals of city life, which opened in 2002. Leisure citizenship was now recast in the form of the *flâneur*, or stroller; citizens became tourists and consumers in their own cities. City 'fathers' sought to remake, rebrand and re-image their cities with mega-events, cultural industries and tourist attractions (Spink and Bramham, 2000). The voices of boosterism, city marketeers and public relations experts silenced earlier democratic demands for local politics and traditional public services. Moreover, mega events could obliterate traditional and/or community leisure spaces, such as allotments, swimming baths or football pitches, and serve as a pretext for designating the land for commercial purposes – the 2012 London Olympics, procured by 'New' Labour' being a prime example (Wagg, 2015).

Leisure scholars were now divided. Some were converted to the new politics of leisure and leisure research funding, notably Coalter (1998, 1999) who challenged domain assumptions behind the original public sector leisure project, citing the resistance of UK leisure studies to the study of commercialised leisure. Both Ravenscroft (1993) and Deem (1999) had provided eloquent defences of both the leisure project and leisure studies. The leisure project was reaffirmed, critically embedded in a politicised social democratic state. Roberts (2004) skilfully circumvented this debate by arguing that the three sectors in leisure provision (the commercial, the public and the voluntary) had always been driven by different 'engines', by different rationales and discourses. With the coming of a new Millennium, national traditions in thinking about leisure had to acknowledge the growing influence of transnational processes and pressures. These processes, both economic and cultural, were captured in theories of globalisation, McDonaldisation (Ritzer, 2004) and Disneyisation (Bryman, 2004). Globalisation forced those thinking about leisure 'to think outside the box', or more accurately, beyond the nation state. For example, reflexive modernisation has placed issues of the environment and green politics nearer centre stage.

Since the 1990s Labour's policies, whether in leisure or elsewhere, show a clear abandonment of previous commitments, however vestigial, to social justice. Inequalities in education, housing and health have widened and social mobility between classes remains minimal despite more fragmented class structuration. Political formations in the guise of the nation state have become increasingly reluctant or impotent to deal with big issues of environment, food safety or health care. One response to global forces has been to strengthen national identity, particularly through sport. It suddenly became essential for cities and indeed nations to stage international events in order to secure global media coverage and thereby to become a popular tourist destination. During the 1990s and 2000s, Labour-controlled local authorities, such as in Manchester, Glasgow and Sheffield, were eager to host sporting events like the World Student Games, the Commonwealth Games or football's European Cup. At a national level, the Labour government promoted *Game Plan*, their sport strategy document of 2002, which called for hierarchies of sports involvement, for a commitment to secure National Lottery funding for elite sports athletes and facilities and for priority to be given to the staging of mega events that might promote a national 'feelgood factor' (Department for Culture, Media and Sport/ Strategy Unit, 2002).[4] The policy now concentrated on those sporting disciplines where Great Britain was likely to gain medals and international recognition. Purported success in global event management now led to the UK securing the franchise to stage the Olympic and Paralympic Games in

London in 2012 and success in Olympic cycling disciplines led to the prologue of the Tour de France being staged in the UK in 2007 and three stages in 2014. (The priority now given to sport spectatorship has not prevented the promoters of sporting mega events such as the Olympics promising that these events will bring a legacy of hugely increased sports participation, although virtually no known evidence supports the likelihood of this outcome.)

For the Labour Party this is more than stealing or inheriting the invisible cloak of 'One Nation Conservatism'. 'New Labour' embarked on a different synthesis of formations of modernity, which some policy commentators such as Anthony Giddens have called 'a third way' in terms of policy (Giddens, 1994). It simultaneously transformed and sustained the Thatcherite project of reshaping politics and culture. One consequence of 'New' Labour's neo-liberal governance has been rhetorically to recast the leisure project as leisure for social inclusion. Cultural projects now came under increasing pressure from the Department for Culture, Media and Sport (DCMS) to demonstrate how they were tackling 'social exclusion'. To quote Long and Bramham (2006a: 50): 'Traditional leisure has gradually lost its holistic social democratic focus on citizenship and has now been refashioned, steeled to demonstrate its distinctive contribution to wider social targets around education, health, crime reduction and employment'.

Bauman's concept of 'liquid modernity' goes to the heart of changes in politics, culture, economy and society. In liquid modernity citizens become seduced into consumerist lifestyles whereas 'flawed consumers', those individuals without resources, i.e. the homeless, poor and unemployed, are subject to states of dependency and surveillance. 'New Labour' simply followed this cultural logic. As Rachel Reeves, Labour's Shadow Minister for Work and Pensions stated baldly in 2015: 'We are not the party of people on benefits. We don't want to be seen, and we're not, the party to represent those who are out of work' (O'Connor, 2015).

Conclusion

In summary, then, in relation to the British Labour Party and the leisure question, we have seen a clear departure from the domain assumptions of social democratic welfarism and the embracing of neo-liberalism. This has entailed abandoning the notion that the state should provide or facilitate improving activities for people in their leisure time and a turn toward commercialised leisure provision and individualised leisure consumption. At both the local and national level, the party now assumes people to be consumers, and not citizens, in their leisure. Moreover, in keeping with one of the central tenets of postmodernism, Labour politicians no longer assume there to be a high culture to be imparted to the uninitiated. Instead they leave matters of cultural discrimination to the individual and to the market, while occasionally scorning the mythic 'chattering classes' for their elitism. But Jennie Lee's legacy can still be detected in the cultural politics of the United Kingdom. In 2015 leading spokespeople marked the fiftieth anniversary of her White Paper by calling for participation in (as opposed to passive consumption of) the arts once again to be made central to British life, not only in the metropolis, but in the regions (Duffy, 2015; Gardner, 2015; Stark *et al.*, 2013; Stark *et al.*, 2014; Warwick Commission, 2015).

Notes

1 For a recent discussion of Clause Four, see Gani, 2015.
2 Lee and Wilson pioneered the Open University, opened in 1969. This university, offering higher education by distance learning and devised for adult students to pursue in their non-work time, was fully in keeping with the then still governing notions of rational recreation and culture for the masses.
3 Quasi-autonomous non-governmental organisations.
4 A number of leisure studies academics were consulted in the preparation of *Game Plan*.

References

Abrams, P. (1982) *Historical Sociology*. Shepton Mallet: Open Books.
Bauman, Z. (1996) 'From pilgrim to tourism – or a short history of identity', in Hall, S. and du Gay, P. (eds) *Questions of Cultural Identity*. London: Sage, 16–34.
Benton, T. (2000) 'Reflexive modernization', in Browning, G., Halcli, A. and Webster, F. (eds) *Understanding Contemporary Society: Theories of the Present*. London: Sage, 97–111.
Bickley, P. (2009) 'The National Lottery: is it progressive?' London: Theos, www.theosthinktank.co.uk/files/files/Reports/NationalLotteryreport.pdf, accessed 22 February 2016.
Black, L. (2006) ' "Making Britain a gayer and more cultivated country": Wilson, Lee and the creative industries in the 1960s', *Contemporary British History* 20(3): 323–342.
Blair, T. (2005) 'We must never concede the politics of aspiration for all', *Guardian*, 18 November. www.theguardian.com/politics/2005/nov/18/schools.education1, accessed 22 February 2016.
Bramham, P. (2006) 'Hard and disappearing work: making sense of the leisure project', *Leisure Studies* 24(4): 379–390.
Bramham, P. (2008) 'Rout(e)ing the leisure project', in Gilchrist, P. and Wheaton, B. (eds) *Whatever Happened to the Leisure Society? Theory, Debate and Policy*. Eastbourne: LSA Publications, 1–12.
Bramham, P. and Wagg, S. (2009) *Sport, Leisure and Culture in the Postmodern City*. Farnham: Ashgate.
Bramham, P. and Wagg, S. (eds) (2011) *The New Politics of Leisure and Pleasure*. Basingstoke: Palgrave.

Bramham, P. and Wagg, S. (2014) *An Introduction to Leisure Studies: Principles and Practice*. London: Sage.

Bryman, A. (2004) *The Disneyization of Society*. London: Sage.

Burrell, Gibson (2013) 'Book review symposium: Scott Lash and John Urry, *The End of Organised Capitalism*', in *Work Employment and Society* 27(3): 537–538.

Butler, J. (2006) *Gender Trouble*. London: Routledge Classics.

Coalter, F (1998) 'Leisure studies, leisure policy and social citizenship: the failure of welfare or the limits of welfare?' *Leisure Studies* 17(1): 21–36.

Coalter, F. (1999) 'Leisure sciences and leisure studies: the challenge of meaning', in Jackson, E. and Burton, T. (eds) *Leisure Studies: Prospects for the Twenty-first Century*. State College, PA: Venture, 507–519.

Clarke, J. and Critcher, C. (1985) *The Devil Makes Work: Leisure in Capitalist Britain*. Basingstoke: Macmillan Press.

Deem, R. (1986) *All Work and No Play? The Sociology of Women and Leisure*. Milton Keynes: Open University Press.

Deem, R. (1999) 'How do we get out of the ghetto? Strategies for research on gender and leisure for the twenty-first century', *Leisure Studies* 18(3), 161–177.

Department for Culture, Media and Sport (2002) *Game Plan: A Strategy for Delivering Government's Sport and Physical Activity Objectives*, www.gamesmonitor. org.uk/files/game_plan_report.pdf, accessed 22 February 2016.

Duffy, S. (2015) 'Fun Palaces 2015: realising the excellence of local communities', *Guardian*, 19 February, www.theguardian.com/culture-professionals-network/ 2015/feb/19/fun-places-2015-excellence-communities-stella-duffy, accessed 22 February 2016.

Gani, A. (2015) 'Clause IV: a brief history', *Guardian*, 9 August, www.theguardian. com/politics/2015/aug/09/clause-iv-of-labour-party-constitution-what-is-all-the-fuss-about-reinstating-it, accessed 22 February 2016.

Gardner, L. (2015) 'Jennie Lee's vision for the arts is as relevant today as it was 50 years ago', *Guardian*, 23 February, www.theguardian.com/stage/theatre blog/2015/feb/23/jennie-lee-policy-arts-white-paper-funding, accessed 22 February 2016.

Giddens, A. (1994) *Beyond Left and Right: The Future of Radical Politics*. Cambridge: Polity Press.

Gilchrist, P. and Wheaton, B. (eds) (2008) *Whatever Happened to the Leisure Society? Theory, Debate and Policy*. Eastbourne: LSA Publications.

Gilroy, P (1987) *There Ain't No Black in the Union Jack*. London: Routledge

Green, E., Hebron, S. and Woodward, D. (1990) *Women's Leisure, What Leisure?* Basingstoke: Macmillan.

Hall, S. (1979) 'The great moving right show', *Marxism Today* January: 14–20.

Hall, S. (1992) 'Introduction', in Hall, S. and Gieben, B. (eds) *Formations of Modernity*. Cambridge: Polity Press, 1–16.

Hall, S. (2003) 'New Labour has picked up where Thatcherism left off', *Guardian*, 6 August, www.theguardian.com/politics/2003/aug/06/society.labour, accessed 22 February 2016.

Haywood, L. (ed.) (1994) *Community Leisure and Recreation*. Oxford: Butterworth Heinemann.

Henry, I. (1999) 'Globalisation and the governance of leisure: the roles of the nation-state, the European Union and the city in leisure policy in Britain', *Loisir et Société* 22(2): 355–379.

Henry, I. (2001) *The Politics of Leisure Policy*, 2nd edn. Basingstoke: Palgrave.

Henry, I. and Bramham, P. (1986) 'Leisure, the local state and social order', *Leisure Studies* 5(2): 189–209.

Hollis, P. (1997) *Jennie Lee: A Life*. Oxford: Oxford University Press.

Hutchinson, R. (1982) *The Politics of the Arts Council: The Making of the English Opera Class*. London: Sinclair Brown.

Jenkins, C. and Sherman, B. (1981) *The Leisure Shock*. London: Eyre Methuen.

Kynaston, D. (2007) *Austerity Britain 1945–51*. London: Bloomsbury.

Lentell, B. (1994) 'Sports development: goodbye to community recreation?', in: Brackenbridge, C. (ed.) *Body Matters: Leisure Images and Lifestyles*. Eastbourne: LSA Publications, 141–149.

Long, J. and Bramham, P. (2006a) 'The changing role of the local state in UK leisure provision', *Journal of Leisure Studies* 30: 43–54.

Long, J. and Bramham, P. (2006b) 'Joining-up policy discourses and fragmented practices: the contribution of cultural projects to social inclusion?', *Policy and Politics* 34(1): 133–151.

Lovett, A. and O'Connor, J. (1995) 'Cities and the night-time economy', *Planning Practice and Research* 10(2): 127–134.

McDonald, I. (1995) 'Sport for all – RIP?', in Fleming, S., Talbot, M. and Tomlinson, A. (eds) *Policy and Politics in Sport, Recreation and Leisure*. Brighton: LSA Publications, 71–94.

Mommaas, H., van der Poel, H., Bramham, P. and Henry, I. (1996) *Leisure Research in Europe: Methods and Traditions*. Wallingford: CAB International.

Morris, N. (2003) 'Kim Howells: plain-speaking minister from the Valleys with few regrets', *Independent*, 13 January, www.independent.co.uk/news/people/_profiles/kim-howells-plain-speaking-minister-from-the-valleys-with-few-regrets-123688.html, accessed 22 February 2016.

O'Connor, J. and Wynne, D. (1996) *From the Margins to the Centre: Cultural Production and Consumption in the Post-Industrial City*. Aldershot: Arena.

O'Connor, R. (2015) 'Rachel Reeves says Labour does not want to represent people out of work', *Independent*, 17 March, www.independent.co.uk/news/uk/politics/rachel-reeves-says-labour-does-not-want-to-represent-people-out-of-work-10114614.html, accessed 22 February 2016.

Ravenscroft, N. (1993) 'Public leisure provision and the good citizen', *Leisure Studies* 12(1): 33–44.

Redhead, S. (1993) (ed.) *Rave Off: Politics and Deviance in Contemporary Youth Culture*. Aldershot: Avebury.

Ritzer, G. (2004) *The Globalisation of Nothing*. Thousand Oaks, CA: Pine Forge Press.

Roberts, K. (2004) *The Leisure Industries*. London: Palgrave Macmillan.

Rojek, C. (1993) *Ways of Escape*. London: Macmillan.

Rojek, C. (2005) 'An outline of the action approach to leisure studies', *Leisure Studies* 24(1): 13–25.

Rojek, C. and Urry, J. (eds) (1997) *Touring Cultures: Transformations of Travel and Theory*. London: Routledge.

Spink, J. and Bramham, P. (2000) 'Leeds: re-imaging the 24 hour European city', in: Collins, C. (ed.) *Leisure Planning in Transitory Societies*. Brighton: LSA Publications, 1–10.

Spivak, G. (2006) *In Other Worlds*. New York: Routledge Classics.

Stark, P., Gordon, C. and Powell, D. (2013) *Rebalancing Our Cultural Capital: A Contribution to the Debate on National Policy for the Arts and Culture in England*, www.artsprofessional.co.uk/sites/artsprofessional.co.uk/files/rebalancing _our_cultural_capital.pdf, accessed 22 February 2016.

Stark, P., Powell, D. and Gordon, C. (2014) *Hard Facts to Swallow: Arts Council England's National Investment Plans 2015–18: Analysis, Commentary and Evaluation*, GPS Culture, static.guim.co.uk/ni/1412872263674/GPS-Hard-Facts-to-Swallow-R.pdf, accessed 22 February 2016.

UN DSEA (United Nations Department of Social and Economic Affairs) (2006) *Social Justice in an Open World: The Role of the United Nations*, www.un.org/ esa/socdev/documents/ifsd/SocialJustice.pdf, accessed 12 February 2016.

Urry, J. (1990) *The Tourist Gaze*. London: Sage.

Urry, J. (1995) *Consuming Places*. London: Routledge.

Wagg, S. (2015) *The London Olympics of 2012: Politics, Promises and Legacy*. London: Palgrave.

Warwick Commission (2015) *Enriching Britain: Culture, Creativity and Growth – The 2015 Report by the Warwick Commission on the Future of Cultural Value*. Warwick: University of Warwick, www2.warwick.ac.uk/research/warwick commission/futureculture/finalreport, accessed 22 February 2016.

Chapter 4

Gender justice and leisure and sport feminisms

Beccy Watson and Sheila Scraton

> The sport nexus is an androcentric sex-segregated commercially powerful set of institutions that is highly visible and at the same time almost completely taken for granted to the extent that its anti-democratic impetus goes virtually unnoticed.
>
> (Travers, 2008: 79)

> It would be a radical move forwards if sport feminists were to explore systematically the links between difference and inequality, and the precise nature of inequality, to ensure that sport feminism does not lose its democratizing potential.
>
> (Hargreaves, 2004: 199)

If ever there was a clear rationale for working towards gender justice in sport then it is succinctly articulated in Travers' account of the 'sport nexus' and Hargreaves' call for sport feminism to contribute to overcoming inequalities. The statements remind us of the pervasiveness of what Travers goes on to refer to as 'hegemonies' in sport (from different theoretical perspectives some might call them 'discourses') and Hargreaves implies that sport feminism needs to 'get back to' addressing inequalities; an assumptive link being that the hegemonies that culminate in the sport nexus are the reasons that inequalities persist. We recognise claims that 'sport feminisms' (Caudwell, 2011; Mansfield *et al.*, forthcoming), in the plural, is perhaps a more accurate label for a movement that is at times divergent in its aims and articulations. We cannot ignore diversity across feminist sport and leisure scholarship; at the same time 'we' (attempting to use a feminist collective pronoun) continue to account for difference and tackle inequality as overarching principles. Our purpose here is not to overview the range and merit of different feminisms, rather it is to make a (continuing) case for aspiring towards gender justice in leisure and sport.

The chapter does this in three key ways. First, it considers a range of key contexts in which gender justice is embedded across leisure and sport feminist scholarship. This is done in order to reinstate the significance of a feminist leisure lens for addressing inequalities across sport, physical activity, active recreation and other activity that takes place under the broad heading 'leisure'. Second, we draw on recent incidents and coverage of women in the UK national cycling team to invoke discussion of how the sport nexus is far from being dismantled. The example of cycling is by no means exhaustive; in short, it is used as a brief illustration to demonstrate that the material-cultural divide within feminist scholarship, within and outside leisure and sport, hinders attempts at naming and overcoming inequalities that different feminisms grapple with. In the final section, drawing on critiques of the 'narrativisation' of feminist theorising, we assert that a politics of gender justice in leisure and sport feminisms, be that implicit or explicit, remains vital to resisting hegemonies and dominant discourses. This includes an assertion (be that a reassertion) that aspirations for achieving gender justice in leisure and sport are not only feminist issues; not only do feminists need to continue towards a collective outcome (despite disparities and differences), it is also incumbent upon those interested in sport and social justice more generally to engage and/or re-engage with sport feminisms.

Concepts and contexts: gender justice and leisure and sport feminisms

Gender justice commonly refers to social, political and economic equality for women and it is often associated with basic human rights on a global scale (Nawaz, 2013). There is usually an implicit and sometimes explicit assumption that equality in this regard is meant as having equality with men. This aspiration is expressed differently depending upon the context in which gender justice is being articulated as well as by whom and for whom (Walby, 2009; Lykke, 2010). That in itself demonstrates that striving to achieve gender justice is not a clear-cut endeavour, either for feminism in general or for leisure and sport feminism in particular. Gender justice arguably remains inextricably linked to other issues that different feminists raise as more or less significant in different ways; for example, the pervasiveness of capitalism (Fraser, 2007, 2012) and ongoing legacies and impacts of colonialism (Yuval-Davis, 2007). To examine, and we would argue more readily embrace, the interrelationships between theory and practice in order to advance a feminist praxis that has gender justice in its sights we need to draw more readily from feminism and feminist theory more broadly, as we and others have noted (Scraton, 2001; Caudwell, 2011; Parry and Fullagar, 2013; Watson and Scraton, 2013; Toffoletti, 2016). Further, our position is premised on the belief that 'leisure' is a critical context for addressing inequalities and improving gender justice. Indeed, we would argue that a feminist leisure lens enables us more fully to understand, account for and take action to challenge gender injustices that persistently marginalise and in some cases exclude participation on the basis of gender across sport, physical activity, active recreation and more.

Making a difference and/or effecting change are often implicit features of interest in diversity, equity and inclusion in sport and leisure (Watson *et al.*, 2013; Fletcher and Dashper, 2014); certainly, they underpin much of the work discussed in this collection. The 'transformative potential' of sport is commonly based on an assertion that sport in its broadest sense is a political project. Transformative potential in this context is conceptualised within a sociological framework that acknowledges agency and the possibility to effect change as a dynamic process of ongoing negotiation of complex subject positions and, at times, the wider rubric of intersecting social relations (Watson *et al.*, 2013). That sounds all well and good, but how and where steps towards achieving gender justice are taken is open to question. To what extent, for example, is gender justice present in calls to promote sport activism? Sport activism *might* result in social change through its (sport's) transformative potential, providing the basis for human development through the intervention of sport projects that engage and promote progressive attitudes to social change for society's most vulnerable groups (Sugden, 2010). Gender *might*, on occasion, be made explicit within those broad aims of social justice. However, the discourse of 'sport for development' (or SFD) is prone to neoliberal rhetoric (McDonald, 2015) that bolsters hegemonies not entirely dissimilar from those identified by Travers (2008). Sport itself still requires fundamental changes if we are to aspire to engage it as a means of enhancing social justice. A humanist aspiration for sport may be a commendable intention, with calls for a refocused philosophy of sport to divert attention away from 'achievement sport' in the 'sports-industrial complex' towards a humanist tradition that is concerned with 'issues such as morality, equity, participation' (Maguire, 2004). Hargreaves (2004) calls for a renewed moral base and a sense of humanism in sport feminism. The two calls sound similar on that basis, yet the calls highlight a disjuncture between a social justice agenda and a gender justice agenda for sport feminism.

Can we adopt a conceptualisation of gender justice that can be applied more locally, be that at national or more micro levels of analysis? We would suggest so, as do others (see, for example, Parry, 2014), and links to broader contexts of leisure are significant in this regard. It is meaningful to conceptualise gender justice in relation to domestic contexts that are the fabric of women's access to leisure, however heterogeneous and complex that might be. National surveys in the UK (e.g. *British Social Attitudes 30*) provide telling statistics (despite any caution we might have regarding big survey data) that 'women still undertake a disproportionate amount of unpaid labour within the home' (Park *et al.*, 2013: 115). Their figures suggest that women (still) do considerably more housework and more childcare every week. By implication they therefore have less time for leisure than the men do.

Of course, leisure time (along with leisure space and leisure identity) is not that simple to quantify or define, especially in the face of problems associated with reaffirming dominant normativities about household makeup and the homogenisation of women as carers. These inequalities in leisure time illustrate that at a basic, rudimentary level there is not gender equality regarding domestic labour, and gender inequalities are (still) easy to highlight. The paid labour market reflects telling disparities in income and opportunities for women (Equal Pay Portal: www.equalpayportal.co.uk). Meanwhile recent reports and strategy documents in the UK remind us that girls and women have persistently low participation rates in sport and physical activity relative to the rates of boys and men, despite ongoing attempts to increase participation and to provide improved opportunities for girls (Women in Sport, 2012) and women (www.thisgirlcan.co.uk). We are acutely aware that a focus on the experiences of women and girls is only one part of a greater whole in terms of addressing gender justice. We also acknowledge that in various guises and at different times there have been feminist statements made from within critical masculinity studies (Connell and Messerschmidt, 2005; Pringle, forthcoming) that are significant to a gender justice agenda. However, it is beyond our scope to detail these here.

Let us, for a moment, draw from a neoliberal, postfeminist populist imaginary, where contemporary woman has access to leisure and sport pastimes that are at once fulfilling, rewarding and appropriately challenging for her worked on, consumerist configured physique (McRobbie, 2008). She, as a given, is white (Wilkes, 2015), middle-class and able bodied, most likely heterosexual, or at least self presents in appropriately acceptable heteronormative ways or possibly acceptable homonormative ways should her social and cultural circuits allow (McRobbie, 2015). She is likely to be upwardly mobile in terms of affluence and disposable income. She has 'chosen' and developed a leisure lifestyle that fits well with her sporting capital (acquired from an early age because she could well be one of the few girls who actually liked, and excelled, at physical education at school) and of course she has a job, perhaps a career, that enables continued engagement in her activities of choice, from gym membership, to body and spa treatments to regular overseas travel and holidays. She has 'chosen' if and when to start a family and her growing responsibilities and dependants are an extension of her competence (compliance?) in her self-articulation of 'having it all'. She is the epitome of the neoliberal, postfeminist sought-after femininity of much current, popular cultural representation (Wilkes, 2015). After all, the dominant discourse within postfeminism is that a new meritocracy allows for 'equality' and empowerment through individual self-determination (McRobbie, 2008, 2015). Where better to work on that than in one's leisure?

This prompts us to revisit some emergent issues in linking gender justice and leisure (and sport). Principles of fairness and each being given their due in terms of social justice, and notions of equality (between men and women) in gender justice, appear to have little currency regarding an 'equal distribution' of leisure. Key theses in the 1980s and early 1990s demonstrated that the context of women's leisure was, at best, one of 'relative freedoms' (Wimbush and Talbot, 1988), and empirical studies questioned whether and how women had leisure at all; *Women's Leisure, What Leisure?* (Green *et al.*, 1990) and *All Work and No Play?* (Deem, 1986) being two particularly significant UK publications from that time. They established that women's leisure was only achieved via ongoing processes of negotiation of pervasive gendered ideologies. Discourses of gender circulate, are produced and construed *within* leisure, and gender does not merely impact upon leisure. These claims were based upon empirical findings that sought to examine and explain women's leisure experiences. It continues to make sense, therefore, to locate sport, physical activity and/or active recreation in broader contexts of leisure, as has been argued previously by leisure and sport feminist scholars.

> Finding out whether women see different forms of sport and physical activities as part of the diverse forms of enjoyment and relaxation which are culturally understood in western societies as notions of leisure, is a key dimension in understanding how gender relations and gender identities help to produce cultural constructions of sport which are largely gender-specific.
>
> (Deem and Gilroy, 1998: 90)

Deem and Gilroy highlight the value of applying feminist analysis that details lived, material relations in the broader context of leisure as culturally constructed and highly significant in informing how gender and leisure have a dynamic influence on sport. Feminist leisure and sport scholars continue to examine how various embodied expressions of sport, leisure, physical activity and active recreation might be deemed as empowering whilst simultaneously constrained by dominant discourses of gender (Scraton and Watson, 2015).

In other areas of feminist scholarship, analysis of discourses that position the body as a signifier of freedom, pleasure and consumption, whilst simultaneously being distinctly and deterministically disciplined around diet and health, for instance, are illuminating. As articulated in their concept of the 'do-diet', Cairns and Johnston (2015: 171) suggest that women 'calibrate' a performance of 'healthy' femininity through 'personal responsibility and moral duty' where 'the feminine body remains a site of surveillance, evaluation, judgement, and regulation'. This is not, they argue, a straightforward means of control, rather women 'choose health' as an expression of 'empowerment through informed consumption' in what Cairns and Johnston (2015) refer to as a context of 'embodied neo-liberalism'. They state that the processes that women engage in are 'deeply shaped by gendered power relations' (ibid.: 172) within 'a gendered discursive terrain'. Their analytical approach is informed by Gill's (2007) 'post-feminist sensibility' which conceptualises post-feminism as a tangible context for scrutiny and enquiry, rather than as a phase of feminism in a conceptual or epistemological sense. This has been taken up by some sport feminists focusing on sport media and we return to this below in relation to women and cycling in the UK and then again in considering the 'narrativisation' of feminist theorising in our final section.

In a desire to achieve and embody 'the perfect' as McRobbie refers to it, what of previous attempts to give credence to the idea of empowerment as a form of embodied resistance to dominant gendered discourses? Surely leisure can offer more potential for women and for feminism than being (just) a context for 'an everyday form of self-measurement' around exercise, eating, maintenance of 'good looks', and a successful balance of paid work, childcare and domestic management (McRobbie, 2015: 9). Feminism has in many ways attached itself 'to an ethos of competitive individualism' (ibid.: 4) and in that context there seems limited scope for feminist concerns with gender justice as a collective enterprise. Little wonder that Hargreaves warns against the loss of the democratising potential of sport feminism, and a decade prior to this Scraton (1994) raised concerns about the consequences of postfeminism for leisure. Outside sport, Nancy Fraser highlights a shift from engagement with materiality and inequalities to a focus on difference and cultural contexts within feminism.

> If the initial thrust of post-war feminism was to 'engender the socialist imaginary', the later tendency was to redefine gender justice as a project aimed at 'recognizing difference'.... The result was a major shift in the feminist imaginary: whereas the previous generation had sought to remake political economy, this one focused more on transforming culture.
>
> (Fraser, 2012: 6)

Cultural feminism and the allure of 'new' rhetoric

How the material and cultural 'play out' remains fundamental in much of what we see in women's experiences of being involved in sport, from grass-roots participation where women and girls have fewer resourced opportunities through to elite and professional sport. Hargreaves (1994) highlighted this over 20 years ago, as did Scraton (1994) in the context of leisure, and Hargreaves (2004) is outspoken in her warning that postfeminist rhetoric fails women and girls, impacts negatively on their experiences of sport, and omits the presence of persistent acts and articulations of sexism, misogyny and gender injustice, both in and outside sport. The sport nexus seems to preserve and reproduce its hegemonies. The challenge for feminism and sport feminism/s is therefore to engage a politics of difference and of inequalities. 'Only by looking to integrative approaches that unite redistribution and recognition can we meet the requirements of justice for all' (Fraser, 2007: 34).

Across our leisure and sport scholarship, we continue to be informed by Avtar Brah's (1996) model of difference; recognising it as simultaneously individual and collective, subjective and emerging from social relations (of inequality). Questions of social and gender justice require sustained consideration as to how to work *with* the dualism of materiality and culturalism rather than against it. In feminist leisure scholarship this claim continues to attract some productive discussion (Aitchison, 2013; Parry and Fullagar, 2013; Watson and Scraton, 2013). It is a tension that persists across feminism, not just when the focus is on sport and leisure. Assessment of the value of different feminisms and their respective contributions has been limited by accounts of feminist theories occurring in linear and/or wave-like ways (Hemmings, 2005; Caudwell, 2011; Parry and Fullagar, 2013; McDonald, 2015). We comment further on the 'narrativisation' of dominant discourses of feminism in our final section.

In the meantime there are numerous examples we might choose to consider in order to illustrate how and where gender injustice persists at material and cultural levels. A justice/injustice dichotomy is problematic, not least because it can misconstrue a simplistic and unrealistic view of gendered power relations. We made reference above to inequalities in the domestic household sphere; we realise that we did so in a generalist way and we are aware that in attempting to identify key issues, we may well be in danger of generalising and/or over simplifying, but we are prepared to accept that for the time being. We are doing so in a move to highlight persistent elements of the sport nexus Travers talks about and as a response to Hargreaves' calls to address inequalities. We are therefore selecting a current issue and highlighting how a struggle for gender justice in sport remains ongoing. The British women's cycling team springs to mind as a useful, illustrative example, not least because Rio 2016 has recently come to a close and a major event or tournament is one of the few times that we see coverage of female athletes in the press on a regular basis (Godoy-Presland, 2014). Some feminist analysis of sport media (e.g. Toffoletti, 2016) employs a postfeminist sensibility that Cairns and Johnston draw on in their analysis of the 'do-diet' above.

> Understandings of female athletes have changed in ways that are consistent with other spheres of social life, so that sportswomen, too, are recast as autonomous and empowered subjects through an ethos of

individual capacity. Importantly for feminist sport scholars, it is the effects of discourses of individualization that are crucial to understanding how female athletes are portrayed. Namely, depictions of sportswomen as sexy and strong deflects responsibility for the sexualization of female athletes away from media institutions and places the burden of representation/self-presentation onto individual sportswomen.

(Toffoletti, 2016: 203)

Toffoletti touches on coverage of women and cycling through reference to Frances Smith's (2012) discussion of Victoria Pendleton (British Olympic cyclist who won nine World Championship gold medals between 2008 and 2012) as an example of a female athlete who is presented by the media as exercising choice and control over ensuing imagery of her. From Smith's point of view Pendleton can be 'read' via a neoliberal lens that resonates with McRobbie's (2008, 2015) critique of postfeminist individualism. In examining the still often objectified 'girl' in sport Toffoletti (2016) suggests that postfeminism is a context that demands further scrutiny rather than dismissal.

Earlier this year (2016) British Cycling came under scrutiny when it was announced that the female athlete, Jess Varnish, was being dropped from the team with the ensuing narrative that she had been told, by the head coach, to 'go and have a baby' (de Menezes, 2016). There were also suggestions that Varnish had been held back by her male coach from moving position within her team and that this was cited as further evidence of a sexist culture in British Cycling. Varnish's experiences and subsequent allegations of sexism within British Cycling prompted other female high-profile cyclists, including Pendleton, to speak out in support of her (Varnish's) claims. Media coverage of this made for good teaching material with both undergraduate and postgraduate (female and male) students and lively debates ensued. Not surprisingly, some students questioned whether the coach did or did not actually say those things, highlighting the 'gossip factor' in media reporting generally. Others suggested that Varnish might have been playing a sexism 'card' as a means of retort at having been dropped from the team. This was expressed in different ways, including an 'angry feminist' type label being attached to Varnish through to a more liberal reliance on a meritocratic discourse of sport to back up a view that maybe she just wasn't good enough and rather than accept rejection in a 'sporting fashion' she looked for ways to lay blame on the context of her sport. Further, it is intriguing, though perhaps not that surprising, that, according to press coverage, it was only other female team mates who spoke out in support of Varnish. Where were the male cyclists coming forward to support their female counterparts? On a resources level, women in cycling have commented on how they do not receive the same perks in terms of training opportunities and continue to compete in fewer and/or less challenging events (de Menezes, 2016). They also receive less in sponsorship endorsements unless they play to dominant discourses that sexualise and objectify (Hargreaves, 1994), the legacies of which persist, whether or not that is read via a postfeminist lens as in the case of Toffoletti (2016).

By the time Rio 2016 was under way, coverage of the women's cycling team's accomplishments made reference to them having 'mirrored the achievement' of the men's team, firmly re-establishing male sports as the bar to be reached (Glendenning, 2016). In the same piece, commentary about one of the female cyclist's heterosexual relationship was the focus for attention, reproducing dominant hetero-normativities of British Cycling. The article ends with a return to the men's performance, reminding us that it is *their* performance and position within the sport that should really be given attention. The dominant discourse that men's achievement is more important (than women's) prevails and acts as evidence that hegemonies of masculinity are left intact within the sports nexus. There are undeniably complexities and contradictions surrounding the representations of the female athlete in sport media and the hegemonies circulating within the sport nexus are not just those of masculinity, or whiteness, or able-bodiedness, or heterosexuality. In the autumn of 2016 British Cycling upheld Varnish's sexism allegations agreeing that there had been gendered discrimination levelled towards her (BBC Sport, 2016). This represents on one hand, steps towards justice in some regards, that is, for her as an individual athlete, whilst on the other it demonstrates how essentialist and stereotypical views of women's abilities and roles in sport are perpetuated and feed into hegemonies and dominant discourses within the sport nexus.

> Sport, like other social institutions that operate to privilege some members of society while marginalizing others, must be transformed away from binary-based biological epistemologies that privilege white corporate masculinity. Applying a queer feminist turn to this strategy for reducing gender injustice by eliminating coercive segregation in sport ensures that the struggle for gender justice includes not only women and girls but gays, lesbians and gender transgressors as well. This makes it possible to generate both concrete, justifiable structural and procedural changes to sport institutions and practices, while retaining sufficient open-endedness to push for ever-increasing parity for all participants.
>
> (Travers 2008: 95)

What might that 'open-endedness' look like in the context of gender justice and what is the potential, for example, for queering sport, as alluded to by Travers? She outlines a feminist strategy for reforming the sport nexus and identifies key tenets of sport feminism from radical to third wave to poststructuralist to queer, suggesting it is the last that is most relevant for challenging hegemonies and hierarchies within sport. Her reference to 'parity for all' echoes Fraser's (2007) calls for 'participatory parity' that is grounded in materialist contexts. It is beyond the scope here to detail how queer feminism might effectively combine both materialism and cultural-ism but it is an important aspect of what sport feminisms offer to prin-ciples of gender justice.

Gender justice and leisure and sport feminisms: ongoing discursive dilemmas

A dominant discourse of neoliberal individualism hinders the prospect of shared and collective goals across and within sport feminisms and this reflects similar concerns in feminist thinking outside sport (e.g. McRobbie, 2015). On that basis, postfeminist sensibilities and queer feminism appear as somewhat polarised, not least because the dominant, neoliberal body described in our opening section is conveyed and constructed as a hetero-sexual, read heteronormative one. Hargreaves has long established (1994, 2004) that the market dominates the appropriateness of bodies and this evidently informs the postfeminist sensibility that Toffoletti (2016) applies to sport media. McRobbie, drawing on Littler (2013), asks whether mer-itocracy has become a substitute for social democracy. Sport of course is all about meritocracy and sits at the heart of the nexus that Travers exposes. Gender justice, we would argue, is about relational inequalities and processes of racialisation, class, sexuality, age, disability, are neither subsumed nor negated by gender; if and where they are in processes of articulation is another reason for leisure and sport scholars to take gender justice seriously and to continue taking it seriously.

We also argue for sport to be located in the context of leisure more explicitly in order to take on and ultimately overcome persistent hegemo-nies that reproduce gender inequalities, albeit in complex ways. There is certainly a place for conceptual development in aspiring towards and attaining greater justice. Brah (1996) argues that understanding difference is a necessary means of achieving justice; that if we do not directly take on what difference is and examine critically how it manifests itself in everyday life then we will not improve gender or social justice agendas. This is quite clearly resonant with Hargreaves' insistence that we address inequalities and it is a necessary part of dismantling the sport nexus. The material con-texts of leisure and sport, be they time, access, resources or the cultural 'circuits' in which female subjects 'perform' their daily lives, require con-tinued engagement and analysis. In the commentary we present here, we are not advocating a postfeminist sensibility, nor are we advocating a third wave feminist approach as a/the 'best' means by which either to explain or eradicate gender injustice (for a useful feminist leisure critique of third wave feminism, see Parry and Fullagar, 2013). In many ways third wave feminism has been proposed as effective in addressing issues of distribution (overcoming inequality) and recognition (engaging with difference). The use of a 'waves' metaphor more generally in feminism and in sport feminisms in particular is however refuted by Caudwell (2011) in her adoption of Hemmings (2005). Hemmings disrupts dominant feminist narratives by rejecting notions of linear development in feminist thinking, arguing that an array of feminist perspectives, not just 'new' or current modes of thinking, continue to inform feminist analysis and she rightfully questions why certain feminist 'voices' and articulations come to be the dominant ones. Caudwell (2011: 122) concludes:

> I suggest that feminist contributions from the past remain relevant to contemporary sport and that feminist ideas *can be* passed down and folded in to, recombined with, the present. Feminist issues in sport studies persist and are persistent [original emphasis].

We advocate some of the potential of intersectionality for feminist leisure scholarship but we do not suggest that is the only means of addressing inequalities and accounting for difference (Watson and Scraton, 2013). Some feminists suggest that interdisciplinary work for justice, through employing an intersectional framework, can be effective in both challenging rhetoric and addressing a lack of resources; to raise and expose difficult questions rather than propelling a simplistic view of interdisciplinary work as a means to get answers (Lykke, 2010). A contextualisation of material that is 'inter-' rather than multi-disciplinary is appealing for gathering 'evidence' about the sport and leisure nexus – with an overarching set of feminist guiding principles for dismantling persistent hegemonies and dominant discourses. The trouble is that what that feminism might be constituted by, and what its theorising tends to reproduce, are dominant discourses of power and privilege. Whiteness for example, is a good case in point. As Bilge (2014) and Wilkes (2015) warn, feminist narratives remain White and Euro/Anglocentric, as is the case in leisure and sport feminisms (see Ratna, Chapter 12 in this volume). As inferred in our opening section, and drawing from Wilkes, postfeminist depictions are entrenched in whiteness. The material and cultural contexts ensuing from White normativity constitute a pervasive hegemony within the sport and leisure nexus (see Hylton and Long, Chapter 11 in this volume). Further, as Bilge articulates, the very attempts at 'un-doing' privilege that intersectionality might aspire to can reproduce White epistemic certainty as opposed to dismantling it and consequently she argues for a critical intersectionality as 'un-disciplinary'.

Puar's (2012) use of the concept of 'heightened demands of bodily capacity' appears to us as a form of effective and meaningful intersectionality.

Her analysis of sexuality, racialisation and disability and the questions she poses regarding bodies and identities in neoliberal contexts is enlightening. In her calls for a rejection of normative and non-normative binaries and a recognition of the significance of affect, not just identity categories or markers, she states (p. 155) 'all bodies are being evaluated in relation to their success or failure in terms of health, wealth, progressive productivity, upward mobility, enhanced capacity'. Different 'bodies' in neoliberal contexts require ongoing recognition and analysis and Puar's thesis prompts new and ongoing challenges for leisure and sport feminist scholarship. Arguably these can inform responses to Travers' calls for a queer feminist opposition to dominant hegemonies within the sport nexus and they might well inform Hargreaves' calls for making a 'radical move' that she claims is required in order for sport feminism to retain its democratising potential. This can be more effectively enabled via a commitment to gender justice and engagement with different feminist theories whose inception may well not follow a linear 'progression' (Caudwell, 2011).

In summary, then, what are the possibilities for effective emancipation from the sport nexus? We agree with Hargreaves (2004) that sport feminism occurs both at intellectual levels and as political action and therefore an oppositional binary between articulation (conceptual) and activism is not helpful, we need both. Sport feminism needs to retain its moral base and a sense of humanism, meanwhile acknowledgement of sport feminisms, in the plural (Caudwell, 2011; Mansfield et al., forthcoming), is a necessary feature of dismantling the sport nexus. We suggest that a feminist leisure lens contributes significantly to that endeavour. Researchers and scholars of leisure and sport who have an interest in social change and sport activism, whatever the basis of their criticality, still have much to gain from feminism 'outside' leisure and sport. Further, we need to continue to convince those feminists and other feminisms how significant leisure and sport contexts are in the insidious aspirations towards 'the perfect' that dominate women's lives in contemporary contexts (McRobbie, 2015). Being (or not being) 'sporty' is more than an expression of the 'can-do' girl masquerade (McRobbie, 2015). In (much) earlier writing, McRobbie and McCabe's edited work (1981) clearly demonstrated that various and varying contexts of young women's leisure are a significant backdrop in which the lived materiality of everyday life as gendered is played out; that observation retains relevance in the current dominant discourses that neoliberalism generates and operates within. With that in mind, there are several feminist discourses and narratives in circulation for our collective appropriation, interpretation and application in continuing to work towards gender justice; it is not always necessary to seek out 'new' ones.

References

Aitchison, C. (2013) 'Gender and leisure policy discourses: the cultural turn to social justice', in: Freysinger, V., Shaw, S., Henderson, K. and Bialeschki D. (eds) *Leisure, Women, and Gender*. State College, PA: Venture, 521–540.

BBC Sport (2016) 'Shane Sutton: Jess Varnish's sexism allegations upheld by British Cycling'. Available from: www.bbc.co.uk/sport/cycling/37804761 (accessed October 2016).

Bilge, S. (2014) 'Whitening intersectionality: evanescence of race in intersectionality scholarship', in: Hund, W. and Lentin, A. (eds) *Racism and Sociology*. Berlin: Lit Verlag, 175–205.

Brah, A. (1996) *Cartographies of Diaspora*. London: Routledge.

Cairns, K. and Johnston, J. (2015) 'Choosing health: embodied neoliberalism, post-feminism and the "do-diet"'. *Theory and Society* 44(2): 153–175.

Caudwell, J. (2011) 'Sport feminism(s): narratives of linearity?', *Journal of Sport and Social Issues* 35(2): 111–125.

Connell, R. and Messerschmidt, J. (2005) 'Hegemonic masculinity: rethinking the concept', *Gender and Society* 19(6): 829–859.

de Menezes, J. (2016) 'British cycling sexism claims: Victoria Pendleton and Nicole Cooke support former team-mate Jess Varnish'. Available from: www.independent.co.uk/sport/cycling/victoria-pendleton-and-nicole-cooke-support-jess-varnishs-claims-of-sexism-at-british-cycling-a7001226.html (accessed September 2016).

Deem, R. (1986) *All Work and No Play? The Sociology of Women and Leisure*. Milton Keynes: Open University Press.

Deem, R. and Gilroy, S. (1998) 'Physical activity, life-long learning and empowerment: situating sport in women's leisure', *Sport, Education and Society* 3(1): 89–104.

Equal Pay Portal. Available from: www.equalpayportal.co.uk/statistics (accessed September 2016).

Fletcher, T. and Dashper, K. (eds) (2014) *Diversity, Equity and Inclusion in Sport and Leisure*. London: Routledge.

Fraser, N. (2007) 'Feminist politics in the age of recognition: a two-dimensional approach to gender justice', *Studies in Social Justice* 1(1): 23–35.

Fraser, N. (2012) *Feminism, Capitalism, and the Cunning of History*, FMSH-WP-2012–17. Available from: https://halshs.archives-ouvertes.fr/halshs-0072 5055/document (accessed September 2016).

Gill, R. (2007) 'Postfeminist media culture: elements of a sensibility', *European Journal of Cultural Studies* 70(2): 147–166.

Glendenning, B. (2016) 'Britain's women surge to gold in Olympic cycling team pursuit', *Guardian*, 13 August. Available from: www.theguardian.com/sport/2016/aug/13/britain-women-gold-olympic-team-pursuit-rio-2016 (accessed September 2016).

Godoy-Pressland, A. (2014) '"Nothing to report": a semi-longitudinal investigation of the print media coverage of sportswomen in British Sunday newspapers', *Media, Culture and Society* 36(5): 595–609.

Green, E., Hebron, S. and Woodward, D. (1990) *Women's Leisure, What Leisure?* London: Macmillan.

Hargreaves, J. (1994) *Sporting Females: Critical Issues in the History and Sociology of Women's Sports*. London: Routledge.

Hargreaves, J. (2004) 'Querying sport feminism: personal or political?' in: Giulianotti, R. (ed.) *Sport and Modern Social Theorists*. London: Palgrave Macmillan, 187–206.

Harris, A. L. (2004) *Future Girl*. London: Routledge.

Hemmings, C. (2005) 'Telling feminist stories', *Feminist Theory* 6(2): 115–139.

Littler, J. (2013) 'Meritocracy as plutocracy: the marketising of "equality" under neoliberalism', *New Formations* 80/81: 52–72.

Lykke, N. (2010) *Feminist Studies: A Guide to Intersectionality Theory, Methodology and Writing*. New York: Routledge.

Maguire, J. (2004) 'Challenging the sports-industrial complex: human sciences, advocacy and service', *European Physical Education Review* 10(3): 299–322.

Mansfield, L., Caudwell, J., Wheaton, B. and Watson, B. (eds) (forthcoming) *The Handbook of Feminisms in Sport, Leisure and Physical Education*. Basingstoke: Palgrave Macmillan.

McDonald, M. (2015) 'Imagining neoliberal feminisms? Thinking critically about the US diplomacy campaign, "Empowering women and girls through sport"', *Sport in Society* 18(8): 909–922.

McRobbie, A. (2008) *The Aftermath of Feminism*. London: Sage.

McRobbie, A. (2015) 'Notes on the perfect: competitive femininity in neoliberal times', *Australian Feminist Studies* 83(3): 3–20.

McRobbie, A. and McCabe, T. (eds) (1981) *Feminism for Girls: An Adventure Story*. London: Routledge and Kegan Paul.

Nawaz, F. (2013) *Global Gender Justice in 21st Century: Lessons and the Way Forward*. Available from: http://dx.doi.org/10.2139/ssrn.2216331 (accessed September 2016).

Park, A., Bryson, C., Clery, E., Curtice, J. and Phillips, M. (eds) (2013) *British Social Attitudes: The 30th Report*, London: NatCen Social Research. Available from: www.bsa-30.natcen.ac.uk (accessed September 2016).

Parry, D. C. (2014) 'My transformative desires: enacting feminist social justice leisure research', *Leisure Sciences* 36(4): 349–364.

Parry, D. C. and Fullagar, S. (2013) 'Feminist leisure research in the contemporary era', *Journal of Leisure Research* 45(5): 571–582.

Pringle, R. (forthcoming) 'On the development of sport masculinities research: feminism as a discourse of inspiration and theoretical legitimation', in: Mansfield, L., Caudwell, J., Wheaton, B. and Watson, B. (eds) *The Handbook of Feminisms in Sport, Leisure and Physical Education*. Basingstoke: Palgrave Macmillan.

Puar, J. (2012) 'Coda: The Cost of Getting Better: Suicide, Sensation, Switchpoints', *GLQ: A Journal of Lesbian and Gay Studies* 18(1): 149–158.

Scraton, S. (1994) 'The changing world of women and leisure: feminism, "postfeminism" and leisure', *Leisure Studies* 13(4): 249–261.

Scraton, S. (2001) 'Re-conceptualising race, gender and sport: the contribution of black feminism', in: Carrington, B. and McDonald, I. (eds) *Race, Sport and British Society*. London: Routledge, 170–187.

Scraton, S. and Watson, B. (2015) 'Leisure and consumption: a critical analysis of free time', in: Holborn, M. (ed.) *Contemporary Sociology*. London: Polity Press, 388–414.

SHEU (Schools and Students Health Education Unit) (2015) *Young people into 2015*. Available from: http://sheu.org.uk/content/page/young-people-2015 (accessed September 2016).

Sugden, J. (2010) 'Critical left-realism and sport interventions in divided societies', *International Review for the Sociology of Sport* 45(3): 258–272.

This Girl Can. Available from: www.thisgirlcan.co.uk (accessed September 2016).

Toffoletti, K. (2016) 'Analyzing media representations of sportswomen: expanding the conceptual boundaries using a postfeminist sensibility', *Sociology of Sport Journal* 33(3): 199–207.

Travers, A. (2008) 'The sport nexus and gender injustice', *Studies in Social Justice* 2(1): 79–101.

Walby, S. (2009) *Globalization and Inequalities: Complexity and Contested Modernities*. London: Sage.

Watson, B. and Scraton, S. (2013) 'Leisure studies and intersectionality', *Leisure Studies* 32(1): 35–47.

Watson, B., Tucker, L. and Drury, S. (2013) 'Can we make a difference? Examining the transformative potential of sport and active recreation', *Sport in Society* 16(10): 1233–1247.

Wilkes, K. (2015) 'Colluding with neoliberalism: post-feminist subjectivities, whiteness and expressions of entitlement', *Feminist Review* 110: 18–33.

Wimbush, E. and Talbot, M. (1988) *Relative Freedoms: Women and Leisure*. Milton Keynes: Open University Press.

Women in Sport (2012) *Changing the Game for Girls*. Available from: www.womeninsport.org/changing-the-game-for-girls-2 (accessed September 2016).

Yuval-Davis, N. (2007) 'Intersectionality, citizenship and contemporary politics of belonging', *Critical Review of International Social and Political Philosophy* 10(4): 561–574.

Chapter 5

Feminist leisure research

Shifts and developments

Samantha Holland

Introduction

In this chapter I begin to examine the strategies and rationales that women employ when seeking to find moments of individual leisure time, despite ingrained and normalised inequalities in accessing leisure. Income and wealth, or even simply access to household income, affects the activities a person is able to undertake, including activities which impact health, well-being, and social and cultural capital. Whereas 'leisure was something struggled over by male employees' (Deem, 1986: 1) women tend to experience their 'leisure' at the same time as they are working (doing domestic or emotional work). For them leisure is not about being able when to choose to go out to perform discrete leisure activities but is about finding pockets of time, literally 'snatched leisure' (Deem, 1986: 49). It is this specific idea which I use as a springboard to ask, can women ensure they find pockets of time for leisure and, if so, how? I compare the women's leisure experiences across three generations of their families to ask if any strategies or rationales are transmitted across the generations. Cross-generational research has proved particularly effective in studies of health and physical activity (for example, Aarnio *et al.*, 1997; Morgan, 1998; Wenger and Burholt, 2001; Burns and Leonard, 2005) but continue to be somewhat under-utilised in sociological research. I discuss some of the methodological issues in accessing and interviewing members of the same family, where matters around privacy could be fraught. Studies such as this have relevance to social justice discourses because women still undertake the bulk of housework and childcare.

In a paper about a different study (Holland, 2009), I examined how three women managed to motivate themselves to attend an exercise class despite the constraints of time and money, and the added dilemmas and pressures around work and family. Ultimately, despite what Clough (2001) calls the 'juggling acts' that women have to perform to balance work, family and leisure, the women in that study found pleasure in overcoming the obstacles; part of the enjoyment and sense of achievement in attending the exercise class was the very act of arriving. Those same kind of limitations and barriers applied here too. To extrapolate that idea, I would argue that the very act of having any sort of leisure time becomes enough *in and of itself*, even if the leisure activity is not strictly *only* leisure, which is why, and how, women's leisure is often conflated with other, more routine, activities.

Feminist leisure theory

Leisure is 'deeply gendered' (Green and Singleton, 2006: 854) which makes studying it, or trying to define it, a mutable, complicated issue; not least because it is embedded in structures of power, both within and outside of the home. As feminist leisure theorists have argued, women's domestic, leisure and work lives tend to overlap (Deem, 1986; Green et al., 1990; Gilroy, 1999; Scraton and Holland, 2006; Karsten et al., 2015). Since the 1980s scholarship about gender and leisure has developed from early beginnings where 'women's leisure could only be understood within the context of unequal structural power relations and the persistence of dominant ideologies of domesticity, motherhood and femininity' (Scraton and Holland, 2006: 234). There is ample existing work around the family, particularly with regard to the changes in family, with new and emerging forms of what constitutes a family; and on literature about ageing and the life-course (Hockey and James, 1993; Arber et al., 2003; Twigg, 2013). Divorce and remarriage, 'blended families', less traditional sorts of families, such as gay couples or single women, and increased social mobility have all destabilised and challenged the idea of what a family is or how long it lasts. The family, including her female relatives, will always affect and shape a woman's leisure life. Some of the most profound effects on women's leisure are when they are in heterosexual relationships, particularly around the gendered division of labour in the home (for example, see Dryden, 1999; Herridge et al., 2003; Hockey et al., 2007; Thébaud, 2010). Feminist scholars began to recognise that women's lives need not be measured only in terms of constraint: that women can find pleasure, creativity and agency within the home, resisting inherent power structures (Shaw, 1994; Henderson, 1996; Wearing, 1998; Pink, 2004; Parry and Fullagar, 2013). So, as well as gendered differences in leisure time/space, in leisure pursuits and in subjectivities and embodiment, women's leisure lives are complex and multi-layered and most likely tied to their relationships, for example, as a mother (Gregory, 1999; Shaw and Dawson, 2001; Arcas et al., 2012), with partners (Herridge et al., 2003; Hockey et al., 2007) or with friends (Pahl, 2000; Smart et al., 2012).

The phrase, and even concept, of 'spare time' or leisure was not accepted by the participants of my study (introduced in the next section), who refuted that they had 'spare' time at all, as Langhamer (2000) also found. Admitting to having any leisure time was understood by my participants to mean that there were acres of spare time in which nothing of any worth was achieved, indicating laziness or a neglect of duty of care. 'I don't have spare time, I always have something I have to do' (Jessie) was a typical response. This necessitated a short period of bargaining or bidding on what I was trying to describe, with the participant responding, until we reached a mutually agreed definition. Certain sorts of activities are 'acceptable' or respectable (Skeggs, 1997) and are seen to be sociable (for example, perhaps paradoxically, watching television); others are seen to be solitary or even selfish and ways must be found to do them, sometimes surreptitiously, amid the demands of work and family. As Green *et al.* (1990: 1–2) warn us, 'the insoluble problem of defining leisure' is never going to be easy because it has a 'chameleon-like quality'. Most commonly, we agreed that leisure is something which happens which is pleasurable, enjoyable, not necessarily productive although sometimes it is, and could be alone or with others. Leisure is not understood to be something that lasts a full day: usually an hour, or an afternoon, are the most that are expected – or needed. This echoes Green *et al*'s (1990: 5) findings:

> The notions of enjoyment and pleasure, particularly the opportunity to 'please yourself', were central to most of the definitions given. Leisure for women is less linked to what are traditionally perceived as leisure activities than to a special state of mind or quality of experience.

Women's leisure suffers because of what Green *et al.* (1990: 116) call 'ideologies of respectability', by which they mean that 'social control is a "normal" feature of women's daily lives' (ibid.: 138) in terms of dress, behaviour and day-to-day activities. So, if women are not expected to be seen in certain places (such as pubs) on their own, and if those places also discourage or ban children on the premises, this immediately significantly limits the sorts of leisure they can do. Beverley Skeggs (1997) also argues that women's lives are constantly policed by ideas about what is acceptable gendered and classed behaviour – notions which shift and change with age, ethnicity, sexuality and marital status – as well as via social and cultural messages. As Diane Parry and Simone Fullagar (2013: 576) argue, 'leisure is a significant site of embodiment through which women's, and other marginalized, identities are shaped by power relations that regulate freedom and possibilities for change'.

By examining women's leisure across generations we begin to build a picture of what, if any, progress has been made in women's ability to access (and to feel able to take) leisure time. However, discrete separate leisure for women in the families I met was still not easily achieved.

The research

I conducted individual interviews with 12 women from four families in Yorkshire (both urban and rural), which were three white families and one white Jewish family. Many people do not now live in the same city or county as their families so any further research would need to take that into account. Obviously with this small sample I do not make generalisations; nor can I make any claims as to the representativeness of it, but arguably it is possible to uncover rich data even in relatively small samples such as this. The age range was between 21 and 84 years old; I stipulated that the youngest participant had to be 21 years or over to facilitate them having had some chance to amass at least a short 'leisure history'. The families were:

> *Family 1*: Irena, 68, three children; Lynn, 44, two children; Donna, 22, one child.
> *Family 2*: Yvonne, 82, three children; Naomi, 53, no children; Chloe, 29, no children.
> *Family 3*: Violet, 84, no children; Marianne, 48, four children; Charlotte, 29, two children.
> *Family 4*: Jessie, 74, four children; Liz, 44, three children; Lucy, 24, two children.

The interviews were recorded (with permission) semi-structured life course interviews; transcribed with pseudonyms, carried out at a place convenient to the participant, so ten were interviewed at their homes and two at their place of work. I had asked the participants to find a few photos that best showed them, at different ages, engaged in some kind of leisure activity, in order to prompt discussion. The photos worked successfully as an ice-breaker, and I started recording the interview after we had looked at and talked about the photos. Almost without exception the photographs showed the participants on holiday, usually on a beach or near a caravan, not at home, illustrating neatly that they didn't consider themselves to perform leisure at home. Rosemary Deem (1996) argues that whilst caravan holidays are not necessarily an opportunity for women to take a complete break from domestic tasks they are, nonetheless, a time when women feel able to slow down and to justify doing less than usual.

The interviews began by asking how much the participant remembered about their own mother's and grandmother's leisure to trace a history of their own and their family history. The first part of the interview would focus on when the participants were young, what did/do they enjoy doing, how much of that have they taken from their childhood and how much of that is learnt from their female family members. The youngest generation had much shorter interviews – a result which had not entirely occurred to me initially but in retrospect seems glaringly obvious. The oldest generation, predictably, had longer narratives so the interviews explored what had changed for them over decades rather than years and, overall, the narratives spanned more than half a century. A transcript of the interview was sent afterwards for comments or clarification.

Basic assurances of informed consent and confidentiality were given; it was crucial to be sensitive about the questions asked, and I was careful to remember who had said what. There were some difficulties which were particular to this specific research. Family lives and relationships are complex, and several participants were concerned about family members discovering information, opinions or incidents about them that they considered private. (Actually most of the private things that they were anxious to shield were, in fact, mentioned by at least one other family member, either as an accepted fact, or as a secret.) Two of the families lived very near their relations and at Jessie's interview her daughter Liz and granddaughter Lucy were both present when I first arrived, and then left together. I conducted their interviews the next day. Lynn was present when I first arrived to interview her mother Irena, although she lived next door and went home after we had had a short conversation; I then followed her to interview her after I had interviewed Irena. It was both informative and pleasant to see the family members all at once like this: I was able to (briefly) observe how they interacted with each other, and how alike they were to each other in looks. Most of the participants asked how their relations had replied to particular questions, both about obviously contentious subjects but also just about day-to-day activities. At no point did I disclose anything that another family member or participant had said to me; instead I would say: 'Well, I cannot tell you what she said about anything, but you can tell me what you think about it'. Jenny Hockey *et al.* (2007) encountered similar difficulties when trying to access couples from different generations in the same families during their cross-generational research about heterosexual relationships and in my research, as in theirs, it affected who was willing to take part.

Research by Berdychevsky *et al.* (2013: 603) about women who go on trips away with friends reported that their participants found their trips therapeutic, relaxing and empowering. They found their trips away were 'an escape from everyday stressors, resistance to social stereotypes and the ethics of care' which gave them a feeling of freedom. For those reasons, in this chapter, I count spending some time alone as leisure time.

Finding 'me' time

All but two of the participants (both were of the youngest generation) stated that simply finding a little time to one's self proved difficult, not to do anything in particular but just to have some time alone to relax or recharge. For example, Liz has three children and her comment is typical:

Sometimes I realise I can't remember when I was last on my own and I really need it or I will go mad, so I go upstairs and watch telly [in the bedroom] for a bit. I say do not follow me I need some time on my own and everyone pulls a face like I asked for the moon!

When I asked what advice the participants would give to other women to ensure they got some leisure time, Marianne, Charlotte, Donna, Liz and Lucy (who have, respectively, four, two, one, three and two children) all said give up on the idea for now and plan for it in retirement. Although their answers prompted some laughter they were also serious about the extent of the difficulties in finding leisure time. They referred here to discrete leisure where time is allotted for particular tasks, such as going to the gym or going out for the day, rather than snatched leisure, which was currently the norm for them. As Deem (1986) argues, women's lives are often dictated by the 'timetables of others'. Similarly, as Gilroy (1999) notes, work is fitted around children; and leisure is fitted around children, husband and work, leaving women's leisure time squeezed out of the picture. However, 'sociable' activities such as watching television, or 'work'-like activities such as sewing or knitting, were not difficult to find space for, for short periods. Interestingly, 'feminised' crafts such as sewing, knitting and crocheting have all seen a resurgence and are fashionable as a lifestyle choice (Burman, 1999; Matchar, 2013).

Green *et al.* (1990) remind us that work and leisure overlap for women which makes perfect sense: if you cannot find much time for leisure you will create time for it wherever and whenever you can. Irena, whose leisure was severely limited by her husband's illness (a fact she openly and frequently referred to), managed to list the following as her leisure interests, despite rarely leaving the house: internet, reading, cross-stitch, rug-making, television, music, radio, and sitting outside with a martini and lemonade (a preference she shared with her daughter, Lynn – both mentioned this as a favourite activity). She longed to join a walking group, and planned to do so when she was widowed (which happened quite quickly after her interview), but had recently joined a reading group which she found extremely enjoyable. Even this, though, was problematic because she felt guilty that she was out for two hours without her husband, and he wasn't really comfortable about her leaving him alone and would sometimes set off to meet her afterwards, even though he wasn't well enough. This angered her, as she repeatedly told him he was too frail to attempt it, and also because it curtailed her time alone. So even this small window of time to herself had become a battleground.

For many participants reading was a hobby that they were determined to find strategies to find time to do. Many, such as Lynn, Charlotte, Naomi and Marianne, loved reading but struggled to find any time to do so. Some of the strategies they had developed to find time to read included reading on holiday and insisting that a certain number of books *must* be read during the time away; reading even when people were visiting, or when cooking or eating; reading on public transport (in fact, choosing to use public transport to enable some reading time); and reading in the bath. However, several participants reluctantly admitted that reading in the bath was problematic, as children and spouses felt able to interrupt, and a lock on the bathroom door, as mentioned above, was seen to be crucial (this was mentioned by Charlotte, Lucy and Liz). This is if the woman or her family does not veto a lock on the door, seeing it as unnecessary or even a safety issue with children around. But even if a lock is fitted, as Liz said:

> You [sic] have to pretend to be deaf! Before I even ran the bath I would go round to make sure everyone and everything could cope without me for half an hour, like, did anyone want a wee? Was the dog fed? Were there any arguments I could sort out first? So it was all sorted. Then I would be in the bath [for] five minutes and they'd all be pounding on the door. Sometimes I would get roaring mad and sometimes I would just cry my eyes out. I used to think, why can't they just let me be on my own, just for a few minutes?!

Liz's daughter Lucy talked about the same time period, during her childhood, and said she was aware even then of her mother's attempts to find time to herself:

> Now I can't even have a shower without everyone wanting to come and talk to me, ask me things, you know, they all troop in. It's like I am having a shower in the kitchen, not in the bathroom, which is meant to be private, really. And I think about my mum and how we never used to let her have a bath on her own. I remember, she used to try to go to read in the bath, she used to say just half an hour, that's all I need, and there was always something that we suddenly needed to ask her. [pause] I feel bad now, to be honest, because now I know how she must have felt. She must have felt really – you know, trapped.

Marianne and Charlotte, mother and daughter, had both had their children in their late teens. Marianne's four children were now grown up, Charlotte's were school age. All of the mother/daughter pairings shared similarities such as these, in life experiences and tastes, which they seemed unaware of, or had chosen to ignore. Charlotte and Marianne shared many of the same concerns about how to find space and time to do what they wanted to do (which was mainly reading and listening to music) and both had found strategies to create pockets of time: Charlotte achieved her wish for solitude through listening to music and the tasks she did whilst doing so. She drove to work in an unheated car because it had a radio, whereas their other car did not, and listened to music while gardening or sorting laundry, fiercely guarding such domestic activities from others because they were the few times she could listen to music uninterrupted:

> So there is a massive big pile of clothes, but I like putting clothes away because I can justifiably put music on and dance around and it actually takes me about three hours to put the clothes away which I think is about ten minutes' work, but I really like doing that because it's really, really hard to listen to any music in my house.
>
> (Charlotte)

Charlotte and Marianne also attended lots of evening classes together, a 'respectable' leisure activity, doubly so because they went together. Charlotte's two children were left on those evenings with her partner; this kind of hard-won negotiation of time for leisure was a common theme in the interviews, indicating that childcare was seen as the woman's job, and to 'get out of it' required a legitimate activity.

Another respectable activity, which arguably, was not even strictly 'leisure', was to go shopping alone: Violet, Charlotte, Jessie, Liz, Lucy, Yvonne, Irena and Donna all cited this as a successful way to find some time to themselves. All four of the eldest generation (Irena, 68, Yvonne, 82, Violet, 84, Jessie, 74) said that during their whole married lives they had used shopping as an opportunity for time alone, which they counted as 'leisure'. Charlotte said that she turned down offers of help from her partner and requests from her daughters to go with her; and a great pleasure of hers was to eat jam doughnuts as she walked around the supermarket: 'Sometimes I spend two hours in there, just being on my own'. Lucy said that the supermarket was

> somewhere I can breathe, I leave the kids with him [partner] or my mum and I go there, I get a coffee in the café bit … er, I don't tell them that. And I stay there ages, just slowly shopping. Then I get back and it's like 'Where's this? Where's that? Oops, I forgot them – never mind, I will just have to go back soon!'

Another, less healthy, way to find a few moments of leisure time was to smoke: Jessie, Liz and Donna all said that they smoked just to allow themselves a 'legitimate' five minutes of leisure time and that even their children respected those moments. As Wearing *et al.* (1994) argue, adolescent girls begin to smoke to signal their rebellion or resistance to gendered ideals; and they argue that smoking fills a gap in the girls' limited leisure experiences. Similarly, a cigarette offers a five minute time-out which otherwise might not be acknowledged by other family members. Smoking was not described to me as an unhealthy pastime, but only as one which was carefully guarded.

Conclusion

This chapter has begun to illustrate that women still find difficulties in accessing regular and meaningful leisure time, including any time alone, highlighting persistent gendered inequalities related to leisure. Within the gendered context of the home, for these women at least, very little has changed between generations. Their efforts to find moments of time to themselves commonly have elements of subterfuge, as they felt their families would otherwise not allow them those moments. Some of the ways in which the participants ensured that they achieved small amounts of leisure time are arguably well-established 'ploys', particularly of working-class women whose ability to pay for leisure is limited; I am thinking, particularly, of smoking. But other strategies fit easily into the gendered expectations around women's work in the home and also around respectability and what is acceptable. Within this framework we see that shopping, laundry, reading and bathing are part of women's lives (no matter what their income level) and to ensure that they experience a small amount of 'leisure' within those tasks, the women must be willing to conflate several responsibilities. This is why so many of their leisure moments are experienced in the home: because that is where their family commitments are. Obviously, the issues about leisure time for women who work full-time are different: women who work full-time out of the home traditionally make more time for discrete leisure; because they are out at work for most of the day their leisure is likely to be regimented as well as snatched. Marianne and Charlotte's attendance at evening classes fits this pattern; they both work full-time so are able to go straight to classes from work, therefore not engaging with family issues beforehand which might prevent their attendance. Middle-class families are perhaps more able to make positive changes around leisure and this is reflected in the leisure histories of family number 2 (Yvonne, Naomi and Chloe) of which the middle and youngest generation did not have children, but, still, the barriers around what is acceptable remain.

My focus here was more about how women 'snatched leisure' for themselves and less about how this was, or was not, transmitted across the generations of their families. However, intergenerational research is valuable for how it can reveal patterns and repetition, as well as changes; it gives us insight into how behaviours are replicated or rejected over decades. It is crucial for our understandings of gendered leisure and, by extension, social inclusion and social justice, that we continue to ground work in empirical data. Overall, there was very little change in women's availability or willingness to 'take' leisure, particularly amongst the participants who had children, and more so again amongst those who did not have a paid job outside the home. The family home, for most of these participants, was still experienced as constraining. As Green *et al.* (1990) found, *women often feel guilt about having any leisure time* [my emphasis], which is quite remarkable. However, of course, the leisure experiences and attitudes of their family members played a part in how women approach and talk about leisure time so there were many parallels and echoes, and some contrasts between women of the same families. In fact, during the interviews, several of the middle or younger generation said that they had just realized how similar their lives had become, or were becoming, to their older relatives. Women do follow the leisure patterns of their older female relatives, whether knowingly or unknowingly, and whilst many of the women refuted being like their mothers they did share broadly similar leisure patterns and experiences, and attitudes to leisure. The oldest generation tended to note similarities between themselves and their younger relatives, rather than differences. And where there were differences, they expected those to recede as the relatives aged and, indeed, on the whole it appears that this is the case. Some progress has been made, chiefly in terms of male partners doing more childcare and housework, but the women in this study still did the majority of both, and it was still viewed (by both partners) as more 'naturally' the woman's job. Being in heterosexual relationships was quite clearly the main gendered impact on the women's leisure lives. So there are still challenges ahead, about changing attitudes to who is the primary carer and caretaker within families, and who is able to perform leisure (even if that leisure entails simply sitting alone with a book for an hour).

References

Aarnio, M., Winter, T., Kujala, U. M. and Kaprio, J. (1997) 'Familial aggregation of leisure-time physical activity: a three generation study', *International Journal of Sports Medicine* 18(7): 549–556.

Arber, S., Davidson, K. and Ginn, J. (2003) *Gender and Ageing: Changing Roles and Relationships*. Maidenhead: Open University Press.

Arcas, M. M., Novoa, A. M. and Artazcoz, L. (2012) 'Gender inequalities in the association between demands of family and domestic life and health in Spanish workers', *European Journal of Public Health* 23(5): 883–888.

Berdychevsky, L., Gibson, H. J. and Bell, H. L. (2013) 'Girlfriend getaways and women's well-being', *Journal of Leisure Research* 45(5): 602–623.

Burman, B. (ed.) (1999) *The Culture of Sewing: Gender, Consumption and Home Dressmaking*, Oxford: Berg.

Burns, A. and Leonard, R. (2005) 'Chapters of our lives: life narratives of midlife and older Australian women', *Sex Roles* 52(5–6): 269–277.

Clough, S. (2001) 'A juggling act: balancing work, family and leisure', in: Clough, S. and White, J. (eds) *Women's Leisure Experiences: Ages, Stages and Roles*. Brighton: LSA, 113–128.

Deem, R. (1986) *All Work and No Play? The Sociology of Women and Leisure*. Milton Keynes: Open University Press.

Deem, R. (1996) 'No time for a rest? An exploration of women's work, engendered leisure and holidays', *Time and Society* 5(1): 5–25.

Dryden, C. (1999) *Being Married, Doing Gender*. London: Routledge.

Gilroy, S. (1999) 'Intra-household power relations and their impact on women's leisure', in: McKie, L., Bowlby, S. and Gregory, S. (eds) *Gender, Power and the Household*. Basingstoke: Macmillan, 155–172.

Green, E. and Singleton, C. (2006) 'Risky bodies at leisure: young women negotiating space and place', *Sociology* 40(5): 853–871.

Green, E., Hebron, S. and Woodward, D. (1990) *Women's Leisure, What Leisure?* Basingstoke: Macmillan.

Gregory, S. (1999) 'Gender roles and food in families', in: McKie, L., Bowlby, S. and Gregory, S. (eds) (1999) *Gender, Power and the Household*. Basingstoke: Macmillan, 60–75.

Gubruim, J. F. and Holstein, J. A. (2002) *Handbook of Interview Research: Context and Method*. Thousand Oaks, CA: Sage.

Gulati, L. and Bagchi, J. (2005) *A Space of Her Own: Personal Narratives of Twelve Women*. London: Sage.

Henderson, K. A. (1996) 'One size doesn't fit all: the meanings of women's leisure', *Journal of Leisure Research* 28(3): 139–154.

Herridge, K., Shaw, S. M. and Mannell, R. C. (2003) 'An exploration of women's leisure within heterosexual romantic relationships', *Journal of Leisure Research* 35(3): 274–291.

Hockey, J. and James, A. (1993) *Growing Up and Growing Old*. London: Sage.

Hockey, J., Meah, A. and Robinson, V. (2007) *Mundane Heterosexualities: From Theory to Practices*. Basingstoke: Palgrave Macmillan.

Holland, S. (2009) 'Preparation and determination: 3 vignettes of gendered leisure', *Journal of Gender Studies* 18(1): 35–45.

Karsten, L., Kamphuis, A. and Remeijnse, C. (2015) ' "Time-out" with the family: the shaping of family leisure in the new urban consumption spaces of cafés, bars and restaurants', *Leisure Studies* 34(2): 166–181.

Langhamer, C. (2000) *Women's Leisure in England 1920–1960*. Manchester: Manchester University Press.

Matchar, E. (2013) *Homeward Bound: Why Women are Embracing the New Domesticity*. New York: Simon & Schuster.

McKie, L., Bowlby, S. and Gregory, S. (eds) (1999) *Gender, Power and the Household*. Basingstoke: Macmillan.

Morgan, B. L. (1998) 'A three generational study of tomboy behavior', *Sex Roles* 39(9–10): 787–800.

Pahl, R. (2000) *On Friendship*, Cambridge: Polity Press.

Parry, D. C. and Fullagar, S. (2013) 'Feminist leisure research in the contemporary era', *Journal of Leisure Research* 45(5): 571–582.

Pink, S. (2004) *Home Truths: Gender, Domestic Objects and Everyday Life*, Oxford: Berg.

Reinharz, S. and Chase, S. (2002) 'Interviewing women', in: Gubruim, J. F. and Holstein, J. A., *Handbook of Interview Research: Context and Method*, 221–238.

Scraton, S. and Holland, S. (2006) 'Grandfathering and leisure', *Journal of Leisure Studies* 25(2): 233–250.

Shaw, S. M. (1994) 'Gender, leisure and constraint: towards a framework for the analysis of women's leisure', *Journal of Leisure Research* 26(1): 8–22.

Shaw, S. and Dawson, D. (2001) 'Purposive leisure: examining parental discourses on family activities', *Leisure Sciences* 23: 217–231.

Skeggs, B. (1997) *Formations of Class and Gender: Becoming Respectable.* London: Sage.

Smart, C., Davies, K., Heaphy, B. and Mason, J. (2012) 'Difficult friendships and ontological insecurity', *The Sociological Review* 60(1): 91–109.

Thébaud, S. (2010) 'Masculinity, bargaining, and breadwinning: understanding men's housework in the cultural context of paid work', *Gender and Society* 24(3): 330–354.

Thomsson, H. (1999) 'Yes, I used to exercise but …: a feminist study of exercise in the life of Swedish women', *Journal of Leisure Research* 31(1): 35–56.

Twigg, J. (2013) *Fashion and Age: Dress, the Body and Later Life.* London: Bloomsbury.

Wearing, B. (1998) *Leisure and Feminist Theory.* London: Sage.

Wearing, B., Wearing, S. and Kelly, K. (1994) 'Adolescent women, identity and smoking: leisure experience as resistance', *Sociology of Health and Illness* 16(5): 626–643.

Wenger, C. and Burholt, V. (2001) 'Differences over time in older people's relationships with children, grandchildren, nieces and nephews in rural North Wales', *Ageing and Society* 21: 567–590.

Chapter 6

Gender justice?

Muslim women's experiences of sport and physical activity in the UK

Rozaitul Matzani,[1] Katherine Dashper and Thomas Fletcher

Introduction

In recent years, partly as a result of such events as those of 11 September 2001 (9/11) and 7 July 2005 (7/7), partly because of rising population numbers and partly as a result of a wider global consciousness of Islam, Britain has witnessed a heightened sense of Islamophobia. This has been sustained via a series of other events throughout Europe over the last decade, including the attack on the satirical magazine *Charlie Hebdo* (January 2015) and, later that year, the Paris shootings (November 2015). According to Ryan (2011: 1046), '[p]ublic discourse on Muslims in Europe is increasingly framed around the alleged incompatibility of Islam and a generalised notion of Western values', which means that Muslims in the West face a number of issues in relation to their identities, religio-cultural norms and values and, ultimately, their citizenship (Abbas, 2011). Writing in a report on minoritised ethnic communities and policing produced by the Runneymede Trust, Tufail (2015) argues that recent British counter-terrorism legislation – particularly the intensification of the PREVENT agenda in the wake of the *Charlie Hebdo* massacre – means that 'Muslims face an often biased and hostile media, an increase in anti-Muslim attacks, consistent demands to integrate, and now, it appears, suspicion and monitoring by their fellow citizens including teachers, lecturers and doctors' (ibid.: 20) He concludes that 'British Muslims are not afforded the same status as other citizens' (ibid.).

The enduring legacy of these events has meant that, worldwide, Muslims have been characterised in blanket, homogenised and caricatured terms such as 'radicals', 'fundamentalists', 'backward' and 'terrorists'. According to Stephenson (2006) anti-Muslim racism and Islamophobia has resulted in the stigmatisation and dehumanisation of all Muslims, regardless of which country they are citizens of and/or their level of adherence to Islam. Ewing (2008) sees this stigmatisation as part of a wider moral panic in Europe, causing renewed emotional investment in a national imagery amidst experiences of terror and social upheaval. Rather than improving, the situation across Europe has deteriorated over the last decade.

The 2011 Census shows that Muslims form 4.8 per cent of the population of England and Wales. The Muslim population in England and Wales has almost doubled from 1,546,626 in 2001 to 2,706,066 people in 2011. The Muslim population is larger than all other non-Christian faith groups put together and is ethnically diverse. Just less than half (47.2 per cent) of the Muslim population is UK-born.

In 2013/14 435,500 international students were registered to study at UK universities (UKCISA, 2015). Figures are not available for the proportion of Muslims amongst this international student cohort, but a level of rhetoric has arisen surrounding so-called bogus students entering the UK for work or other unknown, possibly more sinister, reasons. In a climate of rising Islamophobia and anti-immigration, international students risk being targeted as visible and unwelcome intruders in British universities, towns and cities. This may affect the experiences of Muslim students, and possibly female students in particular, who are visibly 'different' by virtue of dress and other markers.

It is within this context that our chapter is situated. We present oral testimonies from ten women who are Muslim, from a variety of countries, all of whom were studying at university in the UK, on their attitudes towards and experiences of sport and physical activity.[2] The majority of studies into sport, physical activity and women/girls who are Muslim have tended to focus on experiences of belonging to a diaspora. Mindful of the calls of scholars such as Macdonald (2006) to include the voices of women who are Muslim from beyond western diasporas within research on Islam and sport, our sample consisted of women from a variety of ethnic backgrounds and who originated from diverse locations and regions: Libya (two), Malaysia (one), Oman (two), Brunei Darussalam (two), Saudi Arabia (one) and a further two from the UK, who identified themselves as British Indian and British Pakistani respectively. All participants were studying at one of two Leeds-based universities. Our chapter uses a framework of social justice to which we now turn.

Conceptualising social justice

The authors of this chapter are united in their belief that social justice is fundamentally about fairness, and draw on Nancy Fraser's (1998, 2007) conception of social justice to articulate this. Fraser argues for a broad notion of social justice that incorporates two sets of concerns that have often been seen as separate: claims for the redistribution of resources and claims for recognition. For Fraser, both these claims are important and must be satisfied in order to achieve something approaching social justice. On the one hand, traditional concerns of theories of distributive justice, such as poverty, exploitation, access to resources, role within the labour market, class differentials and (re)assessing the value of paid and unpaid labour, must be addressed. At the same time, a useful conception of social justice must also encompass concerns raised within theories of recognition, such as disrespect, cultural imperialism and status hierarchy. Fraser (1998: 1) argues, '[j]ustice today requires *both* redistribution *and* recognition. Neither alone is sufficient'.

Fraser's conception of social justice centres on the principle of parity of participation, which proposes that 'justice requires social arrangements that permit all (adult) members of society to interact with one another *as peers*' (Fraser, 2007: 27, emphasis in original). For this to be possible at least two conditions must be met. First, material resources must be distributed so as 'to ensure participants' independence and "voice"' (ibid.). Social structures and arrangements that institutionalise exploitation and inequality, and result in uneven access to wealth, leisure time and the public sphere limit the abilities of some members of society to interact with others as peers. At the same time participatory parity also requires that 'institutionalized patterns of cultural value express equal respect for all participants and ensure equal opportunity for achieving social esteem' (ibid.). This precludes social patterns and structures that systematically marginalise, and render as 'other', groups and individuals and the categories associated with them. Both of these conditions, (re)distribution of and access to resources *and* cultural recognition, are necessary for parity of participation, and thus for social justice.

Fraser (1998, 2007) recognises that redistribution and recognition are analytically separate and that neither one is directly caused by or reducible to the other. She uses the concept of parity of participation as an 'overarching norm' that can be applied to both conditions, and thus provides 'a single normative standard' (Fraser, 2007: 28) for assessing social justice. Fraser (1998, 2007) applies her concept of social justice to gender in order to illustrate how both these conditions are necessary to achieve something approaching gender justice. Yet she argues that this conceptualisation is also applicable to other axes of social differentiation, including 'race', ethnicity, class and sexuality, all of which can be understood to be two-dimensional categories, 'a compound of status and class' (Fraser, 2007: 27). She illustrates how this conceptualisation of social justice can be used to enable researchers to consider cases in which axes of subordination intersect, such as when claims for cultural recognition of a minority group seem to conflict with gender justice. In such cases the principle of participatory parity must be applied twice: first, to consider the effects of (mis)recognition of cultural practices of minority groups relative to the cultural majority and, second, to assess the effects of these minority practices on groups and individuals within that cultural grouping. This approach offers one way of beginning to address the effects of multiple axes of power on groups and individuals.

Fraser's conception of social justice thus has analytical flexibility to be applied to cases such as that considered in this chapter, in which access to and engagement in sport for women who are Muslim appears to be affected by both distributive issues, access to and ease of use of sporting facilities and associated resources, and issues of recognition, such as the wearing of the veil and desire to practice sport and physical activity in culturally and religiously appropriate ways. Throughout this chapter we use Fraser's two-dimensional conception of social justice to consider some of the sporting experiences of women who are Muslim within the UK, and the extent to which those experiences are mediated by issues of distribution of resources and cultural (mis)recognition.

Sport and women who are Muslim

In the UK (British) Pakistani and Bangladeshi women (many of whom are Muslim) frequently record the lowest levels of participation in sport and physical activity. As such, they are frequently identified as 'at risk' 'target' groups for policy intervention. There are problems with adopting the target-group approach as it tends not to recognise the cause of the estrangement felt by minoritised ethnic groups (Carrington et al., 2016). Rather, it tends to problematise minoritised ethnic groups by explaining relatively low levels of participation as a reflection of their cultural peculiarities, whilst at the same time legitimating a presumed 'normal' level of sporting participation based on unacknowledged sporting practices of White middle-class males (Ratna, 2010). Indeed, early research thrived on stereotypical perceptions of women who are Muslim as socially isolated and passive, colluding in their subordination to a patriarchal domesticity (Walseth, 2003; Walseth and Fasting, 2004; Kay 2006). Such conceptualisations risk over-simplifying Muslim women's sporting experiences, and thus represent a form of cultural misrecognition.

Though there is a growing appreciation of the internal diversity of Muslim communities there has been a tendency to essentialise and homogenise this group. The internal diversity of Muslim communities cannot be reduced to primordial labels of fixed belonging, i.e. 'Pakistani', 'Indian', 'Saudi', 'Qatari' and so on. Nor can this diversity be explained solely in terms of religious identities. Rather it requires an appreciation of what Brah (1996) refers to as 'axes of differentiation', whereby 'race' and ethnicity are not unitary, but multi-dimensional, processual and require meticulous appreciation of power and differentiation. Indeed, according to Brubaker (2013: 2) the term 'Muslim' is both a category of analysis and an increasingly salient, and contested, category of social, political and religious practice.

Early research into the sport and physical activity of women who are Muslim tended to suggest that, due to constraints imposed by religion and culture, the two were anathema (Taylor and Toohey, 2001; Walseth, 2003; Walseth and Fasting, 2004; Kay, 2006). More recent analyses have attempted to interrogate the assumed position of Muslim women/girls as sociocultural Others (Ahmad, 2011; Samie, 2013; Ratna, 2013). These analyses emphasise both the enablers and constraints on Muslim females' involvement in sport by exploring the interrelated factors of family influence, sociocultural expectations of Muslim femininities, patriarchy, ethnic identity and religion (Toffoletti and Palmer, 2015). These factors can be seen to represent both dimensions of Fraser's (2007) conceptualisation of social justice: (re)distribution and (mis)recognition.

Distributive (in)justice, women who are Muslim and sport

There is a popularly held view in the West that Muslim females are discouraged and/or actively prevented from participating in sport by unsupportive family. Kay's (2006) examination of family influence on young Muslim women's participation in sport found that the family was a key component in mediating potential constraints surrounding their involvement in sport. The legacy of their family's country of origin in particular was identified as a point of divergence and conflict. In research conducted in Belgium, de Knop *et al.* (1996) suggested that girls who are Muslim are particularly restricted from playing sports out of fear that they will be badly influenced by Western cultural practices. This can be seen at a variety of levels: from Muslim females being prevented from joining formalised sports teams, to others being withdrawn from PE in schools (Benn *et al.*, 2011). The family could thus be seen as a potential source of distributive injustice for Muslim women, limiting their participatory parity through expectations that they perform domestic work, over sport and leisure, and avoid negative influence of Western cultural practices. However, this would be an overly simplistic view of the role of the family on the experiences of women and girls who are Muslim; Kay (2006) and others (e.g. Benn *et al.*, 2011) argue that families are more likely to support participation if the conditions of participation conform to their interpretation of Islam. Notions of 'acceptability' can be viewed through the duality of religious observance and social respectability.

A number of studies refer to the principle of *izzat* (family honour) and point towards anxiety in many Muslim families of *izzat* being negatively affected through female participation in sport. A primary means of increasing *izzat* is through arranging prestigious marriage matches for the family's daughter(s). This means that, in effect, it is women who are responsible for *izzat* (Bains, 2014). As competitive sports are not seen as promoting an ideal form of femininity, many females who are Muslim refrain, while those who do participate experience disapproval, harassment or sanctions from those who believe participation challenges respectable Muslim femininities (Walseth, 2003; Jiwani and Rail, 2010). This suggests that women and girls who are Muslim are not prevented from participating in sport as long as that participation conforms to cultural and religious ideas about appropriateness. Drawing on Fraser's (2007) conceptualisation of social justice, this suggests that females who are Muslim do not have participatory parity in relation to access to sport, in comparison to either males who are Muslim or non-Muslim males or females. Therefore, the first condition of social justice is not being fully met due to distributive constraints affecting Muslim females' access to sport and physical activity.

Cultural (mis)recognition, women who are Muslim and sport

Islam, through its views towards gender equity, is frequently identified as a barrier to participation. Among other things, expectations to adopt modest dress and maintain segregation from men is believed to hinder Muslim females' uptake of sport (Kloek *et al.*, 2013). However, we must be cautious in discussing Islam in such blanket terms as there is evidence in both the Koran and hadiths that physical activity is encouraged by Islam, for both men/boys and women/girls, as a means of maintaining good health and fitness. In Walseth and Fasting's (2004) study the women who most strongly emphasised the importance of being physically active were those who looked at Islam as a political ideology. By approaching religion and culture as separate, therefore, 'Muslims can argue that Islam supports women's involvement in sporting activities' (Walseth and Strandbu, 2014: 494). Thus, as we will demonstrate below, participation is largely contingent on how women/girls interpret Islam, and how they *apply* such interpretations during everyday social relations. Consequently interpretations of Islam do not necessarily preclude Muslim women's participatory parity in relation to involvement in sport and it is, rather, how religion and culture interact to both enable and constrain that is of primary concern (Walseth and Fasting, 2004; Benn *et al.*, 2011).

Within Western discourses the veil and Muslim women are almost synonymous (Macdonald, 2006).[3] While the veil is normalised in many Islamic countries, such as Saudi Arabia, Afghanistan and Iran, when worn by women who are Muslim in Western and/or secular environments, including the UK, questions have been raised over its appropriateness.[4] While some argue that the veil is a symbol of religious self-expression and female autonomy, others perceive oppressive and patriarchal undertones (ibid.; Walseth and Strandbu, 2014).

Western analyses of women who are Muslim reinforce the veil's repudiation of sexuality and self-expression; 'the image of a veiled Muslim woman seems to be one of the most popular Western ways of representing the "problems of Islam"' (Watson, 1994: 153). Indeed, perhaps more than any other overt embodiment of religiosity, the 'veil' has become symbolic of an impediment to integration. However, as Fraser (2007) argues, such interpretations of the veil do not encompass the complexity of the contested meanings of such symbols within different Muslim communities and may rather be demonstrative of modern forms of colonialism; a view that women who are Muslim need rescuing from the brutality and oppression of Islam and the veil to allow gender justice (MacDonald, 2006; Walseth and Strandbu, 2014).

As Yegenoglu (1998: 115) points out, by constructing veiling as an unusual practice Western analyses imply that unveiling marks a return to a 'natural' and 'normal' body, in that 'the body that is not veiled is taken as the norm for specifying a general, cross-culturally valid notion of what a feminine body is and must be'. Macdonald (2006) has criticised (Western) research for its fixation on the veil, arguing that analyses of the social, economic and political positioning of women who are Muslim within different cultural contexts is inhibited as a result. Consequently, within some Western contexts, including the UK, cultural misrecognition condemns the wearing of the veil as a symbol of Muslim females' oppression, and it is this which denies them participatory parity.

In the context of sport and physical activity it is almost impossible to discuss Muslim females without some reference to the 'veil'. Purely from a functional perspective, the 'veil' (in any form) may hinder physical activity; and second, it is proscribed by the dress codes imposed by many national governing bodies of sport (Amara, 2012).

Contemporary research looks beyond such barriers, instead stressing the relative agency of girls and women who are Muslim in accessing and progressing in sport. Ahmad's (2011) and Ratna's (2013) studies of British Asian female footballers show how ethnic identities are becoming increasingly hybrid, with many negotiating a religious identity around active participation in sport and physical activity. This perspective is further supported by Samie's (2013) examination of Muslim female basketballers, wherein she argues that much of the research has depicted Muslim females as victims of their religion and victims of 'the veil'. She argues that, through sport, many Muslim women are exerting their agency to present their bodies in much the same way as white women. We should not, however, assume that all females who are Muslim have such agency. There are large experiential differences depending upon, among other things, generation, geographic origin and length of residence in the UK.

This brief review of the literature on women/girls who are Muslim and sport suggests that the conditions for participatory parity are not being met on either of the two dimensions put forward by Fraser (1998, 2007). For a variety of economic, social, cultural and religious reasons women and girls who are Muslim often do not have opportunity to access sport in the same ways as other groups. At the same time cultural misrecognition of Islam, within different Muslim and non-Muslim communities, disparages female athleticism and the wearing of the veil, thus denying Muslim women/girls opportunity for respect and achieving social esteem within the context of sport. The conditions for justice would thus appear not to be met for girls and women who are Muslim in relation to sport and physical activity. In the next section we consider this in relation to a specific group of women who are Muslim students at UK universities.

Findings

Islam itself was not seen as a barrier to participation in sport by any of the women within our study, and was actually seen as an enabling and encouraging factor:

> Islam tells you to be active and Islam encourages you to do sports. For me being healthy and active makes me more focused in my studies and religious activities. If you're not active, you'll become lazy.

> Our Prophet Muhammad told us we should teach our children as early as possible to do sports, especially swimming and riding a horse because it makes us healthier.

Several participants spoke of their enjoyment of sport and physical activity:

> I play badminton, netball, football and I go to gym. I have many experiences in sport. I am quite competitive in sport. I used to do athletics, netball, volleyball and badminton.

> I like to run … all the time near my house or go to park.

Contrary to assumptions made by some Western feminists, for some of our participants, families were seen as supportive of their desire to engage in sport:

> I and my family usually played football and cricket at the [park] where there is grass everywhere.

> Yes, my family allowed me to do sports. As long as suitable with me and Islam, they will trust my decision.

The women in our sample all enjoy sport to varying degrees, and there were many factors that enabled their participation. However, as hinted by the participant above, although sport was important to many of these women it was secondary to their commitment to Islam and cultural and religious expectations about acceptable behaviour. For some, this was expressed through wearing the hijab. All of the women in this study who wore the hijab did so because of religion:

> I'm wearing hijab because of my religion.... The hijab is not hard or not comfortable for me. Because I've already used it all time ... I can't do anything without hijab.

There was an agreement that wearing the hijab was 'normal':

> It shouldn't be seen as an odd thing. It is absolutely fine. It is something that, for religion purpose, you have to do ... you just do it. It is like putting your clothes on. Would you practice sports naked? You can't!

However, many of our participants were aware that wearing the hijab marked them out as visually different and felt uncomfortable about the image of the hijab in the West:

> Sometimes people see me wearing hijab while I am doing sports [and] they see me as a strange person.... In here [UK], if I walking in the park, community have no problem looking at me. But if I go to gym, people will look strange at me as I am wearing a hijab. They will ask me, why I am wearing hijab? Because they grow up with idea of what sports attire are suitable to go to gym if I go to gym wearing hijab they will think that I wear wrong sports attire.

> I get uncomfortable and awkward sometimes.... Maybe because I am wearing hijab when I am doing sports where they are wearing short pants and sleeveless in the gym but I am all covered. I don't think they quite understand why I am cover up or why I am wearing hijab.

Wearing the hijab in sport in a non-Islamic country like the UK opens up possibilities for cultural misrecognition, as such cultural and religious artefacts may be incompatible with the majority understanding of suitable sports attire. While all the women believed in the importance of wearing the hijab, many did reflect upon how it can become uncomfortable while undertaking sport. These participants said that they struggle to perform to the best of their ability whilst wearing the hijab:

> At first it was ok ... but when you started playing ... you get sweaty and you start to feel uncomfortable and this can disturb your performance.

I can't do much with wearing hijab. I feel like it gets in the way when I am doing sports. Sometimes I feel uncomfortable because the hijab flies around. It does not necessarily make me not want to do sports. [But] hijab can get in the way.

Mindful of the effects of wearing the hijab this woman said that she consciously reduced the intensity of her performance:

I feel so hot when doing sports, so I used different type of material of hijab that is more comfortable. Or I will change how I wear it. I try not to overdo it so it is easier for me to do sports.

For others, this had implications for the level they could aspire to play at. These comments suggest that, in addition to issues with cultural misrecognition and associated marginalised status in relation to wearing the hijab, this cultural/religious signifier also has potential distributive effects on women's sports performance, possibly limiting capacity to compete on equal terms at higher levels/intensity of sport.

Given these effects the women spoke of the importance of carving out spaces where they can participate without wearing the hijab. Their primary need in this respect was sex-segregated environments:

All the time I am trying to separate from men, just ladies, so that I can take off the hijab.

The importance of sex-segregated spaces was unanimously endorsed and, in many cases, transcended issues related to the hijab:

[T]he hijab has not driven us to stop from participating … ladies or daughter cannot play with the men. Girls cannot play with the boys, touch each other, shake hands, or sit together … especially kids over 15 years old. In my country they are not allowed to mix when they are already big … it is limiting for me to join [clubs] because of the mixed gender. If it is mixed gender then I will not join. As a Muslim, I know I can't do this … this is forbidden…. I believe in my rules. If in Islam it is not allowed, I will not do it.

This clearly sets limits to participatory parity for women/girls who are Muslim in relation to their ability to engage in sport on terms equal to those of males who are Muslim, and females who are not Muslim.

Comparisons between 'home' and the UK illuminated a number of challenges women who are Muslim face. The most common challenge was in relation to facilities and their accessibility in terms of sex-segregation. With the majority of women having originated from Islamic countries, they were used to sex-segregated provision. As similar arrangements are not always available in the UK this made their participation increasingly problematic:

> In my country ... it is different from Leeds where only all ladies do sports. But here, in Leeds, I don't like to do sports together with mixed gender. ... I like to do sports here but because it is mixed gender I can't do the sports.

Other participants identified a reluctance among some facilities and staff to accommodate their religious requirements:

> Yes, any Muslim lady can do sports. But I tell you must wear Muslim hijab. But the problem when doing swimming ... you have to wear the suitable clothes which is not suitable for swimming. I have to cover all my body. In my country I have burkini which I can wear it, but here I was not allowed to wear burkini and the worker ask me to wear special clothes in order for me to do swimming. That's why I can't do swimming and I didn't come again.

> I have experienced in Leeds where I want to go to swimming pool with my kids. However, since I am wearing hijab and Islamic clothes the workers did not allow me and my kids to swim because I am wearing hijab. So I have to take out my kids.

There are clearly issues of both distribution and recognition at play here. Women who are Muslim do not have access to appropriate facilities in order to enable them to participate in sport as they wish (a distributive issue) and their specific needs and modifications, such as wearing a burkini, are not recognised by the (white) cultural majority in Leeds (and doubtless elsewhere in the UK) as being of equal status and acceptability as those of the dominant population (a cultural (mis)recognition issue).

Discussion

Sport has long been understood as a male-dominated domain which women enter as outsiders and second-class citizens, measured and found lacking against an unacknowledged masculine norm (Travers, 2008; Dashper, 2012). Our empirical evidence demonstrates how sports participation may be even more problematic for women who are Muslim, as they face challenges to their involvement on gender, religious, cultural and sometimes ethnic grounds. In our brief discussion in this chapter we have used Fraser's (1998, 2007) conceptualisation of social justice to consider the extent to which the conditions for participatory parity within the context of sport are in place for women who are Muslim.

On Fraser's first measure, that of distribution, we find conditions to be lacking. Women in the UK who are Muslim do not have access to material resources that would give them independence and 'voice' within the sports field. Whilst the category 'women who are Muslim' must not be taken as a homogeneous group and wide variation exists between different interpretations of Islam at group and individual levels, many of the religious and cultural affiliations of Islam, such as the need for sex-segregated spaces and modesty in attire, make sports participation problematic for many women in the UK. Family support for women's sporting activities varies considerably, but the centrality of religion within the lives of many women who are Muslim may work against their capacity and ability to participate in sport on terms equal to non-Muslim women in the UK, especially where Islam and sport are seen to conflict as is frequently the case in relation to sports facilities and provision within the UK. Consequently women who are Muslim do not have parity of participation on distributive grounds in relation to sport in the UK.

On Fraser's (2007) second measure of social justice, that of cultural recognition, we again find conditions to be lacking. Institutionalised patterns of cultural value position women who are Muslim as marginal within the UK sports landscape, framing their specific needs as different and less worthy than those of the cultural majority. Consequently women who are Muslim do not have parity of participation on recognition grounds in relation to sport in the UK. The position of women who are Muslim in the UK is thus lacking on both of Fraser's (2007) measures of social justice, and this may in part help explain the persistently low levels of sports participation amongst this group in comparison to other ethnic groups in the UK.

Notes

1 Now at University of Brunei Darussalam.
2 In this chapter we use the word 'sport' as an all-encompassing term to include all forms of physical activity.
3 The veil is a form of headscarf and a means of maintaining female modesty. In the UK the term 'veil' largely obscures the diversity in body-covering practices undertaken by women who are Muslim. Indeed, 'veiling' varies tremendously: from the hijab which most commonly covers head and neck only, to the burka, a one-piece covering the face and body, often leaving just a mesh screen to see through, which is the most concealing form of veil.
4 In September 2010 the French government banned the wearing of any face covering headgear, including the veil.

References

Abbas, T. (2011) *Islamic Radicalism and Multicultural Politics*. London: Routledge.
Ahmad, A. (2011) 'British football: where are the Muslim female footballers? Exploring the connections between gender, ethnicity and Islam', *Soccer and Society* 12(3): 443–456.

Amara, M. (2012) 'Veiled women athletes in the 2008 Beijing Olympics: media accounts', *The International Journal of the History of Sport* 29(4): 638–651.

Bains, H. (2014) ' "Kabbadi tournaments": patriarchal spaces and women's rejection of the masculine field', in K. Dashper, T. Fletcher and N. McCullough (eds) *Sports Events, Society and Culture*. London: Routledge, 145–159.

Benn, T., Dagkas, S. and Haifaa, J. (2011) 'Embodied faith: Islam, religious freedom and educational practices in physical education', *Sport, Education and Society* 16(1): 17–34.

Brah, A. (1996) *Cartographies of Diaspora: Contesting Identities*. London: Routledge.

Brubaker, R. (2013) 'Categories of analysis and categories of practice: a note on the study of Muslims in European countries of immigration', *Ethnic and Racial Studies* 36(1): 1–8.

Carrington, B., Fletcher, T. and McDonald, I. (2016) 'The politics of "race" and sports policy in the United Kingdom', in B. Houlihan and D. Malcolm (eds) *Sport and Society*, 3rd edn. London: Sage, 222–249.

Dashper, K. (2012) 'Together, yet still not equal? Sex integration in equestrian sport', *Asia-Pacific Journal of Health, Sport and Physical Education* 3(3): 213–225.

de Knop, P., Theeboom, M., Wittock, H. and DeMartelaer, K. (1996) 'Implications of Islam on Muslim girls' sport participation in Western Europe: literature review and policy recommendations for sport promotion', *Sport Education and Society* 1(1): 147–164.

Ewing, K. P. (2008) *Stolen Honor: Stigmatizing Muslim Men in Berlin*. Stanford, CA: Stanford University Press.

Fraser, N. (1998) *Social Justice in the Age of Identity Politics: Redistribution, Recognition, Participation*, Wissenschaftszentrum Berlin für Sozialforschung, Discussion Paper FS I 98–108.

Fraser, N. (2007) 'Feminist politics in the age of recognition: a two-dimensional approach to gender justice', *Studies in Social Justice* 1(1): 23–35.

Jiwani, N. and Rail, G. (2010) 'Islam, hijab and young Shia Muslim Canadian women's discursive constructions of physical activity', *Sociology of Sport Journal* 27: 251–267.

Kay, T. (2006) 'Daughters of Islam: family influences on Muslim young women's participation in sport', *International Review for the Sociology of Sport* 41(3–4): 357–373.

Kloek, M. E., Peters, K. and Sijtsma, M. (2013) 'How Muslim women in the Netherlands negotiate discrimination during leisure activities', *Leisure Sciences* 35: 405–421.

Macdonald, M. (2006) 'Muslim women and the veil', *Feminist Media Studies* 6(1): 7–23.

Ratna, A. (2010) ' "Taking the power back!": the politics of British-Asian female football players', *Young: Nordic Journal of Youth Research* 18(2): 117–132.

Ratna, A. (2013) 'Intersectional plays on identity: the experiences of British Asian female footballers', *Sociological Research Online* 18(1).

Ryan, L. (2011) 'Muslim women negotiating collective stigmatization: "We're just normal people" ', *Sociology* 45(6): 1045–1060.

Samie, S. F. (2013) 'Hetero-sexy self/body work and basketball: the invisible sport-ing women of British Pakistani Muslim heritage', *South Asian Popular Culture* 11(3): 257–270.

Stephenson, M. L. (2006) 'Travel and the "freedom of movement": racialised encounters and experiences amongst ethnic minority tourists in the EU', *Mobili-ties* 1(2): 285–306.

Taylor, T. and Toohey, K. (2001) 'Behind the veil: exploring the recreation needs of Muslim women', *Leisure/Loisir* 26(1–2): 85–105.

Toffoletti, K. and Palmer, C. (2015) 'New approaches for studies of Muslim women and sport', *International Review for the Sociology of Sport*, published online ahead of print.

Travers, A. (2008) 'The sport nexus and gender injustice', *Studies in Social Justice* 2(1): 79–101.

Tufail, W. (2015) 'Policing Muslim communities in partnership: "integration", belonging and resistance', in N. El-Enany and E. Bruce-Jones (eds) *Justice, Resistance and Solidarity: Race and Policing in England and Wales*. Runneymede Trust: London, 18–20.

UKCISA (2015) *International student statistics: UK higher education*, 18 May, www.ukcisa.org.uk/Info-for-universities-colleges--schools/Policy-research-statistics/Research-statistics/International-students-in-UK-HE, accessed 15 December 2015.

Walseth, K. (2003) 'Islam's view on physical activity and sport', *International Review for the Sociology of Sport* 38(1): 45–60.

Walseth, K. and Fasting, K. (2004) 'Sport as a means of integrating minority women', *Sport in Society* 7(1): 109–129.

Walseth, K. and Strandbu, A. (2014) 'Young Norwegian-Pakistani women and sport: how does culture and religiosity matter?', *European Physical Education Review* 20(4): 489–507.

Watson, H. (1994) 'Women and the veil: personal responses to global process', in Ahmed, A. S. and Hastings, D. (eds) *Islam, Globalization and Postmodernity*. London: Routledge, 141–159.

Yegenoglu, M. (1998) *Colonial Fantasies: Towards a Feminist Reading of Orien-talism*. London: Cambridge University Press.

Chapter 7

Lesbian, gay, bisexual and transgender young people's experiences of PE and the implications for youth sport participation and engagement

Scarlett Drury, Annette Stride, Anne Flintoff and Sarah Williams

Introduction

A long-standing rationale for physical education (PE) is that it introduces young people to the knowledge and skills necessary for post-school physical activity and sport participation (Green, 2012). However, evidence suggests that PE leaves many young people feeling deficient in relation to their bodies, identities and physical performances, contributing to a disengagement from physical activity. For example, research with young women, minority ethnic communities, disabled young people and those from working class backgrounds has noted the problematic nature of PE (see Kirk *et al.*, 2006). Yet we know little about lesbian, gay, bisexual and transgender[1] (LGBT) young people's experiences of PE, or their involvement in physical activity upon leaving school. This gap is concerning given Stonewall's (2012) findings that 55 per cent of young lesbian, gay and bisexual (LGB) people experience homophobic bullying in school, 60 per cent report that teachers who witness homophobic bullying never intervene, and only half of LGB students report their schools as saying homophobia is wrong. It is important to note that Stonewall's research did not include transgender young people's experiences, highlighting a further and significant gap in our understandings. Such evidence strengthens Carless' (2012) call for 'gay and bisexual stories' (and we would add transgender) to be shared to help understand young people's experiences, and to inform PE and youth sport practice.

Given the sensitivity of addressing issues of sexual identity with young people, previous research has tended to ask young *adults* to reflect *back* on their school experiences (e.g. Caudwell, 2014; Sykes, 2011), or used fictional or auto-ethnographic narratives (Carless, 2012; Sparkes, 1997). This chapter, likewise, draws upon data from young adults (aged 17–21) reflecting back on their experiences of PE and sport at school. The data were generated as part of a wider initiative by the Rugby Football League (RFL)[2] to help inform policy and practice around issues of diversity, equity and inclusion. As part of this wider agenda, the RFL consulted with a number of under-represented communities, including a group of LGBT young people, to understand their experiences and perceptions of the game. Although the data generated through these discussions were not intended for the purposes of academic research, their reflections, particularly those about school PE, motivated us to write this chapter. Its aim is to consider LGBT young people's experiences of PE and school sport, how these experiences may influence their current involvement in physical activity and, importantly, highlight the implications for inclusive PE and youth sport practice.

Identities, categories, queer theory and social justice

Before presenting literature on gender and sexuality in PE, it is useful to outline some of the key theoretical debates including the complexities around terminology related to gender, sex and sexuality. While we use the term LGBT, we are mindful of the potential tensions that emerge from its use. Identity categories, such as 'gay', 'lesbian', 'woman' or 'black and minority ethnic' have been used as important political tools to highlight the *shared* nature of discrimination and to fight for social justice for oppressed groups based on one aspect of identity. However, less useful are the ways in which such categories work to *homogenise* groups of people, downplaying the differences amongst individuals within a group that result from their intersecting identities (Bonnett and Carrington, 2000). In relation to the term LGBT, Caudwell (2014) argues that we must move beyond homogenised understandings that imply a shared *LGBT* identity and experience. She suggests such thinking can reinforce a 'hierarchy of (in)visibility' in which LGBT is used to refer predominantly to the needs of lesbian and gay individuals, resulting in bisexual identities rarely being considered and transgender issues either overlooked altogether or tokenistically positioned as an additive to non-normative *sexual* identities (Caudwell, 2014). In this sense, the uncritical use of the term LGBT is problematic because it has the potential to conflate issues of *gender*, which relate more closely with transgender individuals, and *sexuality*, which are more commonly a concern for lesbian, gay and bisexual individuals. This is an important distinction to make as Lucas-Carr and Krane (2011: 533) note: 'while there are some common experiences among LGBT individuals, issues surrounding gender identity differ from those related to sexual orientation'.

A further issue associated with the use of identity categories is that they risk *reproducing* rather than challenging the very binaries around which discriminatory practices are based. For example, in relation to sexuality, the dominant position of heterosexuality is dependent upon the existence of a marginalised oppositional 'other', in this case homosexuality. This means that the claiming of a homosexual identity results in reasserting heterosexuality as normative. Identity politics-based approaches towards social justice using LGBT or individual identities such as 'lesbian', 'gay', 'bisexual' and 'transgender' may therefore be limited in their aim of overcoming discrimination.

Acknowledging these caveats over the use of identity categories for social justice, here we draw on queer theory since it provides a framework that acknowledges the fluidity of identities, and is useful for examining the discourses that produce binary ways of thinking about gender and sexuality. In turn, this enables a critique of the dominance of heterosexuality and cisgender[3] identities in discourse and practice. Another benefit of adopting a queer perspective is that it enables a shift in focus from an emphasis on challenging homophobia, towards an examination of the interplay between discourses of homophobia *and* heteronormativity. Homophobia is generally understood to refer to 'the irrational fear or intolerance of lesbians, gay men, and bisexual people' (Griffin, 1998: xv). Heteronormativity refers to 'the institutions, structures of understanding, and practical orientations that make heterosexuality not only coherent – that is organised as a sexuality – but also privileged' (Berlant and Warner, 1998: 565). The discourse of heteronormativity not only insists on the normativity of heterosexual relationships, but reasserts a binary gender logic that positions men and women in relationships of opposition. Thus, heteronormativity is concerned with the regulation of *gender* identities and *sexualities*, and is therefore connected with transphobia, 'the dislike, fear or hatred of transgender people' (Clarke, 2013: 89). We now turn to how some of these issues have been addressed in PE.

Feminist scholars have provided important insight into the ways in which homophobia is used to police gender boundaries, (re)producing patterns of inequality in PE contexts (Clarke, 2013). More recently, Anderson's (2012) research on masculinity and sexuality in PE has indicated that homophobia *may* be diminishing as young people become more accepting of non-normative sexual identities. Anderson (2012) suggests that shifts in the nature of contemporary masculinities have resulted in a decrease in homophobia, 'homo-hysteria' and a widespread tolerance of homosexuality in PE and school sport contexts. If this is indeed the case, it is a positive shift; however, there remains a need to be cautious in assuming that the absence of homophobia equates to an environment that is inclusive of all non-normative sexualities and gender identities. Research underpinned by queer theory questions the *types* of gay identities afforded social acceptance. There is evidence to suggest that gay men are still expected to embody hegemonic masculinity built around heteronormative gender ideals if they are to be accepted (Wellard, 2006). Indeed, efforts to tackle homophobia are often premised on the notion that stereotypes of gay men as weak and effeminate, or lesbian women as butch and masculine must be dispelled. This has significant implications for all young people who do not conform to dominant gender norms, but particularly those who are non-heterosexual[4] or transgender. The discussions presented within this section demonstrate a need to move beyond a sole focus on homophobia to consider also the impact of heteronormativity and transphobia. Queer and feminist theories of gender and sexuality provide frameworks to challenge and question the normativities associated with the social construction of gendered and sexual identities.[5]

Understanding gendered and sexual experiences in PE

There has been a sustained focus on how the content, organisation and pedagogy of PE creates particular sets of conditions that advantage and value some young people, whilst disadvantaging and rejecting others (Penney and Evans, 2000). Although a focus on disability, race and intersectional identities have been more evident in contemporary research, earlier research in PE focused upon gender as a key difference. For example, Scraton (1992) highlighted how the promotion of 'acceptable' femininities within girls' PE operates through teachers' expectations, coupled with a narrow range of curriculum activities, both of which serve to alienate many girls. Single-sex environments have also been highlighted as problematic in reinforcing ideologies of masculinity and femininity. However, alternatively, mixed-sex settings can also marginalise girls' involvement and reproduce gendered power relations through boys' physical and verbal domination (Hills and Croston, 2011; Oliver and Hamzeh, 2010).

Research also demonstrates that many boys have a problematic relationship with PE. Tischler and McCaughtry (2011) point to the complex processes of negotiating masculine identities within PE. They note that only a small number of boys are able to embody hegemonic masculinity, and benefit from the ways PE is constructed and delivered. Research about boys' experiences also highlights the prevalence of homophobia as a tool for policing the boundaries of 'appropriate' masculinities in PE. This has significant implications for many young boys, but particularly those who do not identify as heterosexual. PE is a particular school setting where dominant discourses of gender and sexuality are magnified, and homophobia and heteronormativity are pervasive (Block, 2014; McCaughtry et al., 2005). As Clarke (2013: 90) identifies:

> Schools in general, and PE departments in particular, are sites for social and moral regulation wherein gender and gender roles are produced against a dominant heterosexuality, and marginalised, often

vilified, homosexuality. These gender roles and relations are constructed along narrow, highly demarcated lines which are exemplified through normative and stereotyped expectations about what it is to be or become male or female.

Despite arguments that homophobia is diminishing in some sporting contexts, Anderson (2012) recognises that homophobia in PE may be linked to the competitive sport-based approaches that dominate its provision where hegemonic masculinity and normative bodily ideals are valorised. Both Sykes (2011) and Larsson *et al.* (2011) note the ways in which the physical movements of the body are read and interpreted in ways that imply gendered and sexual identities. Gay males are persistently positioned as the antithesis of athletic physicality (O'Brien *et al.*, 2013) and women involved in sports, as indicated, are commonly labelled as lesbian (Griffin, 1998). Although this is problematic for all young people in PE, it has a particularly damaging impact on young LGBT students who can face feelings of isolation within education (Block, 2014). In the UK, these issues have been compounded by the legacy of legislation, particularly Section 28, which created a climate in which LGBT issues were (and continue to be) not always appropriately addressed within schools (Clarke, 2013). Research demonstrates that teachers are inadequately prepared to support LGBT students, and many do not challenge homophobic and transphobic discrimination appropriately (Clarke, 2013; Stonewall, 2012).

Methodology

We draw on data gathered as part of a Rugby Football League (RFL) initiative, aimed at increasing the inclusivity of the game for LGBT communities. The RFL has a particularly strong record for its inclusive practice,[6] and one of us (Sarah), as the former Equality and Diversity manager of the RFL, was centrally involved in the initiative.[7] A series of activities were organised with a small group of LGBT young people aged 17–21 based in the north of England. Session 1 involved discussions around their experiences of PE and sport at school and within the wider community, including their experiences and perceptions of rugby league, and barriers to participation. Session 2 involved the young people attending one game at the Four Nations[8] tournament. The final session involved a skills and touch rugby session followed by a focus group discussion about their experiences of the initiative, and the ways in which the RFL could work towards inclusive practice for LGBT people.

As highlighted above, our motivations for writing this chapter are to contribute to countering the invisibility of LGBT young people's experiences of PE. By drawing on the issues raised during the focus group discussions and broader literature, we represent these data in the form of three short, melded, fictional narratives: Ben, who identifies as a young gay man; Kate, a young woman who sees her sexual identity as fluid and chooses not to label herself; and Amber, who identifies as a transgender woman. Narratives are a useful tool in social justice work as they provide an opportunity to give voice to absent stories (Johnson and Parry, 2016). They also allow connections to be made between the daily lived social realities of individuals, their multiple identities, and the macro societal relations of power in which they are constituted (Carless, 2012; Dowling, 2012). They can also act as a persuasive means of opening readers' minds to perspectives that may be different from their own (see Dowling, 2012).

Stories from LGBT youth

Amber's story

Team sports are just not for me, in fact I don't think sport is, full stop. But my mates were all really keen to come to the game so I sit here, getting colder, looking forward to the drive home and the chance to catch up on the gossip. I know why team sports don't interest me, I was never any good at them. End of. My early memories of football and rugby in boys' PE so horrendous they refuse to become part of a dim and distant past. I remember my last encounter with football, the inter-form tournament where I was cajoled, then threatened and forced into goal to make up the numbers. Then, the humiliation as my uncoordinated effort was put on display for all to see. But, as if that wasn't enough, there was the verbal stuff. The chants come flooding back, refusing to be quieted. 'Why've ya got that poof in goal? She'd be better with the cheerleaders!', 'What's the queer doing here? Do ya wanna lose or what?', 'IT, IT, IT is shit. IT, IT, IT is shit', their voices getting louder and louder competing with the roars of the crowd in the stadium. I try to banish their chants from my head, but a prickle of annoyance works its way across my scalp as I give myself a hard time for still being bothered.

And then we got the green light. After months of campaigning in the school, I was given permission to switch PE classes. Great news I thought, the school have finally recognised my right to get changed with the girls and do activities with them. I remember the relief I felt at not having to go back to Mr Clark's class, escaping boys' PE, with its smelly changing rooms, the rough, physical activities, and loud, cliquey groups of boys, bullying anyone different. But my optimism was short lived because of the PPP crew as they called themselves, Posh, Pretty and Perfect. The constant name calling remained, as did the refusing to work with me. Luckily, I had some girlfriends so I was never stuck on my own like in the boys' class. But they never made it easy for me, the PPP's, Pretentious, Painfully Stupid and Pretty Awful as we renamed them. I smile at that memory. The changing rooms were the worst. All eyes seemed to be on me, piercing me with their stares; accusing, loathing, hate, fear, pity evident in those looks. So, I developed some strategies. Arrive first, bag one of the corner spots so I was partially hidden from prying eyes on both sides. But that didn't stop them screaming in horror whenever Miss' back was turned or she left the room. Then, ultimate humiliation, she asked me to change in the store cupboard like some circus freak. Didn't say a thing to the PPP lot, like it was all my fault.

Ben's story

The excitement of the crowd swells as the winger charges down the line, every muscle straining as he clutches the ball to his chest. His other arm stretches out to ward off the huge centre bearing down from the left flank. But too little too late as the wiry number 2 throws himself into the air, suspended for eternity before he hits the ground. Then, triumphantly he jumps to his feet, slamming the ball down. His teammates huddle round and he is momentarily lost amongst the crowd of back slaps and grinning faces until he emerges, thumping his chest, looking to the crowd for their approval. Roars of appreciation echo around the stadium. I'm envious of their camaraderie, their easy physicality, their enjoyment from a sport that brings me nothing but bad memories. It wasn't the game as such. Given half a chance I'd have liked to be more involved, the chance to push myself, get rid of my pent up aggression, experience the camaraderie of a team. And I think I'd have been quite good – I've got the build and I'm speedy when I put my mind to it.

No, it was all the other stuff I had to put up with that ruined rugby for me – well most games in PE, thinking about it. Like classmates refusing to work with me, openly verbalising their 'concerns'. 'Sir, I don't wanna be groped by him', they'd whine, acting all innocent, like I was some sort of perv wanting to catch a feel. No one passed me the ball in rugby, worried they'd have to tackle the 'poof'. Mind you, that didn't stop their sly punches in the scrum, and the late tackles in football. Huh, what was that if not unwanted touching? To make things worse, Mr Robson, my old PE teacher, did nothing, implicitly siding with the bullies with his 'ignorance is bliss' attitude. On a 'good' day he might acknowledge what was going on with a shrug of exasperation and a 'what do you expect?' look directed towards me. It was the same in the other activities, football, basketball, and worse in gymnastics and dance, everyone avoiding me in case we had to hold hands. Of course, they all expected the 'gay boy' to excel but I hated it – got two left feet my mum says! To be honest, I used to forget my kit when it got really bad, accidentally on purpose like. And old Robbo wasn't bothered. You could see the relief on his face when I turned up without kit. He'd let me just hang out in the changing rooms or go to the library…. Things could have been a lot different.

Kate's story

We make our way to the minibus, jostled by the crowds fighting to get from the stadium. We wade through discarded chip papers and kick at plastic cups, their last dregs of lager frothing onto the pavement. A fine drizzle has begun and the oncoming car lights sparkle in the misty rain. I was kind of dreading coming to the game if I'm honest, my apprehension fuelled by recollections of PE, memories I'd rather forget. Looking back it was kinda weird 'cause I was OK at sport, used to play football outside school. But PE was like, completely different. Only boys got to play cool sports like football, rugby and basketball. Girls had to do netball, hockey and badminton which I hated. A couple of us asked Miss once if we could have a go at rugby. I can hear her now in that prim and proper voice: 'Girls are not allowed to play rugby in our school because they might get a nose bleed.' Seriously? After that me and my mate had to put up with a load of verbals from the rest of them calling us 'Lezza' and 'Dyke'. So original! If they'd known I played football that would've been it. Only 'chavvy lezzas' play football they used to say. I clamber into the back of the minibus, grabbing a window seat, wanting to be lost in my thoughts.

No, PE wasn't a good time for me. Like the whole business of getting changed. I shudder at the thought and instinctively wrap my arms around my body. It was enough to put me off before the lesson began. The minute I walked into the changing rooms the noise levels would drop and Clare Marlow's gang would quickly turn round and face the walls, sniggering to themselves. Then there'd be the furtive looks to see if I was checking them out. As if? I've got more taste than that. It was all so embarrassing. In the end Miss used to turn a blind eye when I sidled into the toilets to get changed. And she let me go to the changing rooms five minutes before class ended so I'd be out of the showers before the rest of them came back. I don't think she could cope with their screams of horror and protests of having to be seen naked by a lesbian. Looking back, I'm sure Miss thought she was doing me a favour but really she should have said something to them. There was none of that at the football club. When I first joined I felt welcome straightaway. It was a really positive environment, no one bothered if you were gay or straight. And the coach was ace, helped develop my skills, built my confidence. But then he left and the new one was a bit more serious, giving us training plans, and a couple of my mates left so I stopped going.

Discussion

The narratives raise a number of issues about LGBT young people's experiences that have significant implications for the provision of PE, and how this supports their out-of-school sport experiences, which are considered next.

The gendered PE curriculum

The narratives illustrate the ways in which many of the practices of PE (at least in England) work to construct rather than challenge gendered binaries of girl/boy (Penney and Evans, 2000). Competitive team games dominate the curriculum, with gendered forms offered separately to girls and boys. For boys like Ben, the games are rugby and football, and although comfortable and confident of his own capabilities, his opportunities to develop a viable athletic identity are undermined by other students' readings of his sexuality. This provides testimony to the way in which gay male sexuality, regardless of the extent to which it conforms to normative masculinity, is positioned at odds with heteronormative notions of male athleticism. Similarly, Kate's story reflects the continuing stereotyping of physical activities as 'female' or 'male' by some PE teachers, and their power to close down or limit girls' learning experiences on the basis of these. Her story further illustrates the ways in which gendered stereotypes around physicality are closely linked to those of sexuality (Green and Scraton, 2000). Out-of-school footballing opportunities present safer spaces for her engagement in the game than PE contexts, where homophobic bullying is prevalent.

These young people's experiences of a gendered curriculum are exacerbated by the sex-segregated nature of PE provision, still common in many schools in England. Whilst in some instances single-sex PE can provide safe spaces for particular groups of young people (see Hills and Croston, 2012), they can also be problematic in reinforcing binary ways of thinking around gender. This is particularly apparent in boys' PE, known to be a key site for the reproduction of hierarchies of power shaped around hegemonic forms of masculinity. Single-sex classes for PE can also be particularly problematic for transgender young people like Amber. Her reflections point to the ways in which the interactions between students in the informal spaces of PE (such as the changing rooms) can contribute to the policing of rigid conceptions of gender, as well as to the limited resources available on which teachers are able to draw to address transgender students' needs, issues we discuss below.

Unsafe spaces

The narratives point to the importance of acknowledging the cultural and social dimensions of PE spaces. As Banks (2005: 187) argues, space is 'a dynamic social site where power struggles occur, hierarchies are established, and identity-informing interactions take place'. Spaces can be sites that promote normative ways of being, leading to discrimination and exclusion. As Valentine (2007: 19) notes:

> When individual identities are 'done' differently in particular temporal moments they rub against, and so expose, these dominant spatial

orderings that define who is in place/out of place, who belongs and who does not ... [to] produce moments of exclusion for particular groups.

The narratives highlight how LGBT identities 'rub against' the 'dominant spatial ordering' of heternormativity and 'ideal' notions of masculinity and femininity to define these students as 'out of place' in PE.

The narratives of Amber and Kate single out the changing room as a space that creates opportunities for bullying that often goes unchallenged. Much of this bullying stems from the implicit policing of bodily norms by peers at a time when young people are most likely to express anxieties around the appearance of their bodies (Gorely *et al.*, 2003). This situation is exacerbated by the open and communal nature of many school PE changing rooms where the body is most 'on show' (O'Donovon and Kirk, 2007). This can create significant discomfort for those transgender students who are concerned about the ways in which their bodies are 'read' and interpreted by others. Amber's narrative highlights the complex issues that a gender-rigid PE poses for transgender young people and the challenges for teachers in trying to work for their inclusion and safety.

Teachers' pedagogies

The narratives also point to the importance of teachers' pedagogies in reinforcing gender and sexuality norms which can, in turn, play a significant part in how LGBT young people come to understand themselves. For Kate, the teacher's messages about 'appropriate' activities for girls reinforce students' beliefs about the 'type' of girl that participates in so called 'boys' sports. It is therefore not surprising to see that she keeps secret her out-of-school involvement in football. However, as well as *what* activities are on offer to girls and boys in the curriculum, the nature of the pedagogy and *how* these are taught, is also significant. Flintoff (2008) shows how a sport performance pedagogy continues to dominate secondary PE practice, creating environments in which many young people come to understand themselves as 'lacking' physical abilities. Kirk and Gorely (2000) have argued for the importance of an educational, task-based, pedagogy, rather than one orientated towards sports performance. In a task-based pedagogy, success depends on doing the best you can, compared with 'ego'-oriented performance pedagogy, where success depends upon being better than others. It is the former kind of pedagogy, they argue, that is needed to develop young people's lasting involvement in sport.

In all three stories, the negative memories of PE recall experiences of verbal abuse left unchallenged by teachers. These reinforce the findings of Stonewall (2012) that teachers are insufficiently equipped to deal with homophobic and transphobic bullying. In failing to address bullying between students, teachers' (in)actions serve to sanction the abuse. Teachers have an influential role in creating equitable and non-discriminatory PE cultures through their pedagogies and everyday interactions with their students. Larson *et al.* (2011) shows how it *is* possible for teachers to 'queer' their pedagogy in PE, and so create more inclusive learning environments. Yet teachers' apathy and/or inabilities to deal with bullying serves to reinforce the view that such interactions are acceptable. Whilst teachers' inactions have implications for their enjoyment in PE whilst at school, they also have far reaching effects on young people's motivation for involvement in physical activity post school, and their general health and well-being as our narratives show.

Conclusions

Our findings raise significant implications for PE and youth sport practice. Despite changes in educational policy, and a notable shift in societal attitudes towards acceptance of LGBT people in recent years, the needs of LGBT young people in schools merit further consideration. Whilst acknowledging again the importance of recognising that LGBT young people are not a homogenous group with the same experiences and perceptions of PE, nevertheless a number of common themes cut across the experiences explored here. In our research these included the gendered nature of the curriculum, the 'unsafe' spaces created by the spatial and structural organisation of PE, and teachers' practices that leave heteronormative thinking and homophobic abuse unchallenged. Our research points to the need for a more critical questioning of the pervasiveness of normative discourses of gender and sexuality within PE contexts. This may involve improving the education of teachers about issues affecting non-heterosexual and non-gender conforming young people and more adequately equipping them with the resources to tackle homophobic and transphobic bullying. We would also argue for a radical rethink of traditional approaches that continue to shape the provision of PE in many schools, including the taken-for-granted practices of sex-segregation and ubiquitous use of a competitive, sporting pedagogy. Rethinking PE practice in this way may result in a more engaging and inclusive learning experience not just for LGBT young people, but for all young people. If an important rationale for PE is that it provides young people with the opportunities to develop the physical skills, abilities and motivation to choose to participate in physical activity post-school, such a radical rethink is long overdue.

Notes

1 We acknowledge the complexities associated with defining gender and sexual identities, not least the use of such categories in research and policy/practice, and return to this below. Here we adopt the term 'transgender' as an inclusive term to refer to individuals whose gender identities are perceived as different from the gender norms typically associated with the sex ascribed at birth. This may include people who identify as transgender, transsexual, trans*, intersex, androgynous, third gender, genderqueer, or those who choose not to define their gender identity in accordance with binary gender logic.

2 The RFL is a large sports governing body in the United Kingdom.

3 Cisgender is the term used to refer to individuals whose gender identity matches up with the sex they were ascribed at birth.

4 Taking into account queer debates around identity, we use the term non-heterosexual in the same way as Elling and Janssens (2009) denoting the rejection of an exclusively heterosexual identity and subsequent positioning as non-normative in relation to dominant discourses of sexuality.

5 Although importantly, we recognise these have tended to focus on gender and insufficiently acknowledge the intersections with ethnicity and disability.

6 See www.rugby-league.com.

7 Anne, Annette and Scarlett were not involved in the initiative or data gathering, but in the discussion and analysis of the data with Sarah, we felt the findings about PE were important to share with a wider audience, hence our inclusion of them here.

8 The Four Nations tournament is a rugby league tournament between Australia, England, New Zealand and a qualifying fourth nation.

References

Anderson, E. (2012) 'Inclusive Masculinity in a Physical Education Setting', *Journal of Boyhood Studies* 6(2): 151–165.

Banks, C. A. (2005) 'Black Girls/White Spaces: Managing Identity through Memories of Schooling', in: Bettis, P. J. and Adams, N. G. (eds) *Geographies of Girlhood: Identities In-Between.* New Jersey: Lawrence Erlbaum Associates, 177–194.

Berlant, L. and Warner, M. (1998) 'Sex in Public', *Critical Inquiry* 24(4): 547–566.

Block, B. A. (2014) 'Supporting LGBTQ Students in Physical Education: Changing the Movement Landscape', *QUEST* 66: 14–26.

Bonnett, A. and Carrington, B. (2000) 'Fitting into Categories or Falling between Them? Rethinking Ethnic Classification', *British Journal of Sociology of Education* 21(4): 487–500.

Carless, D. (2012) 'Negotiating Sexuality and Masculinity in School Sport: An Autoethnography', *Sport, Education and Society* 17(5): 607–625.

Caudwell, J. (2014) '[Transgender] Young Men: Gendered Subjectivities and the Physically Active Body', *Sport, Education and Society* 19(4): 398–414.

Clarke, G. (2013) 'Challenging Heterosexism, Homophobia and Transphobia in Physical Education', in: Stidder, G. and Hayes, S. (eds) *Equity and Inclusion in Physical Education and Sport.* London: Routledge, 87–101.

Dowling, F. (2012) 'A Narrative Approach to Research in Physical Education, Youth Sport and Health', in: Dowling, F., Fitgerald, H. and Flintoff, A. (eds)

Equity and Difference in Physical Education, Youth Sport and Health: A Narrative Approach. London: Routledge, 37–59.

Elling, A. and Janssens, J. (2009) 'Sexuality as a Structural Principle in Sport Participation: Negotiating Sports Spaces', *International Review for the Sociology of Sport* 44(1): 71–86.

Flintoff, A. (2008) 'Targeting Mr Average: Participation, Gender Equity and School Sport Partnerships', *Sport, Education and Society* 13(4): 393–411.

Gorely, T., Holroyd, R. and Kirk, D. (2003) 'Masculinity, the Habitus and the Social Construction of Gender: Towards a Gender-Relevant Physical Education', *British Journal of Sociology of Education* 24(4): 429–448.

Green, K. (2012) 'Mission Impossible? Reflecting upon the Relationship between Physical Education, Youth Sport and Lifelong Participation', *Sport, Education and Society* 19(4): 357–375.

Green, K. and Scraton, S. (2000) 'Gender, Coeducation and Secondary Physical Education: A Brief Review', in: Green, K. and Hardman, K. (eds) *Physical Education: A Reader*. Oxford: Meyer & Meyer Sport, 272–290.

Griffin, P. (1998) *Strong Women, Deep Closets*. Leeds: Human Kinetics.

Hills, L. A. and Croston, A. (2011) ' "It Should Be Better All Together": Exploring Strategies for "Undoing" Gender in Coeducational Physical Education', *Sport, Education and Society* 17(5): 591–605.

Johnson, C. W. and Parry, D. C. (eds) (2016) *Fostering Social Justice through Qualitative Inquiry: A Methodological Guide*. London: Routledge.

Kirk, D. and Gorely, T. (2000) 'Challenging Thinking about the Relationship between School Physical Education and Sport Performance', *European Physical Education Review* 6(2): 119–134.

Kirk, D., Macdonald, D. and O'Sullivan, M. (eds) (2006) *The Handbook of Physical Education*. London: SAGE.

Larsson, H., Redelius, K. and Fagrell, B. (2011) 'Moving (in) the Heterosexual Matrix: On Heteronormativity in Secondary School Physical Education', *Physical Education and Sport Pedagogy*, 16(1): 67–81.

Lucas-Carr, C. B. and Krane, V. (2011) 'What Is the *T* in LGBT? Supporting Transgender Athletes through Sport Psychology', *The Sport Psychologist*, 25: 532–548.

McCaughtry, N., Dillon, S. R., Jones, E. and Smigell, S. (2005) 'Sexually Sensitive Schooling', *QUEST* 57(4): 426–443.

O'Brien, K. S., Shovelton, H. and Latner, J. D. (2013) 'Homophobia in Physical Education and Sport: The Role of Physical/Sporting Identity and Attributes, Authoritarian Aggression, and Social Dominance Orientation', *International Journal of Psychology* 48(5): 891–899.

O'Donovon, T. M. and Kirk, D. (2007) 'Managing Classroom Entry: An Ecological Analysis of Ritual Interaction and Negotiation in the Changing Room', *Sport, Education and Society* 12(4): 399–413.

Oliver, K. L. and Hamzeh, M. (2010) ' "The Boys Won't Let Us Play": Fifth-Grade Mestizas Challenge Physical Activity Discourse at School', *Research Quarterly for Exercise and Sport* 81(1): 38–51.

Penney, D. and Evans, J. (2000) 'Dictating the Play: Government Direction in Physical Education and Sport Policy Development in England and Wales', in: Green, K. and Hardman, K. (eds) *Physical Education: A Reader*. Oxford: Meyer & Meyer Sport, 84–101.

Scraton, S. (1992) *Shaping up to Womanhood: Gender and Girls' Physical Education*. Buckingham: Open University Press.

Sparkes, A. (1997) 'Ethnographic Fiction and Representing the Absent Other', *Sport, Education and Society* 2(1): 25–40.

Stonewall (2012) *The School Report: The Experiences of Gay Young People in Britain's Schools in 2012*. Cambridge.

Sykes, H. (2011) *Queer Bodies: Sexualities, Genders and Fatness in Physical Education*. New York: Peter Lang.

Tischler, A. and Mcaughtry, N. (2011) 'PE Is Not for Me: When Boys' Masculinities Are Threatened', *Research Quarterly for Exercise and Sport* 82(1): 37–48.

Valentine, G. (2007) 'Theorising and Researching Intersectionality: A Challenge for Feminist Geography', *The Professional Geographer* 59(1): 10–21.

Wellard, I. (2006) 'Exploring the Limits of Queer and Sport: Gay Men Playing Tennis', in: Caudwell, J. (ed.) *Sport, Sexualities and Queer/Theory*. London: Routledge, 76–89.

Chapter 8

Working towards social justice through participatory research with young people in sport and leisure

Annette Stride and Hayley Fitzgerald

Introduction

As critical researchers within sport and leisure our work centralises the experiences of those who are often excluded, marginalised and disadvantaged within these settings. Our research is implicitly informed by a number of the principles of social justice as outlined by Miller (2005) in Chapter 2 of this book by Wetherly *et al.* In acknowledging these principles we have reflected upon the ways in which we engage in the research process and with our participants. We concur with McNamara (2011), Fox (2013) and Bradbury-Jones and Taylor (2015) that there is a need to interrogate more fully the claims researchers make about researching and the ways in which research is undertaken. Our reflections have led us to reconsider how we generate data, and in much of our research we have favoured using more participatory approaches. In this chapter we offer some preliminary thoughts on engaging with participatory approaches, including the challenges experienced and the benefits these bring. In the spirit of extending this debate we draw on reflective accounts in our research diaries and consider the extent to which participatory approaches are achievable in sport and leisure research. We hope this chapter prompts researchers to reflect on their engagement with young people within the research process and also promotes thinking around notions of participation in sport and leisure research. Next, consideration is given to recent shifts in thinking regarding engaging young people in research, including the emerging trend to undertake participatory research and the possibilities this brings.

Researching young people in sport and leisure

Contemporary society has seen a shift in the way young people are understood. In part, this re-articulation has emerged from ideas associated with a social justice agenda, including the importance of fairness, equity and citizenship (Miller, 2005). This kind of thinking has led to an increasing recognition that there is a need to value and listen to the voices of young people to get a better understanding of their experiences. Young people have become positioned as 'experts' in their own lives, rather than deemed incapable of making useful observations about themselves and the world they occupy (Clark and Moss, 2011). This way of thinking has found purchase internationally through human rights (for example, the United Nations Convention on the Rights of the Child). At a national level, legislation (for example, the Children Act, 2004) and policy (for example, Every Child Matters, 2004) has echoed a need to recognise and engage with young people about their lives. Research, particularly that situated within childhood studies, has also advocated the merits of including and the need to include young people (James *et al.*, 1998; Save the Children, 2000). Moreover, within the broader context of empowerment and self-advocacy, a growing number of educational projects and community youth settings are engaging young people and involving them in decision-making (Barnardo's, 2002; Robinson and Taylor, 2013; Weller, 2007). According to Alderson (2008), these kinds of development have extended the nature of responsibility for young people from protection and provision to 'participation rights'.

In adopting a position that aims to promote fairness, equity and citizenship, researchers have recognised the need to reconsider the ways in which research is undertaken. As Greig *et al.* (2007) note, assumptions that regard young people as unable to contribute meaningfully to research has both influenced the research questions asked and delayed the development of methods to which young people can relate. Clark and Moss (2011) concur, advocating an imaginative rethinking of the more traditional approaches that are often adopted when researching young people's experiences. In this regard, sport and leisure research has begun to embrace the trend towards using what some consider to be participatory approaches to research. It is argued that these approaches can offer possibilities to shift the emphasis away from research *on* young people to research *with* and *by* young people (Azzarito and Kirk, 2013; O'Sullivan and MacPhail, 2010). Within sport and leisure, researchers have adopted a range of strategies in their endeavours to support participation including: photo elicitation (Azzarito and Hill, 2013; Stride, 2014); drawings (Fitzgerald, 2012); media exploration (Enright and O'Sullivan, 2013; Hamzeh and Oliver, 2012); and scrap books and journals (Hamzeh, 2011). By researching in what could be considered by some as less conventional ways, scholars are beginning to grapple with and better understand a range of issues that more positively support the participation of young people within research. It is this issue of participation that has attracted the interests of researchers and we consider this next.

Participatory research

Researchers have differing conceptions of what it means to enable young people to engage in participatory research. Indeed, earlier thinking about participation was guided by Hart's (1992) 'ladder of participation'. This ladder focuses on the varying degrees of collaboration with young people and how involvement in research can be supported. Participation from this perspective was considered in relation to the research process and is akin to McNamara's (2011) outlook that participation should move beyond tokenistic involvement and attend to the active involvement of young people in research. Later, Hart (1997) critiqued the ladder for being a simplistic metaphor for what is a complex process. For example, the ladder can imply that young people operating at the higher levels are involved in superior projects, which may not be the case. Moreover, while the ladder provides a crude measure of 'how much' young people are enabled to participate, it does not problematise 'who' is being enabled to participate (Holland *et al.*, 2008). In this respect, Holland *et al.* (2008) argue that participatory research privileges those who are already privileged, those considered to be emotionally literate and those for whom White, middle-class (and we would add non-disabled) means of communication are the norm. What the ladder fails to acknowledge is that 'young person' as a social category interplays with other identity markers including disability, ethnicity, sexuality, gender and class. It is this interplay that creates categories of difference and inequalities within society. From a research perspective, when these identity markers intersect with institutional structures of power, equality and fairness in research participation can be compromised (Dentith *et al.*, 2012).

The need to extend consideration beyond those who are already privileged becomes apparent with regard to some of the young people with severe learning disabilities that we have worked with, including those who do not communicate verbally. These young people are all too often excluded from a research project where the preferred approach to data collection involves interviews. This restricted view of listening, and inflexibility in research design, often means many people with disabilities who engage using augmented forms of communication are presumed to be unable to make meaningful contributions to research. This perspective is often not questioned as it merely replicates wider views within society that position disabled people as less able than non-disabled people. We have found engaging with young disabled people becomes far more productive when proper consideration is given to the young person's communication needs. Participation in this context is fundamentally about ensuring fairness and equity in the research design and data collection strategies that reflect the research participant's preferred means of communication.

More recently, Dentith *et al.* (2012) have proposed a number of features that participatory research should encompass. In part, these features attend to the criticisms levelled at Hart's (1992) ladder in relation to 'how' and 'who' is enabled within research. These features include: (1) researchers and participants co-conceptualising and implementing research; (2) collective reflection and critique on practice, relationships and interpretation; (3) communitarian politics where change is aimed at social justice and participant satisfaction; and (4) research and education involving the development of skills for organising, disseminating and fostering social change which takes place in partnership between the researcher and participants. Next, we reflect upon our experiences of engaging with participatory research by considering the extent to which we were able to work (or not) in participatory ways.

The (im)possibilities of participatory research

Engaging in participatory research can be a very exciting and attractive proposition for researchers. However, the reality of attempting to undertake participatory research is less straightforward. By drawing on reflective accounts from our research diaries we have found a number of recurring issues that contribute to the debates around the possibilities and challenges of participatory research. Next, we discuss four of these issues: 'what is participation?'; 'where's the data?'; 'time'; and 'exhilarated and exhausted'.

What is participation?

As outlined earlier, participatory research and participation in research has been interpreted in different ways. For some, participatory research involves ensuring research participants are engaged with interactive data collection methods. As Hayley (HF) reflects, her concern was about stimulating the interest of students: 'What can I do that will switch the students on so I get a glimpse of their lives?' This is in contrast to simply completing a questionnaire or responding to interview questions. In Annette's (AS) research young women were invited to share their experiences of PE and physical activity by taking photographs, drawing, writing and mapping. Here the emphasis is on the data collection phase of the research process and utilising collection methods that promote active engagement. Annette's diary reflects a recognition that interactive approaches to data collection may be more appealing than traditional approaches as they offered the girls in her study some degree of flexibility in their engagement.

> The girls' responses to the 'brief' I had given them were a little different from what I was anticipating. I envisaged them using the cardboard boxes as physical repositories to place objects, e.g. kit, and/or reflections about PE. As they placed these items in the box I thought we could talk about why these were included to open up discussions

about their experiences. Instead, the girls enthusiastically grabbed the felt tip pens and started to decorate the boxes quite openly with their likes and dislikes about the subject. I was pleasantly surprised during this session at how many of the girls seemed at ease chatting about PE, but also how some of them demonstrated a deeper level of critical reflection regarding the subject. For example, they critiqued curriculum content and classroom dynamics and linked these to broader issues around sexism and bullying.

(AS)

Annette highlights how the young people involved in her research seemed to respond well to the research activities they were asked to undertake. While there is some evidence of promoting 'collective reflection', there is less emphasis on the other features of participation identified by Dentith *et al.* (2012).

Participation in research can also be extended to other phases of the research process. For example, in Annette's research the young women developed questions and interviewed each other in a series of 'Big Sister' style interviews. Similarly, Hayley has conducted research where students developed questions and interviewed their teachers and practitioners in community sport. While this may seem to be a more collaborative endeavour that promotes involvement progressing upwardly on Hart's (1992) ladder of participation, it was clear to both of us that these activities were rather tokenistic, something we were trying to avoid.

I've got the students interviewing teachers. They seem really up for it and have even helped with the questions. We've practiced and practiced. I can see they are excited about doing this. Sam[1] sees it as a big responsibility and talked about it to his form group. Tom keeps going on about how they will be in charge and the teachers have to answer them. I do wonder though if I've catapulted them into this. I'm not sure they understand why they are doing the interviews, how it fits with the research, and what will happen with what they find out.

(HF)

In this instance, although participation extended into data collection, we would consider this kind of participation to be somewhat limited. For example, when considered alongside the criteria of Dentith *et al.* (2012) the students were less involved in conceptualising research and little attention was directed towards collective reflection and action towards social change. On reflection, our attempts were more akin to a quick fix to participation that was premised on our terms and concerns, rather than those of the young people we were working with.

Where's the data?

Unlike the research projects reflected on above we have both attempted to adopt a more holistic approach to participation that aligned to the key features of participation proposed by Dentith *et al.* (2012). This has led to some interesting outcomes. For example, by co-conceptualising research you have to be prepared to forgo a preconceived agenda for research that you may favour. In this respect the research focus and kinds of data generated may not be what you anticipate collecting.

> This isn't the data I wanted to collect. The disabled students have decided they want to do research on their non-disabled classmates. That's not the group I wanted to collect data from. I've found this hard to come to terms with but I do have the flexibility to go with what they want to do. And I suppose I can't claim to be involving the disabled students if it's on my terms all the time.
>
> (HF)

As Hayley reflects here, the direction the research ended up taking was not what she had anticipated. Consequently, her expected outcomes in terms of finding out about the disabled students' experiences would not materialise. Hayley reluctantly accepted that her plans would be somewhat compromised. We recognise that this way of approaching research may be challenging, particularly for those researchers who are not prepared and/or unwilling to compromise. Yet, we believe researchers wishing to work in socially just ways need to be open and flexible in their research endeavours.

Another issue that emerges concerning participatory research relates to the distractions that take us away from the generation of data. Indeed, we have found that the planning of research related activities wrapped around the data collection sometimes becomes more important than the data collection.

> I've spent hours on this display, I think it's taken me longer to put together than doing the research with the students. It does feel like it's a focal point, something to show what we've been doing. Well you can't miss it. A lot of time has been invested in it, but I'm beginning to see how it's helping to make a statement about the research and the importance of positioning the students as informants about themselves and their PE experiences.
>
> (HF)

We have both reflected on spending more time on a range of activities to the extent that generating data seemed incidental. Similarly, we recognise the incredible amount of work that is required to support students to be co-researchers when researching in participatory ways. For example, as Hayley reflects, she spent weeks helping a small group of students in developing an interview schedule and practising interviewing; although, by her own admission, she believes she naively underestimated the research competence of the young people and the challenges of equipping them with the necessary skills to become co-researchers (Bradbury-Jones and Taylor, 2015).

> I've really underestimated my role in helping the students to develop research skills. I have to remember I'm not working with undergraduate students, these are 12 and 13 year olds. Even explaining the notion of research took a lot of thinking. They liked the idea of them being a 'news reporter' and I went with that. Developing the questions took some time. I don't think I managed to make that activity interesting. But they loved doing practice interviews and actually became good at listening and probing. This part of the research has taken weeks but on reflection I shouldn't have expected it to be any different.
>
> (HF)

On other occasions we reflected on how the research activities we had planned did not lend themselves to generating data. Here, Annette contemplates how the combination of working with the girls at lunchtime and bringing pizzas to the school did not provide the most conducive environment in which to engage the girls in research. Ironically, Annette was convinced that this context would generate rich data but in reality the pizzas and timing created an unwelcome distraction from her agenda.

> I'll be lucky if I get anything from today, feel like the visit over there was a waste of time. When you think about the time spent planning the activities, 90 minutes round trip, collecting of pizzas, and all they did for the hour was talk about the pizzas, boys and who had fallen out with whom. There was no getting them on (my) agenda today. I had to respect this was their time and let them vent their frustrations over what's important to them.
>
> (AS)

This account illustrates how, in attempting to work in participatory ways, Annette recognised the importance of creating spaces that facilitate the girls' agency. However, working in this way heightened Annette's frustrations around the limited data generated. These frustrations were compounded by the considerable amount of time that had gone into the planning of her research activities. As we next discuss, time is a commodity that can sometimes impinge on the possibilities of engaging in participatory research with young people.

Time

As we have already indicated, beyond the 'normal' time of collecting data thought needs to be given to the ways in which data are to be collected. This takes careful planning as captured in Annette's diary.

> I cannot believe the time and effort that has gone into this and still no data collected – reading up on making research interesting; thinking of activities; sourcing cameras; ordering stationery; then establishing each girl's postcode, photocopying local, regional, national and inter-national maps; creating workbooks to help them reflect, not to mention constructing interview schedules. I just hope these ideas appeal to the girls or all this may be for nothing.
>
> (AS)

Of course, time is a precious commodity in the life of an academic. Finding time for research can be a rare luxury that is grabbed at amongst teaching commitments, administrative duties, endless meetings, paperwork and trialling the latest education initiative. When that research takes extra time to plan, execute and disseminate, we recognise that for some academics it is far easier just to collect the data and run. While we encourage researchers to explore opportunities to work in participatory ways with their research participants, we are also pragmatic and recognise the need to be realistic about what can be achieved within the time available.

Negotiating time to be with potential research participants can also be challenging. In our school-based research we have found the time we have typically been offered would result in the participants being taken out of PE. This is something we have both tried to avoid.

> I've just got a message from Paul telling me the students are going to be pulled out of PE. I've gone with this before when it's been a one-off rush job. But I'm going to have to talk to him. It's not right pulling them out of PE when I'm asking them to talk about PE and sport.
>
> (HF)

At other times we have been afforded the opportunity to work with young people in other curriculum areas such as Annette's work with girls in their Personal, Social, Citizenship, Health and Education (PSCHE) lessons. Working with young people in curriculum time adds legitimacy to the research project for the students, parents and the school. However, we also recognise that undertaking research in school time can be problematic and as Annette reflects, may limit student choice.

> I question the extent to which these girls perceived they had choice over whether to be actively engaged in the production of the research artefacts. The fact that these activities were located in PSCHE lessons,

and part of the girls' formal education, will no doubt have influenced their decision to engage and did little to help break down power relations between myself and the girls. Nevertheless, I worked hard to create non-authoritarian and informal relationships, using additional strategies to distance myself from the teacher identity. For example, I answered their questions about my life, and their eating of sweets and texting on mobile phones, not permissible in class, went unchallenged.

(AS)

While we recognised other pockets of time we could draw upon in the school day, including lunch times, break times, before and after school, we were mindful that this too is precious for many young people.

After spending some time in the school (form, break, lunch and PE lessons) I realise that finding time to spend with the girls will be difficult. Form time is 20 minutes and from my experience is very busy and hectic, break time is also short as are lunch times and these are the few opportunities girls get to spend with their friends. I also get the impression from the teachers that the girls will be reluctant to stay behind and/or come into school earlier to be involved in my research.

(AS)

These kinds of negotiations regarding accessing students and getting time have contributed to the emotional rollercoaster we have experienced and it is to these kinds of issues that we next turn.

Exhilarated and exhausted researcher

A recurring theme in our diaries concerns the exhilaration experienced in our attempts to support participatory research.

I feel a huge sense of relief, don't know what I was so worried about, thinking that nobody would want to do my research. I've got 90 out of 120 girls wanting to be involved! My only dilemma now is that I can't work with this many.

(AS)

What a day, I'm delighted with how it's gone. I'm beginning to feel like everyone's on board and we all seem to be having a good time, including me!

(HF)

At times we felt exhilarated when we saw students positively engaging within the research process, when students felt they had been successful or in response to moments where we had helped students to think a little differently.

> There's been a real breakthrough, James is finally getting involved. It's taken him ages to realise this isn't a normal lesson and I'm not a teacher. He's beginning to buy into the idea that he, along with the others, can shape the direction of the research.
>
> (HF)

> I think they are finally beginning to think more critically. Today one set of girls talked about the differences in activities undertaken in boys' PE compared to their own. Interestingly, they began to question the explanations given to them for these differences by their teachers. Some girls articulated teachers' beliefs were out of date and stereotypical, with others claiming the situation was both unfair and sexist.
>
> (AS)

This sense of exhilaration was also tempered with frustration, when things we thought were going well did not continue. We have come to realise that this is just part of the process of researching in participatory ways.

> On paper I look organised and planned but in practice this goes out of the window. I had developed a two week interview timetable, detailing which girls to see, either in form period or at work placement.... Two of the girls I have been to see at their placements were not there.... Bebo was not in form this morning and Messa didn't turn up till last five minutes for form interview.... Re-scheduled her interview for lunch but she got into trouble on way to first lesson and so had to go to lunch time detention.... Noticed a note on teacher's desk to say Borat is on placement, news to me as she was one of the girls I was going to interview in school this week! Beginning to panic, only done one physical activity interview! Time is running out.
>
> (AS)

When our plans or research related activities with young people did not go well our diaries reveal a greater awareness of the work that we were putting into the research. As Annette reflects, sometimes this was coupled with a sense of exhaustion.

> I'm exhausted by the constant getting up early to get into school, the adrenaline rush before going to class, the monotony of having to listen through the audio files to capture questions to ask in the following session, and then doing it all over again the following day and trying to keep a handle on which girls are up to date with their work and

whose outstanding what. I am also coming in at least one day at the weekend and working later than usual so think this is all taking its toll.

(AS)

Despite these frustrations and low points in our research journeys, the accompanying highs seem to feed our continued commitment to participatory approaches. As we conclude, our research diaries have been integral to our critical reflections and serve as a key resource for guiding our attempts to research in participatory ways.

Conclusions

In the first two chapters of this book it is contended that social justice matters fundamentally to leisure and sport. The essence of this argument focuses upon issues of access to and participation in sport and leisure opportunities. In this chapter we have extended this argument to include participation in and access to research. Moreover, we would add that it should not be presumed that researchers working on social justice projects will be researching in socially just ways. We have found it useful to draw upon participatory approaches as a means of working fairly and equitably within our research. Yet, as we have also outlined, working with young people in participatory ways is not straightforward, and can be challenging. For example, it requires a researcher who questions and reflects upon ideas about the possibilities of participation, what it is and what it could be. We believe that researchers attempting to work in a participatory manner to promote social justice should be cautious about the claims they make. We would encourage researchers to engage in open dialogue regarding not only the extent of contributions made by their participatory approach but also the limitations and challenges encountered.

Another challenge to consider concerns the time commitment required when working with participatory approaches. As we have reflected within this chapter, our own experiences illustrate the considerable time required to plan, organise and deliver research activities. When research participants are actively involved in the research this may require significant time to develop their skills to enable them to contribute meaningfully to the process. On occasions, the development of the research participants takes on more significance than the generation of data. This can leave the researcher confused and panicking about the lack of data. It is at times like these that we have come to value our research diaries. They have served as a useful reminder of the social justice agenda we are working towards. Our diaries have also offered an effective means of reflecting on the power we hold, not only in the choice of research topic, and who is chosen to be researched, but also in the ways in which research questions are posed and how the results are disseminated. As we work towards social justice using participatory approaches we will continue to scribe in our diaries to help us to reflect critically upon the ways in which we research.

Note

1 In both Annette's and Hayley's research the names of those involved in the research have been changed and in some cases the names have been chosen by the research participants.

References

Alderson, P. (2008) *Young Children's Rights: Exploring Beliefs, Principles and Practice*. London: Jessica Kingsley Publishers.

Azzarito, L. and Hill, J. (2013) 'Girls looking for a "second home": bodies, difference and places of inclusion', *Physical Education and Sport Pedagogy* 18(4): 351–375.

Azzarito, L. and Kirk, D. (eds) (2013) *Pedagogies, Physical Culture, and Visual Methods*. Abingdon: Routledge.

Barnardo's (2002) *The Spark Centre: Barnardo's Consultation with Children and Young People*. London.

Bradbury-Jones, C. and Taylor, J. (2015) 'Engaging with children as co-researchers: challenges, counter-challenges and solutions', *International Journal of Social Research Methodology* 18(2): 161–173.

Clark, A. and Moss, P. (2011) *Listening to Young Children: The Mosaic Approach*. London: National Children's Bureau.

Dentith, A. M., Measor, L. and O'Malley, M. P. (2012) 'The Research Imagination amid Dilemmas of Engaging Young People in Critical Participatory Work', *Forum: Qualitative Social Research* 13(1).

Department for Education and Skills (2004) *Every Child Matters: Change for Children*. London: HMSO.

Enright, E. and O'Sullivan, M. (2013) ' "Now, I'm magazine detective the whole time": listening and responding to young people's complex experiences of popular physical culture', *Journal of Teaching in Physical Education* 32(4): 394–418.

Fitzgerald, H. (2012) ' "Drawing" on disabled students' experiences of physical education and stakeholder responses', *Sport, Education and Society* 17(4): 443–462.

Fox, R. (2013) 'Resisting participation: critiquing participatory research methodologies with young people', *Journal of Youth Studies* 16(8): 986–999.

Greig, A., Taylor, J. and MacKay, T. (2007) *Doing Research with Children*. London: Sage.

Hamzeh, M. (2011) 'Deveiling body stories: Muslim girls negotiate visual, spatial, and ethical hijabs', *Race Ethnicity and Education* 14(4): 481–506.

Hamzeh, M. and Oliver, K. L. (2012) 'Because I am Muslim, I cannot wear a swimsuit', *Research Quarterly for Exercise and Sport* 83(2): 330–339.

Hart, R. A. (1992) *Children's Participation: From Tokenism to Citizenship*. London: Earthscan/UNICEF.

Hart, R. A. (1997) *Children's Participation: The Theory and Practice of Involving Young Citizens in Community Development and Environmental Care.* New York: UNICEF.

Holland, S., Renold, E., Ross, N. and Hillman, A. (2008) *Rights, 'Right On' or the Right Thing to Do? A Critical Exploration of Young People's Engagement in Participative Social Work Research.* London: ESRC.

James, A., Jenks, C. and Prout, A. (1998) *Theorizing Childhood.* Cambridge: Polity Press.

Miller, D. (2005) 'What is social justice?' in: Pearce, N. and Paxton, W. (eds) *Social Justice: Building a Fairer Britain.* London: Politico's, 3–20.

McNamara, P. (2011) 'Rights-based narrative research with children and young people over time', *Qualitative Social Work* 12(2): 135–152.

O'Sullivan, M. and MacPhail, A. (eds) (2010) *Young People's Voices in Physical Education and Youth Sport.* Abingdon: Routledge.

Robsinson, C. and Taylor, C. (2013) 'Student voice as a contested practice: power and participation in two student voice projects', *Improving Schools* 16(1): 32–46.

Save the Children (2000) *Children and Participation: Research, Monitoring and Evaluation with Children and Young People.* Belfast.

Stride, A. (2014) 'Let US tell YOU! South Asian, Muslim girls tell tales about physical education', *Physical Education and Sport Pedagogy* 19(4): 398–417.

Weller, S. (2007) *Teenagers' Citizenship: Experiences and Education.* London: Routledge.

Chapter 9

Cypher Wild

Leisure, hip-hop and battles for social justice[1]

Brett D. Lashua and Matthew Wood

Introduction: the cypher

During the Canadian summer months, every Thursday evening from 6 p.m. to 9 p.m., a corner of Edmonton's central municipal plaza, Churchill Square, is transformed. Bordered by citadels of civic power (Edmonton City Hall, Central Library, a performing arts centre and art gallery) Churchill Square sits at the very heart of Edmonton. It is the namesake of the main station in the city's light-rail transit (LRT) system; from this hub buses connect to the rest of the city. As such it is a meeting space, but often for those only passing through. As municipal space, Churchill Square is inscribed with the power and prestige of its official surroundings; it is also highly ordered and sanitized: young people and other marginalised groups such as the homeless are often policed out of Churchill Square. But on summertime Thursday evenings up to 100 people stop and gather: hip-hop music booms from the loudspeakers, breakdancers jump and spin on a makeshift dance floor, DJs take turns on the turntables, and a microphone is at the ready for anyone wanting to rhyme or sing. Some participate, some just watch, and for a few hours this corner of Edmonton's central square is alive. This is Cypher Wild YEG[2] (see Figure 9.1).

In hip-hop culture, a cypher is a social gathering, usually circular and often public, in which participants contribute to a collective creative experience via performance (Saucier, 2014). Cyphers draw from the blueprint of the initial 'block parties' where hip-hop culture emerged in the early 1970s, primarily those in Brooklyn associated with DJ Kool Herc (Forman, 2002). Cypher performances can include improvised rhyming vocals (freestyle rapping or emceeing), DJ-ing (turntablism), beat boxing and breakdancing (b-boy/b-girl-ing). Cyphers may also include street art, such as graffiti, and street entrepreneurialism,[3] as well as offer opportunities to engage in the sharing of hip-hop knowledge and culture. They are, as stated in Figure 9.1, exercises in *community building*. As part of hip-hop's 'street corner society' cyphers 'articulate urban worlds as they are seen through the eyes of those who live within these social environments'

Figure 9.1 'Building up the community' – promotional material for Cypher Wild YEG (courtesy of Matthew Wood).

(Barron, 2013: 532). Developed from the concept of Paulo Freire's 'culture circle' to raise consciousness about social issues (MacDonald, 2012: 101), the cypher, then, is a powerful space, one that is symbolic of broader hip-hop culture and the social justice issues, such as poverty and racism, which hip-hop often articulates, often via highly racialised terms. Since its advent in the 1970s, the symbolic 'circle' of the cypher has expanded as hip-hop has been embraced globally, with diverse local inflections (Huq, 2007; Mitchell, 2001). Hip-hop's global uptake positions its set of practices as perhaps the most popular, powerful and potentially transformational youth leisure activities in an increasingly urban and youthful world (Marsh, 2012; Nitzsche and Grunzweig, 2013; Saucier, 2014). While 'rap music' has become a highly commercialized global product, hip-hop culture has settled into something more broadly resembling grassroots political activism (Forman and Neal, 2012).

This chapter explores youth leisure and hip-hop as postcolonial prac-tices (Braidotti *et al.*, 2012) via a case study of urban hip-hop with First Nations[4] youth in Edmonton. Through a case study of one hip-hop cypher, the chapter evaluates leisure as a central site in broader conversations and struggles for social justice, which we argue is *also* a kind of cypher. In doing so, the chapter advocates participatory research practices, such as collaborative projects that embrace social justice aims, following the imperative of Denzin and Giardina (2009: 13) who argued we are no longer called 'to *interpret* the world [...] we are called to *change* the world and to change it in ways that resist injustice' (emphasis in the original). First, the chapter discusses Cypher Wild YEG within the wider historical context of colonial injustices in Canada. Social justice has become some-thing of an academic buzzword in recent years (Johnson and Parry, 2015), and demands careful attention to relations of historical breadth and com-plexity. Mantie (2009: 90) argued that, particularly for music education initiatives, 'social justice doesn't come easy', and social justice is perhaps 'more effectively conceptualized in terms of *complex equality* where the lines between various spheres of activity are recognized and accounted for in arriving at whatever we call *justice*'. Accordingly, the chapter next builds from Brett's doctoral work (2002–05) in Edmonton with 'The Beat of Boyle Street' music program (Lashua, 2005) and its successors, show-casing the significance of hip-hop in the lives of many Aboriginal-Canadian young people in Edmonton, one of whom at the time was Matt. Overall, this chapter advocates hip-hop performances in public spaces as showcases for social justice practices by Aboriginal-Canadian young people.

'Native lives matter'?[5] Canadian indigeneity and social justice

As in many postcolonial settler states (Johnson, 2011), in Canada the voices and views of Aboriginal people have largely gone unheard outside Indigenous communities. Representations of Aboriginal people have historically been controlled by the government, and have been based on geographical and genetic identification markers (such as which Nation or reserve one hails from, or status based on bloodlines), as well as presumed, dominant Franco-English Canadian norms and values (Fox, 2006). Stereotypes of 'Indians' abound, both in popular media and public discourse, perpetuating views of Indigenous people as backward, uncivilized and troublesome, a burden on the State. Were it not for these negative stereotypes, some might believe First Nations people no longer existed, consigning Indigenous people to history books.

Statistics alone show this 'vanishing' to be unfounded. There are more than 600 First Nations in Canada, numbering over 1,400,000 people. According to Statistics Canada (2015), the Aboriginal population has been increasing markedly in recent years: in 2011, Aboriginal people represented '4.3% of the total Canadian population. Aboriginal people accounted for 3.8% of the population enumerated in the 2006 Census, 3.3% in the 2001 Census and 2.8% in the 1996 Census'. The Aboriginal population increased by 20.5 per cent from 2006 to 2011, in comparison to a 5.2 per cent growth rate for the non-Aboriginal population. In the urban environment of Edmonton, over 18,000 Aboriginal people reside and comprise 1.6 per cent of the total population (Edmonton has the second largest urban Aboriginal population after Winnipeg, which has approximately 25,000 Aboriginal residents or 3.6 per cent of its total population). It is urban centres that have the fastest growing population of Aboriginal people, and many of these are young: almost 50 per cent of Canada's Aboriginal population is under 25 years old, and over 50 per cent now reside in cities (Statistics Canada, 2015). The predominance of the young is due in part to high 'fertility rates' but also shorter life expectancy (Statistics Canada, 2015). Such statistics also point to the many challenges and difficulties confronting Aboriginal-Canadian people, from racism and poverty, lack of equitable access to education and healthcare, as well as higher rates of incarceration, violence (both as victims and perpetrators), addictions, depression and suicide. These issues have long been borne out in national media, including numerous accounts of health crises, incidents of teen suicide, sexual abuse and police brutality. These issues are grim, enduring legacies of colonialism.

As elsewhere in the world (Johnson, 2011), Indigenous people in North America continue to struggle for social justice. After centuries of violence, since the 1990s a number of official initiatives have aimed to redress, both symbolically and economically, the wrongs that have been perpetrated through colonial subjugation of Indigenous people. In 2015, one such step was a long-anticipated report issued by the Canadian Truth and Reconciliation Commission (TRC). Titled *Honouring the Truth, Reconciling for the Future*, the report opened with the admission:

> For over a century, the central goals of Canada's Aboriginal policy were to eliminate Aboriginal governments; ignore Aboriginal rights; terminate the Treaties; and, through a process of assimilation, cause Aboriginal peoples to cease to exist as distinct legal, social, cultural, religious, and racial entities in Canada. The establishment and operation of residential schools were a central element of this policy, which can best be described as 'cultural genocide'.
>
> (TRC, 2015: 1)

The Truth and Reconciliation Commission was the second[6] Canadian federal commission organised to redress the relations between Canada and First Nations. The TRC's mission was to open a pathway to reconciliation through a full acknowledgement of the violence of Canadian government policy carried out via residential schools from 1870 to 1996. Through these schools, 'the government took Indigenous children from their families in order to "kill the Indian in the child"' (Couture-Grondin and Suzack, 2013: 100). In residential schools:

> The children were separated from their brothers and sisters; they were prohibited to speak their mother tongues; and they suffered psychological, spiritual, physical, and sexual abuses. This violence was part of a systemic plan of assimilation, which is rooted in a long history of colonialism.
>
> (Couture-Grondin and Suzack, 2013: 100)

Residential schooling was a central component in the cultural genocide of Aboriginal people. The TRC (2015: 1) defined 'cultural genocide' as the destruction of social practices that define a group, including the free movement, use of language, spirituality, as well as the disruption of those practices that allow 'the transmission of cultural values and identity from one generation to the next'. Speaking to the Canadian House of Commons regarding the establishment of residential schools in 1883, Canada's first Prime Minister, Sir John A. Macdonald, stated:

> When the school is on the reserve the child lives with its parents, who are savages; he is surrounded by savages, and though he may learn to read and write his habits, and training and mode of thought are Indian. He is simply a savage who can read and write. It has been

strongly pressed on myself, as the head of the Department, that Indian children should be withdrawn as much as possible from the parental influence, and the only way to do that would be to put them in central training industrial schools where they will acquire the habits and modes of thought of white men.

(Quoted in TRC, 2015: 2)

Here the erasure of Indigenous culture is laid bare. Although residential schools were gradually phased out and finally closed in 1996, they are emblematic (as in MacDonald's comments above) of much broader and deeply entrenched racist views in (neo)colonial thought; they endure in far too many ways. Aboriginal-Canadians and allies continue to work against these racist discourses, and leisure, recreation and sport have become important areas to contextualise, celebrate and collaborate for more just cultural views and practices (Fox, 2006, 2007; Giles, 2001; Giles *et al.*, 2010; Johnson and Halas, 2011; Rose and Giles, 2007; van Ingen and Halas, 2006).

Although often sites for reproducing (post)colonial discourses (Wagg, 2005), leisure, sport and recreation also offer contexts to challenge and transgress dominance and oppression (Paisley and Dustin, 2010). This makes sport and leisure potentially significant as practices that are more than largely symbolic forms of reconciliation and 'transitory justice' (Couture-Grondin and Suzack, 2013) with little immediate impact in the daily lives of young Aboriginal-Canadians. Although the residential schooling system is no longer in operation, many Indigenous people continue to feel the impress of its legacy, not least in education (Leard and Lashua, 2006), and many 'young people are living in poverty and confronting other challenges, ranging from learning disabilities, drug addictions, teen parenting, poor parenting, racism, violence, homelessness, and the vicissitudes of life "on the streets"' (Lashua and Fox, 2006: 394). In Edmonton, due to these challenging social issues, the city is widely and derisively labelled 'Deadmonton' – a morose sobriquet that those active in its hip-hop community hope to shake off. For this community, social justice requires a more active stance, and more active movements: hip-hop provides a set of activist practices to make a stand against injustice.

Aboriginal hip-hop: from the Beat of Boyle Street to Cypher Wild YEG

Hip-hop is widely recognized as a cultural battleground, a culture that is 'burdened by its contradictions' (Marsh, 2013: 117) of cultural resistance, containment and reproduction; it is a contested terrain where young people engage in radical acts of political performance (Forman and Neal, 2012; Storey 1997). As a space of political performance, as noted by MacDonald

(2012: 95), 'hip-hop emerged during the decline of both the [American] civil rights and Black Power movement' in response to the need of marginalised groups to express opposition to dominant hegemonic cultural forms (Rabaka, 2013). Despite its many contradictions, 'for many youth of colour, rap music is not seen as a destructive force; it's seen as an asset. It provides an outlet for expression' (Alvarez, 2012: 123). An increasing number of scholars have highlighted the political significance of hip-hop in the lives of Canada's Indigenous youth (Fox and Lashua, 2010; Fox and Riches, 2014; Krims, 2000; Lashua, 2007; Lashua and Fox, 2006; Lashua and Kelly, 2008; MacDonald, 2012; Marsh, 2013; Pearson and Yazdanmehr, 2014; Wang, 2010). This scholarship centralises the local, collaborative and participatory politics of hip-hop.

In research in Regina (Saskatchewan), Marsh (2013: 111) sought to contest the ways that Aboriginal young people are seen through a 'colonialist lens most closely associated with a contemporary discourse on Aboriginal youth living in Canada as bodies in crisis – gang-affiliated, drug-addicted, linked to crime, prostitution, and poverty, or lacking in education, motivation, and initiative'. Her collaborative music projects illustrated that hip-hop offers a way to speak up about 'real' experiences, 'offering meaningful contextualizations, as well as problematizing stereotypical representations' of Aboriginal-Canadian youth that 'tells it like it is' (Marsh, 2013: 111). That is, her work shows how young people are actively resisting negative stereotypes as they use hip-hop music, dance, style and fashions to discuss the troubling social issues that suffuse their lives (see also Lashua, 2013). In this, Marsh's work echoed many of the themes that Brett discussed through his research in 'The Beat of Boyle Street'.

In 2002, working in collaboration with Boyle Street Education Centre, an inner-city charter school serving disadvantaged young people, and the University of Alberta, Brett helped to initiate 'The Beat of Boyle Street', an in-school electronic music project designed to teach inner-city Aboriginal youth (ages 14–20) to use computers to create music (Lashua, 2006, 2007; Lashua and Fox, 2006, 2007; Lashua and Kelly, 2008). Given their intensely urban cultural focus, most of the music created by students was hip-hop. Brett's analyses highlighted the powerful space of hip-hop, where 'young people engage with him in discussions of race, class, and gender, and talked to each other about ways that begin to expose and unravel ways that some ideologies work' (Lashua, 2006: 406) through music in urban contexts. In these exposures and unravellings, hip-hop practices offered 'small victories [that] inform larger hegemonic processes of social change, cultural hybridity, and border crossings, where young people make and remake popular culture into meaningful aspects of their everyday lives' (Lashua, 2006: 406).

The Beat of Boyle Street is just one youth music programme among a handful in Edmonton, including a range of programmes offered by iHuman

Youth Society, and Sun and Moon Visionaries Aboriginal Artisan Society that aim to engage with urban youth. In another example, MacDonald (2012) initiated a gathering in Edmonton called 'Cipher5' via a local university to provide 'a space where personal identity can be cultivated through the elements of Hip Hop' (Pearson and Yazdanmehr, 2014). Reading across these programmes, organisations and events, Fox and Riches (2014: 226) argued that

> Urban Aboriginal hip hop provides a voice and presence for Aboriginal people who grew up and live in low-income areas with all of the struggles and triumphs of living on and off reservation, on the margins of non-Aboriginal society, and blending traditional and 'modern' practices.

One of the young people who not only excelled in The Beat of Boyle Street but also became an active leader within Edmonton's hip-hop community, is Matt Wood, also known as Cree-Asian. Over ten years ago, Matt told Brett (Lashua, 2005: 112):

> Hip-hop made me the person who I am today. I think I'd be selling drugs, I'd be in jail, or either I'd probably be dead right now without that stuff. And I'm not one of those gangstas, I'm not a negative person, I'm straight-up positive. Yeah, that's who I be, I'm half Native and half Vietnamese. So, my boy was sitting there, and he knew that I was half Native and half Asian, he was like, 'yo, you know what would be a sick name for you? "Cree-Asian" – You know? Like, a word 'creative', like 'creation' or two races that click together, you know? Like, it does the same thing with hip-hop, there's no certain race you have to be in hip-hop, there's no certain skin colour, it's all about what's inside you: the creativity.

As a hip-hop dance instructor, DJ and community activist, Matt is also now an instructor in The Beat of Boyle Street. As someone who embodies and enacts hip-hop, Matt aims to deliver the Zulu Nation[7] message: 'Each one, teach one'. Matt is a committed advocate for hip-hop as a transformational practice for young people. On social media, he has argued that the world needs 'DJs that don't just push buttons they push boundaries. DJs who turn heads instead of just knobs. DJs that … you get the point.' Through a number of local, national and international initiatives, Matt is part of a broader community of hip-hop activists who seek to develop opportunities for young people to thrive through hip-hop. He is one of the initiators of Cypher Wild YEG.

Supported in part by the Edmonton Arts Council and iHuman Youth Society, Cypher Wild YEG is a free community event that celebrates hip-hop culture and aims to build community by bringing people together in a weekly block party-style event. For Matt:

> [The cypher] takes over and you start speaking whatever language you speak, whether it is dance, music, art. Doesn't matter from what direction you come, what religion you believe in, or colour of skin, we are all the same people when you get in the cypher [...]. We are destroying barriers and stereotypes, [but] you can't sugar-coat things; it is the inner city. We try to maintain it and let people know that this is a family event, and to let them know not to bring that negative energy here.
>
> (Edmonton Arts Council, 2014, para. 1)

Hip-hop culture and Aboriginal traditions sync in the cypher: 'The circle is where we [Indigenous peoples] share art, stories, language. The cypher is a circle too, so it just spoke to me naturally' (ibid.). For Matt, being an artist in Edmonton is a challenge, but it was this challenge that motivated him most:

> I am tired of hearing it called Deadmonton. I'll admit, I used to call it that. I was almost sick of my city. But then I started waking up [realizing] 'I got to do things myself; I'm not going to wait around for people to do events like this. I'm going to do it'.

In a press release to celebrate a documentary film he directed about Cypher Wild YEG, titled 'Cypher Wild: Keep the Circle Strong'[8] Sean 'Pharush' Arceta stated:

> CypherwildYEG is premised on Hip Hop's central tenets: love, peace, unity, and having fun. It has reclaimed Hip Hop's original purpose of engaging youth and transforming negative energy to positive expression. CypherwildYEG's infectious rhythms and positive energy radiates from the space and welcomes all – but especially marginalized communities such as Indigenous young people and the homeless.
>
> ('Keep the Circle Strong' – CypherwildYEG documentary screening, 2016)

Through its public hip-hop events and other creative practices (such as film making), Cypher Wild YEG becomes a site of radical performances that resonate with battles for social justice, as dancers, rappers and hip-hop artists converge to celebrate visions for greater social equity.

Coming full circle: leisure research and battles for social justice, from hip-hop to hip-hop(e)

Finally, then, we turn toward visions and realisations of social justice through leisure and hip-hop with Aboriginal young people. Clearly, as Marsh (2013: 112) cautioned, it is important to understand the 'variety of contradictory, yet also productive reasons' that social justice resonates through hip-hop activities with Indigenous youth: although many programmes are empowering, some organised hip-hop initiatives can be part of broader attempts to regulate and discipline young people. Further, while we remain critical and do not wish (as Matt stated above) to 'sugar-coat things', hip-hop offers an idealistic vision for social change. For Johnson and Parry (2015: 8, original emphasis), 'Social justice is built on a commitment and action to *make it better*!' Such idealism is echoed in the words of Freysinger *et al.* (2013: 553), who advocated

> a vision of society where the distribution of resources is equitable and all members are physically and psychologically safe and secure. In this society, individuals are both self-determining and interdependent. Justice involves a sense of one's own agency and a sense of social responsibility towards others, and for society as a whole.

For scholars, researchers and educators, this responsibility extends from individuals into communities of practice, and hip-hop cyphers are one site where this vision can be enacted, drawing people together to communicate with one another. For Wang (2010: 61), hip-hop is 'close to spoken word and focuses on lyrics with a message, reviving local traditions of song that tell histories, counsel listeners, and challenge participants to outdo one another in clever exchanges'.

Community-mindedness, as with the celebrated block parties where hip-hop started, is crucial for cyphers to remain rooted in the ground, in their localities. From there, a broader symbolic circle extends outwards, to include local governments, educators, youth workers, police and academic communities. Accordingly, academic work has a social justice responsibility too: 'the processes and outcomes of scholarship must move beyond academic discourse to benefit communities or groups that are treated unfairly in the social world' (Johnson and Parry, 2015: 12). In practice, it is crucial that social justice inquiry 'attends to inequities and equality, barriers and access, poverty and privilege, individual rights and the collective good, and their implications for suffering' (Charmaz, 2011: 359). For social justice research to matter, it is crucial to address social inequities. While some markers of social identity have been increasingly addressed in leisure scholarship, such as racialisation, sexuality and gender, many issues remain under-addressed in the research literature in regard to social justice.

For example, in his treatise on 'love', Johnson (2014) argued that, for social justice practice, leisure scholarship must work harder to address inequities of socio-economic class (see Rose, 2013).

Beyond the need to maintain a critical focus on identity politics, social justice scholarship argues for a shift in the kinds of research relations that researchers with their inquiry, moving towards becoming 'activist-scholars'. For Parry *et al.* (2013: 83):

> With a social justice research agenda, participants are not distant objects of study, but rather neighbors, lovers, friends, family members and/or allies. Knowledge is built from the lived experiences of people as opposed to distant or objective scholarly claims. Understanding this lived experience is essential because the social justice researcher becomes an additional spokesperson or advocate for causes and issues, helps people articulate enduring and emergent problems, or brings together key stakeholders for community discussions/actions.

Therefore, the cypher can be seen as a vivid illustration of this formulation. While individual freedoms matter, social justice depends on wider collaborative efforts (e.g. Cypher Wild YEG is supported by Edmonton Arts Council and iHuman Youth Society) in order to address, collectively, longstanding and complex issues (Mantie, 2009). This includes addressing historical and ongoing injustices that Aboriginal communities continue to battle, and represents a broader, global struggle for human rights, recognition and dignity (Kalsem and Williams, 2010). Here again, we argue for the significance of hip-hop in such global battles (Saucier, 2014), as spaces and practices for celebration, joy, resistance, reconciliation and renewal. For many young Aboriginal people now living in cities, the era of residential schools is part of an abstract past, often removed from their daily lives by generations, even if its legacy continues to shape their lives in concrete ways. While the Truth and Reconciliation process acknowledges the continuing impress of colonial injustices, how and where social justice is enacted and felt concretely in young people's lives is another matter. From the global to the local and back again, in examples such as Cypher Wild YEG (and also in many other cities), hip-hop cyphers present community-building practices that can lead, as Porfilio and Biola (2012) argued, from hip-hop to hip-hop(e).

Notes

1 We would like to thank Cypher Wild YEG organisers and participants, The Beat of Boyle Street, and all who are active in Edmonton's hip-hop community.
2 YEG is the airport code for Edmonton. Rather than the telephone area codes in the US, or the postcodes identified in the UK, Canadian hip-hop often employs airport codes to intone the locality of its hip-hop cultures.

3 Street entrepreneurialism generally refers to the creative, self-motivated, commercial aspects of hip-hop. In the past some might say that a street entrepreneur is someone who 'has game' or is a 'hustler' – another term is a 'natural salesperson'. This would include self-promotion of someone's talents as an artist, DJ, dancer, or performer; it could also mean selling hip-hop related items such as clothing or artwork. Lastly, it involves skills that are learned 'on the street', rather than in formal education (especially where opportunity structures preclude participation in formal education).

4 First Nations is the preferred term for most Indigenous Canadians, along with Inuit, and Métis groups. Aboriginal-Canadian is widely used as a collective term too. Here we use the term First Nations, unless referring to Aboriginal-Canadians more broadly.

5 Set against the 'Black Lives Matter' (and counterpoint uses of other 'lives' that 'matter', e.g. the pro-police 'Blue Lives Matter'), some have called for increased attention to the racism against Indigenous people in North America. Millet (2015: para. 13) outlined outrageous levels of injustice, including police brutality, depression, suicide, poverty and infant mortality rates in Indigenous communities:

> At this moment, when black Americans are speaking up against systemic police violence, and their message is finally being carried by virtually every major news source, it's time we also pay attention to a less visible but similarly targeted minority: the people who lived here for many thousands of years before this country was founded, and who also have an unalienable right to respect and justice.

6 The Royal Commission on Aboriginal Peoples (1991–96) was the federal commission organised after the Oka crisis in 1990 in an attempt to improve relations with First Nations communities.

7 The Zulu Nation is an international hip-hop awareness organisation initiated in the 1970s by hip-hop pioneer Afrika Bambaataa.

8 The film is available on YouTube: www.youtube.com/watch?v=FUIq6_8ucgg.

References

Alvarez III, T. T. (2012) 'Beats, rhymes, and life: rap therapy in an urban setting', in: Hadley, S. and Yancy, G. (eds) *Therapeutic Uses of Rap and Hip Hop*. New York: Routledge, 117–128.

Barron, L. (2013) 'The sound of street corner society: UK grime music as ethnography', *European Journal of Cultural Studies* 16(5): 531–547.

Braidotti, R., Hanafin, P. and Blaagaard, B. (eds) (2012) *After Cosmopolitanism*. London: Routledge.

Charmaz, K. (2011) 'Grounded theory methods in social justice research', in: Denzin, N. K. and Lincoln Y. E. (eds) *The Sage Handbook of Qualitative Research*, 4th edn. Thousand Oaks, CA: Sage, 359–380.

Couture-Grondin, É. and Suzack, C. (2013) 'The becoming of justice: indigenous women's writing in the pre-truth and reconciliation period', *Transitional Justice Review* 1(2): 97–125.

Denzin, N. K. and Giardina, M. D. (eds) (2009) *Qualitative Inquiry and Social Justice: Towards a Politics of Hope*. Walnut Creek, CA: Left Coast Press.

Edmonton Arts Council (2014) 'The voice of Edmonton's *CypherWild*: DJ Creeasian', http://yegarts.tumblr.com/post/88583775368/the-voice-of-edmontons-cypherwild-dj-creeasian, accessed 1 April 2016.

Forman, M. (2002) *The 'hood Comes First: Race, Space, and Place in Rap and Hip-Hop*. Hanover, NH: Wesleyan University Press.

Forman, M. and Neal, M. A. (eds) (2012) *That's the Joint! The Hip-Hop Studies Reader*, 2nd edn. New York: Routledge.

Fox, K. M. (2006) 'Leisure and indigenous peoples', *Leisure Studies* 25(4): 403–409.

Fox, K. M. (2007) 'Aboriginal peoples in North American and Euro-North American leisure', *Leisure/Loisir* 31(1): 217–243.

Fox, K. M. and Lashua, B. D. (2010) 'Hold gently those who create space on the margins: aboriginal young people and the rhythms of leisure', in: Mair, H., Arai, S. and Reid, D. (eds) *Decentering Work: Critical Perspectives on Leisure, Social Policy, and Human Development*. Calgary: University of Calgary Press, 96–104.

Fox, K. M. and Riches, G. (2014) 'Intersecting rhythms: the spatial production of local Canadian heavy metal and urban aboriginal hip hop in Edmonton, Alberta, Canada', in: Lashua, B. D., Spracklen, K. and Wagg, S. (eds) *Sounds and the City: Popular Music, Place and Globalization*. Basingstoke: Palgrave Macmillan, 322–341.

Freysinger, V., Shaw, S., Henderson, K. and Bialeschki, D. (eds) (2013) *Leisure, Women and Gender*. State College, PA: Venture.

Giles, A. R. (2001) '(An)Other is the (un)making: participation in sporting opportunities for aboriginal peoples in Canada', *AVANTE-ONTARIO* 7(2): 84–91.

Giles, A. R., Castleden, H. and Baker, A. C. (2010) ' "We listen to our Elders. You live longer that way": examining aquatic risk communication and water safety practices in Canada's North', *Health and Place* 16(1): 1–9.

Huq, R. (2007) *Beyond Subculture: Pop, Youth and Identity in a Postcolonial World*. London: Routledge.

Johnson, A. C. and Halas, J. (2011) 'Rec and read mentor programs', *Reclaiming Children and Youth* 20(1): 20–24.

Johnson, C. W. (2014) ' "All You Need Is Love": considerations for a social justice inquiry in Leisure Studies', *Leisure Sciences* 36(4): 388–399.

Johnson, C. W. and Parry, D. C. (eds) (2015) *Fostering Social Justice through Qualitative Inquiry: A Methodological Guide*. Walnut Creek, CA: Left Coast Press.

Johnson, M. (2011) 'Reconciliation, indigeneity, and postcolonial nationhood in settler states', *Postcolonial Studies* 14(2): 187–201.

Kalsem, K. and Williams, V. L. (2010) 'Social justice feminism', *UCLA Women's Law Journal* 18(1): 131–193.

Keep the Circle Strong – CypherwildYEG documentary screening (2016) 'Press release', www.mailoutinteractive.com/Industry/LandingPage.aspx?id=2068192&p=1, accessed 1 April 2016.

Krims, A. (2000) *Rap Music and the Poetics of Identity*. Cambridge: Cambridge University Press.

Lashua, B. D. (2005) *Making Music, Re-Making Leisure in the Beat of Boyle Street Music Program*. PhD thesis, University of Alberta.

Lashua, B. D. (2006) ' "Just another Native?" Soundscapes, chorasters, and bor-
derlands in Edmonton, Alberta, Canada', *Cultural Studies Critical Methodologies* 6(3): 391–410.

Lashua, B. D. (2007) 'Making an album: rap performance and a CD track listing
as performance writing in the Beat of Boyle Street music programme', *Leisure
Studies* 26(4): 429–445.

Lashua, B. D. (2013) 'Community music and urban leisure: The Liverpool One
Project', *International Journal of Community Music* 6(2): 235–251.

Lashua, B. D. and Fox, K. M. (2006) 'Rec needs a new rhythm "cause rap is where
we're livin' " ', *Leisure Sciences* 28(3): 267–283.

Lashua, B. D. and Fox, K. M. (2007) 'Defining the groove: from remix to research
in the Beat of Boyle Street', *Leisure Sciences* 29(2): 143–158.

Lashua, B. D. and Kelly, J. R. (2008) 'Rhythms in the concrete: re-imagining the
relationships between space, race, and mediated urban youth cultures', *Leisure/
Loisir* 32(2): 461–488.

Leard, D. W. and Lashua, B. D. (2006) Popular media, critical pedagogy, and inner
city youth. *Canadian Journal of Education* 29(1): 244–264.

MacDonald, M. B. (2012) 'Hip-hop citizens: local hip-hop and the production of
democratic grassroots change in Alberta', in: Porfilio, B. and Biola, M. J. (eds)
*Hip-Hop(e): The Cultural Practice and Critical Pedagogy of International Hip-
Hop*. New York: Peter Lang, 95–109.

Mantie, R. (2009) 'Take two aspirins and don't call me in the morning: why easy
prescriptions won't work for social justice', in: Gould, E., Countryman, J.,
Morton, C. and Rose, L. S. (eds) *Exploring Social Justice: How Music Education
Might Matter*, Vol. 4. Waterloo, Ontario: Canadian Music Educators' Association, 90–104.

Marsh, C. (2012) 'Bits and pieces of truth: storytelling, identity, and hip hop in
Sasketchewan', in: Hoefnagels, A. T. and Diamond, B. (eds) *Aboriginal Music in
Contemporary Canada: Echoes and Exchanges*. Montréal: McGill-Queen's Uni-
versity Press, 346–371.

Marsh, C. (2013) ' "Don't call me Eskimo": representation, mythology and hip hop
culture on Baffin Island', *Musicultures: The Canadian Journal for Traditional
Music* 36: 108–129.

Millet, L. (2015) 'Native lives matter, too', *New York Times*, 13 October. http://
mobile.nytimes.com/2015/10/13/opinion/native-lives-matter-too.html?smid=tw-
share&_r=1&referer=http://t.co/vnMXqfLxBE, accessed 1 April 2016.

Mitchell, T. (2001) *Global Noise: Rap and Hip-Hop outside the USA*. Middleton:
Wesleyan University Press.

Nitzsche, S. and Grunzweig, W. (eds) (2013) *Hip-Hop in Europe: Cultural Identities and Transnational Flows*. Berlin: LIT Verlag.

Paisley, K. and Dustin, D. (eds) (2010) *Speaking up and Speaking out: Working for
Social and Environmental Justice through Parks, Recreation and Leisure*. Champaign, IL: Sagamore.

Parry, D., Johnson, C. W. and Stewart, W. (2013) 'Leisure research for social
justice: a response to Henderson', *Leisure Sciences* 35: 81–87.

Pearson, D. and Yazdanmehr, R. (2014) 'Edmonton hiphop kulture: techniques of
self and cultural sustainability', *Earth Common Journal* 4(1), www.inquiries
journal.com/a?id=952, accessed 1 April 2016.

Porfilio, B. and Biola, M. J. (eds) (2012) *Hip-Hop(e): The Cultural Practice and Critical Pedagogy of International Hip-Hop*. New York: Peter Lang.

Rabaka, R. (2013) *The Hip Hop Movement: From R & B and the Civil Rights Movement to Rap and the Hip Hop Generation*. Plymouth: Lexington Books.

Rose, A. and Giles, A. R. (2007) 'Alberta's Future Leaders Program: a case study of aboriginal youth and community development', *The Canadian Journal of Native Studies* 27(2): 425–450.

Rose, J. (2013) 'Contesting homelessness: public nature, political ecology, and socioenvironmental justice', in: Schwab, K. and Dustin, D. (eds) *Just Leisure: Things that We Believe in*. Urbana, IL: Sagamore Publishing, 58–66.

Saucier, P. K. (2014) 'Continental drift: the poetics and politics of African hip hop', in: Lashua, B., Spracklen, K. and Wagg, S. (eds) *Sounds and the City: Popular Music, Place and Globalization*. Basingstoke: Palgrave Macmillan, 196–208.

Statistics Canada (2015) 'Aboriginal Peoples in Canada: First Nations People, Métis and Inuit', www12.statcan.gc.ca/nhs-enm/2011/as-sa/99-011-x/99-011-x2011001-eng.cfm, accessed 1 April 2016.

Storey, J. (1997) *An Introduction to Cultural Theory and Popular Culture*. London: Pearson.

TRC (Truth and Reconciliation Commission of Canada) (2015) *Honouring the Truth, Reconciling for the Future: Summary of the Final Report of the Truth and Reconciliation Commission of Canada*, www.trc.ca/websites/trcinstitution/File/2015/Honouring_the_Truth_Reconciling_for_the_Future_July_23_2015.pdf, accessed 1 April 2016.

van Ingen, C. and Halas, J. (2006) 'Claiming space: aboriginal students within school landscapes', *Children's Geographies* 4(3): 379–398.

Wagg, S. (ed.) (2005) *Cricket and National Identity in the Postcolonial Age: Following on*. London: Routledge.

Wang, E. L. (2010) 'The Beat of Boyle Street: empowering aboriginal youth through music making', *New Directions for Youth Development* 125: 61–70.

Chapter 10

Integration or special provision?

Positioning disabled people in sport and leisure

Hayley Fitzgerald and Jonathan Long

The *European Sport for All Charter* was established in 1975 and since then the idea of 'Sport for All' has gained significant momentum in policy and practice in the UK. The broad philosophy of Sport for All is underpinned by a recognition that inequalities exist in sports participation and that some people are denied ready access. As well as national campaigns, many local initiatives and programmes have been developed under the auspices of Sport for All and aim to support participation for diverse groups, including disabled people. Despite these initiatives Sport England (2016) acknowledges that the *Active People Survey* records people over 16 years old with a long-term limiting illness, disability or infirmity as only around half as likely as the general population to participate in sport at least once a week.

It is this broad idea of Sport for All that this chapter focuses upon. It does so within the wider context of sport and leisure more generally, as similar discussions also arise in the arts and people's other recreational interests regarding access and participation. Matters are thrown into particularly stark relief in sport however because of its celebration of physical prowess. Recognition that disabled people should be supported to engage in sport and leisure prompts questions around *who* should facilitate these opportunities and *how* provision should be offered. It is arguable whether the interests of disabled people are best served by offering specialist (separate) provision or encouraging participation with everyone else (integration). For example, the principles of inclusion might lead us to presume that full integration should be the goal, but what might be intended as integrated provision may serve to separate disabled people frustrated by being sidelined or unable to compete.

In order to contextualise these two overarching approaches to provision we begin by considering the dominant understandings of disability found within society: the medical and the social model. Despite a somewhat simplistic binary, these models offer a useful means of exploring the relationship between disability and sport/leisure. This speaks to the different ways in which disabled people are 'visible' in sport and leisure. Attention then focuses on separate and integrated provision and we consider the different circumstances and identify the problems and merits associated with each type of provision. In doing this, it is not our intention to present one type of provision as better than the other and our coverage is not exhaustive. Rather we hope this chapter offers an insight into the possibilities and challenges that emerge when enabling disabled people to participate in sport and leisure.

Understanding disability within sport and leisure

Debates regarding understandings of disability commonly centre around two key models, the medical and social models of disability. The exact nature of these models and their implications for disabled people are the source of much debate (Goodley, 2011).

Impairment is central to the understanding of disability within the medical model. An individual's impairment is considered to cause disability by restricting their ability to undertake activities that are viewed as 'normal' (Oliver, 2009). From the medical perspective, it is evident that disability and impairment are seen as a problem having an 'adverse effect' on the individual and is considered to be a 'personal tragedy', limiting and restricting a person's quality of life. Disabled people are consequently subject to medical intervention through medical and professional services designed to diagnose, cure and/or treat illness and abnormality. The aim of such medical intervention is to restore normality, ensuring that individuals can participate in society and live the 'fullest life possible' (Barnes and Mercer, 2010). The negative connotations associated with disability tend to lead to negative views being associated with disabled people and the focus is often on what disabled people cannot do rather than what they can (Barnes and Mercer, 2003). Given the physical demands made of people in most sports as they have been formulated, it is not surprising that the medical model has some currency in this area. When applied to sport and leisure, the perspective of the medical model of disability may lead to the assumption that people are not capable of participating in activities because of their disability and are therefore excluded, given special assistance or offered separate provision. Within sport and leisure a 'therapeutic recreation' discourse dominates academic research and this emphasises how engaging in these activities will make disabled people 'better'. This outlook reinforces the negatives of the medical model focusing on what people cannot do rather than recognising other aspects of participation such as enjoyment, skill development or competition.

The social model of disability emerged as an alternative to challenge the medical model. It was developed by disabled people in response to the view that all problems faced by disabled people are a consequence of their impairment (Oliver, 2009). Instead, advocates of the social model argue that it is society that disables people through imposing restrictions and barriers and through attitudes which exclude disabled people from full participation in society, which together lead to their marginalisation and oppression (Barnes and Mercer, 2010). The social model shifts the focus from impairment to disabling environments within society. Proponents of the social model believe that the solution to disablement is not through medical intervention but through the removal of disabling barriers such as inaccessible transport, buildings and amenities, lack of opportunity and prejudicial attitudes. When applied to sport and leisure, the perspective of the social model of disability may lead those responsible for facilities and activity sessions to consider how their resources, programmes and staff restrict rather than enable disabled people to participate. Here the focus is on identifying barriers and working to reduce these in sport and leisure. However, the challenge for many sports and some leisure activities is that the foundations of these activities are premised on a non-disabled norm. This is particularly the case in sport, where taking a social model perspective could bring into question the very nature of the sport and position the very essence of sport as a disabling barrier.

Useful though this binary is between impairment and disability, there has been a concern, particularly within the critical disability studies movement, that it gives insufficient attention to the specific context of individuals who are also defined by class, gender, ethnicity and other characteristics (Goodley, 2013). By taking an intersectional lens it is claimed that the fluid and diverse constructions of people's identities can be better understood. For example, scholars within sport and leisure drawing on an intersectional perspective have recognised how gender and class are enmeshed within racial identities (Dagkas, 2016; Watson and Scraton, 2013). Less attention has been paid to disability within these intersectional discussions in sport and leisure – something that is symptomatic of the lack of attention that disability receives generally within these fields of study (Fitzgerald, 2009). When a critical disability studies perspective is adopted in sport and leisure it may lead those supporting participation to recognise that disability need not always define participation and that in different settings other characteristics can contribute to engagement in sport and leisure. Of course, taking an intersectional lens adds complexity to the theoretical debates and practical decision-making that revolve around how best to support different people and account for difference in sport and leisure (Flintoff and Fitzgerald, 2012).

Locating disabled people in sport and leisure

DePauw (1997) identified three locations that disabled people occupy in sport. Although DePauw contextualises her thinking within sport the way she locates disabled people in different situations is relevant to broader leisure settings as well. In the first 'location' some are excluded from sport and leisure through the 'invisibility of disability'. Sadly, by this she does not mean that disabled people are so well integrated that no one notices their disability, but that the needs of disabled people are overlooked. This and the well-documented barriers and challenges to participation emphasise how sport and leisure can be a site of exclusion. For example, research undertaken by Rankin (2012) found that barriers to participation could be grouped into three categories: logistical, physical and psychological. Logistical and physical barriers can also be described as external (or physical and structural) barriers to participation. These environmental barriers include inaccessible sporting provision due to geographical location, cost and associated transport difficulties; a failure to provide the required support for participation (e.g. people trained to use specialist equipment such as hoists); and a failure to communicate information about opportunities effectively.

Much the same barriers were identified by the Arts Council of Northern Ireland (2007) regarding disabled people's participation in and access to the arts. Beyond active participation in sport and leisure it should also be recognised that the lack of representation in management, coaching and volunteering can also impact on the 'invisibility of disability' in sport and leisure. With the exception of the Paralympics, this invisibility extends to media representation (Jackson *et al.*, 2015). Similarly, representation within wider leisure contexts such as museums may be absent or reinforce old stereotypes of disability (Dodd *et al.*, 2006). Sport and leisure institutions can construct disability in ways that perpetuate exclusion. Just as physical and structural barriers create disablement so too do attitudinal barriers to sport and leisure participation by disabled people.

The second 'location' outlined by DePauw (1997) is where disabled people may be visible as disabled participants, that is, the 'visibility of disability' in sport and leisure. In this location, disabled people are made visible but their position is considered inferior to that held by non-disabled people. For example, disability sport adapted from a mainstream version (e.g. wheelchair basketball and hand cycling) may be seen as secondary to the original activities. In this position disabled people engaging in sport and leisure are perceived as holding a lesser position than their non-disabled counterparts. After all, they are not capable of participating in the mainstream versions of these activities and therefore have to undertake an 'easier' form of the activity. Research conducted prior to the 2012 Paralympics at the Centre for Diversity, Equity and Inclusion reveals how the inferior positioning of elite disabled athletes extends to broader aspects of their lives and encompasses negative views about gaining employment, relationships, achievement at school and physical appearance (Fitzgerald, 2012). This inferior positioning of disabled people has echoes of the medical model by focusing on what people cannot do.

Finally, DePauw (1997) argues that disabled people may be visible in sport, viewed as any other participant. The athletes are recognised for their ability and their disability is rendered invisible: the '(in)Visibility of disAbility'. In 1997 DePauw saw this as an aspirational location that would require sport to be transformed to be more inclusive. This more radical location requires sport to change significantly and positively account for difference rather than focusing on the negatives of disability. Since the late 1990s developments in legislation and policy have led to more structured opportunities for disabled people to participate in sport and leisure. Whilst these are positive moves forward we would argue they are essentially marginal advances rather than transformative changes to sport.

Integrated and separate provision

The three locations of disabled people in sport and leisure offered by DePauw (1997) help to shed light on the ways in which they are understood and valued within these settings. In relation to these locations two approaches have typically been adopted to support sport and leisure participation for disabled people: encouragement to integrate with non-disabled people or to participate in separate provision. We do not seek a simplistic resolution, but recognise a range of issues when policymakers, providers and practitioners deliberate over integrated and separate provision. In their discussion of integration DePauw and Gavron (2005) argue that disability sport needs to address three key issues: first, whether sport should be grouped by ability or disability; second, whether sport is for participation or competition; and, finally, whether sport competitions should be integrated. Each of these issues can be seen as a continuum; for example, sport can be classified by disability at one end and at the other end by ability with no consideration of disability. Similarly, the integration/separation continuum can be seen as having integrated competition for non-disabled and disabled people at one end, while the other end of the continuum separates competitions for disabled people (e.g. Paralympics, Special Olympics, Deaflympics) or by specific disability grouping.

Each of the three issues identified by DePauw and Gavron (2005) has implications for the way in which sport and leisure is managed and delivered. For example, at an organisational level separate bodies have been established to manage opportunities for particular groups of disabled people (e.g. Gateway Clubs and RNIB Clubs) and offer distinct programmes, initiatives and participant pathways. Alternatively, mainstream organisations (e.g. some governing bodies of sport) can offer separate sport and leisure provision specifically for disabled people (programmes, initiatives and participant pathways). Mainstream organisations can also support disabled people to integrate with non-disabled people and in this way work to provide opportunities for non-disabled and disabled people to participate recreationally or competitively together. There is much debate about what constitutes integration and this is often confused with the notion of inclusion. Scholars within education continue to be significant in contributing to this debate and argue that integration signifies the placement of disabled people with non-disabled people and minor adjustments to activities or offering extra support. In contrast, inclusion is seen as a process and understood as a means of increasing participation and engagement by all through the removal of all forms of exclusionary practice (Slee, 2011). This inclusive aspiration is premised on a social model view of disability that seeks to eliminate the structures and practices that exclude and in the context of sport this brings into question the very essence of sport. To become inclusive would require a significant change in order to work towards De Pauw's (1997) aspiration of the '[in]Visibility of disAbility'. Such a re-positioning may not appeal to those content with the current state of sport and leisure.

The picture that we paint here for separate and integrated provision is not straightforward and research conducted at the Centre for Diversity, Equity and Inclusion indicates how disabled people may crosscut these differing types of provision (Fitzgerald, 2005; Fitzgerald and Kirk, 2009; Fitzgerald and Stride, 2012). Drawing on this body of research we offer two scenarios to illustrate how disabled people may crosscut provision and opportunities. For example, consider Sam, who is 16 and started to play wheelchair tennis after having been introduced to the sport at a disability leisure club. From here she was directed to a disability tennis camp and then began to train once a month with a local disability tennis coaching group. She wanted to train and play more regularly, so joined a mainstream tennis club and is having coaching sessions with non-disabled junior players. She has been selected to train with the regional tennis development squad and is training to compete in the national wheelchair tennis junior championships. Sam also enjoys swimming and attends a weekly mainstream swim lifesaving club. John is 26, visually impaired, and has been competing in athletics since he was ten years old. He has always trained at the same mainstream city athletics club. He competes for the club in open events and also regularly coaches junior athletes. Until last year, John represented Great Britain in a number of disability sport athletics competitions. He competed in the 200 metres and 400 metres (visually impaired classification) and gained medals at national and international championships. In the past two years John has taken up judo and trains at a local mainstream judo club, where he is working towards his blue belt. As these examples of separation and integration illustrate Sam and John are participating in different sports, in cross-cutting contexts (mainstream and disability clubs, competitions and teams) and at different levels of participation.

More broadly, the acts of defining, categorising and classifying in providing sporting and leisure opportunities also serve to separate and divide.

In the sporting world this is evidenced in the classifications of different levels of physical disability designed to make competition more equal. There is also a longstanding rift between the movements to represent people with learning disabilities and those with other disabilities. At an elite level this was exacerbated when ineligible athletes competed in the learning disability category in the Paralympics, leading to the exclusion of all learning disabled athletes from subsequent Paralympics. Moreover, a recent case highlighted how top-level competition is difficult to find for athletes with Developmental Coordination Disorder (dyspraxia) because they are not included within the International Paralympic Committee classifications (Griffiths, 2014).

There is a strong voice in the literature that being deaf is not a disability, yet there has been a desire among deaf people for their own sporting and leisure organisations, including what is now the International Committee of Sports for the Deaf (ICSD) and the Deaflympics. According to Atherton (2009) deaf clubs are important settings in which a sense of community and normality are experienced by deaf people. Ammons and Eickman (2011) rehearse the argument that deaf people do not properly fit the category of either non-disabled or disabled and recognise the concern of people in the deaf community that their needs are overlooked when they are assigned to either category. These acts of separation may have been initiated in the spirit of promoting fairness that is celebrated by some but they also emphasise difference in a way that may be construed in negative terms by others.

Challenges of supporting separate and integrated provision

Either option, separate or integrated, brings challenges. Separate sporting provision can be problematic as some disabled people do not identify with being 'disabled' and so may be reluctant to use provision specifically for disabled people. This was particularly evident among some of the deaf participants in research undertaken by Rankin (2012). They would not attend sporting events for 'disabled' people as they do not consider themselves to be 'disabled', insisting that the only barrier to accessing integrated provision is accessible communication. Conversely, others held a preference for separate provision because they felt that participating alongside 'similar' people with comparable levels of ability can provide a supportive and understanding environment (Rankin, 2012). However, within any one geographical area it can be difficult for a sport to get sufficient numbers of disabled people to set up separate sports clubs/teams. The result can be sporadic provision or the need to travel large distances.

Having separate provision may lead some mainstream providers to assume they are not responsible for, or need to prioritise, sport and leisure opportunities for disabled people. After all, it is the separate organisations specifically supporting disabled people who have the experience and expertise to deliver these opportunities. While it may indeed be the case that these separate organisations have expertise, that is not grounds for assuming that theirs should be the only outlet for participation by disabled people.

The current distinction made between disability sport (sports developed specifically for disabled people or adapted versions of mainstream sports) and mainstream sport also serves to emphasise the separation between disabled and non-disabled people and can reinforce a view that disability sport requires separate specialist providers. By offering separate provision the status quo is reinforced, normalising the separation of disabled people within society. More broadly, disability activists have contested this kind of orientation towards the medical model on the grounds that the consequence is exclusion, and have instead been campaigning for a more inclusive society. The separation promoted through sport and leisure could be counterproductive to these kinds of wider concerns to address exclusion within society, or may serve to increase participation by disabled people in sport and leisure.

We can also readily identify a number of problems in providing integrated sport and physical activity. A common theme within the literature is that participating or competing alongside non-disabled people can reinforce feelings of low self-confidence, low self-esteem and feelings of 'difference' among disabled people (Rankin, 2012; EFDS, 2014). This is fuelled by the fear among some disabled people that they will not be able to keep up with non-disabled people, a feeling that they will 'stand out' and risk humiliation. Research conducted at the Centre for Diversity, Equity and Inclusion has shown how physical education can be a key setting in which young disabled people feel different when they undertake PE separately from the main class, do different activities, receive exemptions and their skills and abilities are not valued by PE teachers (Fitzgerald, 2005; Fitzgerald and Stride, 2012).

Integrated provision can be hindered by the attitudes of both disabled and non-disabled people. Research undertaken by Rossow-Kimball and Goodwin (2014) in a Canadian leisure context found that older non-disabled people 'tolerated' sharing a leisure space (in this instance a senior citizen recreation centre) with disabled people and felt uncomfortable actively interacting with them. Integration was also hindered by non-disabled people getting frustrated when disabled people did not perform activities to expected levels of proficiency, reinforcing the perception of weakness and normative views about the nature of performance. In this example integrated provision emphasised differences rather than similarities (Rossow-Kimball and Goodwin, 2014). Rankin's (2012) research revealed how deaf people find hearing people unwilling to make adaptations to involve them, but at the same time deaf people were reluctant for hearing groups to participate in activities due to a fear of losing the opportunity to compete on their terms.

The success of integrated provision also depends upon the nature of impairment and associated needs. Research evidence tends to suggest that integrated provision may be more problematic for people with moderate to severe learning disabilities and those with hearing impairments due to issues with communication. Research undertaken by Diva Creative (NHS, 2012) identifies a perception among service providers that those with learning disabilities will have difficulty understanding the requirements of participation and that providing the appropriate level of support would detract from 'keeping other participants happy' (NHS, 2012: 13). Tellingly, the report by 2CV on behalf of the English Federation of Disability Sport (EFDS, 2014) presents this communication issue as a problem of service providers not possessing adequate levels of skill to tailor information to meet the needs of the audience. The report by Diva Creative (NHS, 2012) identified how the training of service providers limited the scope for integration of people with learning disabilities into mainstream provision. They also found, however, that carers were quite positive about the inclusion of people with learning difficulties into mainstream activities. They were reported as believing that inclusion is possible if conducted gradually, progressing through stages: for example, observing sessions, taster sessions, alternation between mainstream and isolated activities, and the use of a volunteer buddy system. We do not seek to minimise the difficulties in making appropriate provision, but examples exist to demonstrate how trained staff can deliver opportunities for involvement in sport and leisure that result in enhanced self-esteem.

In some of the more recent literature, practising professionals and researchers have been considering the implications of 'reverse integration', a process that refers to non-disabled athletes competing alongside disabled people in sports which have been traditionally known as disability sports (Spencer-Cavaliere and Peers, 2011). This operates on the basis that it is easier to secure integration by including people without any significant disability in 'disability sport' than vice versa. If conducted sensitively, reverse integration can empower disabled people by facilitating activities that can be undertaken with equal levels of competence, reducing gaps between non-disabled and disabled people in arenas where it is disabled people who are expert. This idea of reverse integration can also be adopted in leisure contexts, for example *Dialogues in the Dark* (Cohen, 2006) was an exhibition in which blind guides led visitors in complete darkness through what they describe as 'a parcours' of different environments (e.g. harbour, bar, forest, city, market). The associated longitudinal research identified that it left a lasting impression on visitors. Five years later, 58 per cent still stated that as a result of the exhibition their perception of blind people had changed radically.

In another leisure setting Jeanes and Magee (2010) reviewed the development of an inclusive playground in Northern Ireland that was built on the grounds of a special school in consultation with parents and young people from the school. Interviews with parents identified a number of factors which led to the success of the playground, including the location of the playground in the grounds of a special school. This led to a feeling of 'belonging' amongst disabled children and their families based on a feeling that they had a 'right' to use the facility (Jeanes and Magee, 2010). Moreover, parents felt that, because people were used to seeing disabled children in the area, it normalised disability rather than highlighting differences. Parents also felt that the playground enabled disabled children to play freely alongside non-disabled children, bridging gaps between the two groups.

Of course the idea of reverse integration is not without its difficulties and Rankin's (2012) study highlights that the very nature of reverse integration may lead to the marginalisation of disabled people as non-disabled people take over their domain. Research conducted at the Centre for Diversity, Equity and Inclusion highlights a number of issues that require consideration before supporting reverse integration within physical education, including establishing what purpose this is serving, how these activities are embedded within the curriculum, considering the nature of the pedagogy underpinning reverse integration and determining how similar experiences can be extended beyond the formal school curriculum (Fitzgerald and Kirk, 2009).

Another approach to integrated provision concerns dismantling the distinction between disability sport and mainstream sport. This approach is not dissimilar to the traditional approach to integration outlined earlier in relation to encouraging disabled people to participate in mainstream sport with non-disabled people. However, a key aspect of this alternative approach would be to ensure disabled people are automatically included in activities rather than their inclusion considered as an afterthought. By eliminating the categories distinguishing mainstream and disability sport, attention would be given to how sports, and those participating, could be more equally valued. Carter et al. (2014) commend the Cheetahs sports club as an example of providing wheelchair-based activities on equal terms to disabled and non-disabled children. Interestingly, Carter et al. (2014) report that the club facilitated the 'invisibility of disability'; because all the children were in wheelchairs it was sometimes difficult to distinguish between disabled and non-disabled children. The use of wheelchairs in the activities broke down the negative social constructions of wheelchairs as signifiers of disability and (lack of) accessibility, and replaced them with more positive ideas about wheelchairs as facilitating equipment. Overall, Carter et al. (2014) explain that the success of the sports club was due to it shifting the focus from 'disability' to fun, participation, engagement and inclusion in an environment where the children did not have to consider their disability. To some extent this kind of response to sports provision is working towards DePauw's aspiration for the '[in] Visibility of disAbility'. The club is labelled neither a 'disability only' club nor 'adapted mainstream club'; instead, the only criterion for joining was that 'you were a child who wanted to play sport in a wheelchair' (Carter *et al.*, 2014: 13). This kind of approach to provision lies closer to the idea of inclusion as it attempts to reconsider practice in a manner that removes barriers and minimises difference. Of course wider acceptance of disability in everyday life, as well as sport, is also needed if disabled people are to have more equitable experiences. Like other spheres of life, sport and leisure has a pivotal role to play and needs to take responsibility for helping to shift understandings about disability.

Conclusion

At the beginning of this chapter we posed two questions about sport and leisure for disabled people around *who* should facilitate provision and *how* it should be offered if the Sport for All rhetoric is to become reality. That obliges a consideration of the extent to which provision should be underpinned by a philosophy of integrating disabled people into sport and leisure activities with non-disabled people. Further debate also arises regarding separate provision and the extent to which this is counterproductive to broader concerns for an inclusive society. In particular, maintaining the status quo leaves intact endemic institutional and structural barriers to participation in sport and leisure. In grappling with these issues we have come to recognise that neither approach to provision is intrinsically right or will work for all. Decisions are taken conditional on the complex circumstances of life in a society not yet accustomed to accommodating the needs of disabled people. It is a combination of approaches supporting integration, reverse integration, separation or inclusion that offers the possibilities for a diversity of provision and opportunities such that disabled people feel free to participate on their own terms. It is perhaps the unintended consequences of each approach to provision that policymakers and providers should be more attentive to. For example, if supposed integration leaves disabled people feeling alienated by being unable to perform at the same level as others it is likely to separate instead. Conversely, if choices to participate separately are prompted less by a desire to participate with other disabled people and more as a pragmatic response by an individual who feels other options are unavailable or unrealistic, sport providers are failing those involved.

Our interest in Sport for All is not meant to suggest that disabled people 'ought' to participate in sport, or any other leisure activity, but if they wish to participate they should not be denied the opportunity. Moreover, beyond that, if disabled people do not want to participate it may say more about the construction of sport and the reach and impact of Sport for All rather than about them as individuals. Our proposals for a genuinely multi-modal response of sensitive separatism, integration and reverse integration are presented as being essential to inclusion, yet we cannot avoid the added complexity and cost involved. However, we want to encourage the provision of such opportunities and exhort those charged with supporting participation by disabled people in sport and leisure to facilitate the kind of variety of engagement enjoyed by our research participants, Sam and John.

References

Ammons, D. and Eickman, J. (2011) 'Deaflympics and the Paralympics: eradicating misconceptions', *Sport in Society* 14(9): 1149–1164.

Arts Council of Northern Ireland (2007) *Barriers to Disabled People's Participation in and Access to the Arts in Northern Ireland*. Belfast.

Atherton, M. (2009) 'A feeling as much as a place: leisure, deaf clubs and the British deaf community', *Leisure Studies* 28(4): 443–454.

Barnes, C. and Mercer, G. (2003) *Disability*. Oxford: Blackwell.

Barnes, C. and Mercer, G. (2010) *Exploring Disability*. Cambridge: Polity Press.

Carter, B., Grey, J., McWilliams, E., Clair, Z., Blake, K. and Byatt, R. (2014) ' "Just kids playing sport (in a chair)": experiences of children, families and stakeholders attending a wheelchair sports club', *Disability and Society* 29(6): 938–952.

Cohen, O. (2006) *Dialogue in the Dark: What are Its Consequences and how can They be Proved?* Hamburg: Orna.

Dagkas, S. (2016) 'Problematizing social justice in health pedagogy and youth sport: intersectionality of race, ethnicity, and class', *Research Quarterly for Exercise and Sport* 87(3): 221–229.

DePauw, K. P. (1997) 'The (In)Visibility of DisAbility: cultural contexts and "sporting bodies" ', *Quest* 49(4): 416–430.

DePauw, K. P. and Gavron, S. J. (2005) *Disability Sport*. Champaign, IL: Human Kinetics.

Dodd, K. J., Hooper-Greenhill, E., Delin, A. and Jones, C. (2006) *'In the past we would just be invisible': Research into the Attitudes of Disabled People to Museums and Heritage*. Leicester: University of Leicester Research Centre for Museums and Galleries.

EFDS (English Federation of Disability Sport) (2014). *Motivate Me: Understanding What Motivates and Appeals to Disabled People to Take Part in Sport and Physical Activity*. Loughborough.

Fitzgerald, H. (2005) 'Still feeling like a spare piece of luggage? Embodied experiences of (dis)ability in physical education and school sport', *Physical Education and Sport Pedagogy* 10(1): 41–59.

Fitzgerald, H. (2009) 'Bringing disability into youth sport', in: Fitzgerald, H. (ed.) *Disability and Youth Sport*. Routledge: London, 1–8.

Fitzgerald, H. (2012) 'The Paralympics and knowing disability', *International Journal of Disability, Development and Education* 59(3): 243–255.

Fitzgerald, H. and Kirk, D. (2009) 'Physical education as a normalising practice: is there a space for disability sport?', in: Fitzgerald, H. (ed.) *Disability and Youth Sport*. Routledge: London, 91–105.

Fitzgerald, H. and Stride, A. (2012) 'Stories from young people with disabilities about physical education', *International Journal of Disability, Development and Education* 59(3): 283–293.

Flintoff, A. and Fitzgerald, H. (2012) 'Theorising difference and inequality in PE, youth sport and health', in: Dowling, F., Fitzgerald, H. and Flintoff, A. (eds) *Equity and Difference in PE, Sport and Health: A Narrative Approach*. Routledge: London, 11–36.

Goodley, D. (2011) *Disability Studies: An Interdisciplinary Introduction*. London: Sage Publications.

Goodley, D. (2013) 'Dis/entangling critical disability studies', *Disability and Society* 28(5): 631–644.

Griffiths, A. (2014) 'Swimmers with dyspraxia fall foul of Paralympics bureaucracy', *Guardian*. Available from: www.theguardian.com/society/2014/may/13/swimmers-dyspraxia-fall-foul-paralympics-bureaucracy (accessed 29 May 2014).

Jackson, D., Hodges, C. E. M., Molesworth, M. and Scullion, R. (eds) (2015) *Reframing Disability? Media (Dis)Empowerment and Voice in the 2012 Paralympics*. London: Routledge.

Jeanes, R. and Magee, J. (2010) 'Social exclusion and access to leisure in Northern Ireland communities: examining the experiences of parents with disabled children', *Loisir et Société/Society and Leisure* 33(2): 221–249.

NHS (National Health Service) (2012) *Social Marketing Insight into Increasing Access to Mainstream Sport and Physical Activity for Adults with Learning Disabilities*. Sheffield: DIVA Creative.

Oliver, M. (2009) *Understanding Disability: From Theory to Practice*. Basingstoke: Palgrave Macmillan.

Rankin, M. A. (2012) *Exploring Why Disabled People and Deaf People Do and Don't Participate in Sport*. Loughborough: English Federation of Disability Sport.

Rossow-Kimball, B. and Goodwin, D. L. (2014) 'Inclusive leisure experiences of older adults with intellectual disabilities at a senior centre', *Leisure Studies* 33(3): 322–338.

Slee, R. (2011) *The Irregular School: Exclusion, Schooling and Inclusive Education*. London: Routledge.

Spencer-Cavaliere, N. and Peers, D. (2011) ' "What's the difference?" Women's wheelchair basketball, reverse integration, and the question(ing) of disability', *Adapted Physical Activity Quarterly* 28(4): 291–309.

Sport England (2016) *Sport and Disability*. Available from: www.sportengland.org/research/encouraging-take-up/key-influences/sport-and-disability (accessed 12 September 2016).

Watson, B. and Scraton, S. (2013) 'Leisure studies and intersectionality', *Leisure Studies* 32(1): 35–47.

Chapter 11

'Knowing me, knowing you'

Biographies and subjectivities in the study of 'race'

Kevin Hylton and Jonathan Long

Introduction

Dealing with a normative concept like social justice it is easy to presume that our own norms prevail. However, it is clear that, though there is often consensus that social justice should be a fundamental principle, it is vital that we critique what these principles mean for individuals and key stakeholders in society. Importantly, our critical gaze should not exclude turning on our own subject positions. When critical research seeks to promote social justice we must address questions of what social justice looks like in the arena of sport and leisure. In part, this is contingent on people's own social position so, in the context of repeated demands for reflexive research, we consider the implications of our selves, two academics, one Black,[1] one White,[2] with diverging and converging backgrounds, researching vexed issues of 'race' in sport and leisure. We do this by returning to an exercise conducted some time ago with two of our co-researchers[3] that has led to related publications on the place of 'race' in research (Hylton and Long, 2016) and by interrogating our biographies in the context of our sensitivity to the use of problematic political approaches, labels, ideas and experiences surrounding 'race' and ethnicity (Long and Hylton, 2014). Having enjoyed the advantages of working in multi-ethnic teams where others have challenged the assumptions we did not even know we were making, we now address some of the key themes we believe are central to our understanding of racialised processes in research, theory and practice. To demonstrate their significance for a continued critical approach to social justice we draw on these reflective narratives to identify links to issues emerging from our empirical research.

One of the points made by Arai and Kivel (2009) in their reflections on social justice and researching 'race' is that the categorical nature of 'race' and ethnicity often leaves research participants, and subsequently whole categories, open to stereotyping. The failure to problematise those categories makes research vulnerable to essentialising forces that perpetuate oppression. However, it is in that paradoxical space of engaging with the lived realities of those socially constructed identifiers of 'race', ethnicity and nationality that we have been able to work with and against racial categories (Long *et al.*, 2009, 2014; Hylton, 2015a; Hylton and Long, 2016), what Gunaratnam would describe as a 'treacherous bind' (Gunaratnam, 2003). It is our contention in this chapter that examining our own biographies makes us more aware of the forces at play and therefore helps us to challenge such essentialising categories which we would argue significantly improves approaches to social justice.

In the following section the italicised text represents extracts from our original narrative accounts, while in ordinary text we offer some reflections that are informed by the original comments offered by the others in the project team.

Our stories: responses and reactions

Kevin's story and reflection

(Song). 'The world is black, the world is white, together we learn to read and write, to read and write.' It's primary school in Leeds, assembly, and my class is singing its heart out. Whilst I am singing I am wondering if 'they' are thinking the same thing as 'us' (well, by 'us', I mean me and Brian James, the only other Black person in the class). I hated this song because it was one of those times that made me shift from being Kevin to being 'Black', different. For a seven-year-old this is very disconcerting and could be viewed as one of the 'awakenings' that young Black people face as their superficial dissimilitude is emphasised by primary school songs, by school plays (my brother played the 'Black Knight' in a primary school play, and we also watched 'Please Sir', 'Love Thy Neighbour' and 'Rising Damp' that provided me with images of myself, or at least people in my image, that remained unproblematised by my family and me for many years because they were … ahem, funny?)

My parents came from Jamaica in the 1950s and we travelled 'up north' to Leeds in the 1960s for new jobs (Yorkshire Television and Nursing). My parents never spoke of 'race', or racism. It was not a rule, it just was not an issue discussed in the house. Occasionally, however, I would be reminded of my Blackness and, as mentioned earlier, it could be funny on television, or it could be very different in the centre of Leeds while avoiding threats of National Front racist violence in the 1970s.

Reading my reflective biography my colleagues expressed views that my sense of self and ethnicity were marked at a *very* early age; partly through my African-Caribbean heritage and working-class northernness coupled with a reading of my 'otherness'. The irony of the symbolic multicultural-ism in the song that made me so uncomfortable, and the power of the media to shape images of Blackness, reflect the environmental tensions experienced by young Black people like me in the 1960s and 1970s. I wrote later in my account of my critical sociological awareness emerging at uni-versity, part of a process of 'becoming' Black. On reflection, this 'becoming' occurred *very* early, but it was through developing more of a critical race consciousness that I became comfortable in articulating, defending and championing issues of 'race' and Blackness which my earlier experiences of education stymied through ignorance or utopian colourblindness.

It was clear to one of my co-authors that my account was almost the polar opposite of Jonathan's in relation to how visible Blackness was, how it was signified through song, play and the media. It was also apparent that my primary identity was my Blackness rather than class or nationality, which seemed to take a more prominent place in Jonathan's reflective recount (below).

The notion of colourblindness and meritocracy followed me into the world of work as I progressed into local authority sport development. Local authority sport often mimicked my experience(s) of education; for example, how Black people were absent from influential positions. As I wrote about my continuing feelings of exclusion and alienation in educa-tion and in local government my co-authors reflected on the way racism shifted from my parents' experiences of overt explicit manifestations to more coded and subtle systemic forms in public and institutional dis-courses; that is, the racisms are still there but have become more slippery, ambiguous and pernicious. Their observations also helped me to a better understanding of my father's claims that racism has dissipated since he arrived in the 1950s to witness 'no blacks' signs in public places and guest houses. Indeed, as they packed to go back to Jamaica, my father recounted how we could never have lived in the area they were leaving when they first arrived in Leeds due to racism and our class position; hence his assess-ment that racism was much less of an issue for him now.

I embrace my raced identity as it is part of my development as a produc-tive social being. However, I despise my experiences of racism because it necessarily requires an additional level of reflexivity in light of the poten-tial of everyday racialised microaggressions. It forces me to recognise the continued legacy of Du Bois' recognition of and how Black and minori-tised ethnic[4] people develop a heightened awareness of themselves in White dominated societies. However skilfully I might manage everyday racism, control can be surrendered at any moment. The perpetual awareness of the racialised self is a necessary but tiring aspect of Blackness. As Du Bois (1994: 1) argued, 'being a problem is a strange experience'.

The experiences that have led me to where I am today point to the ontological root of my research, that retains an orbit around 'race' and challenging racism as means of pursuing social justice. I continue to privilege the Black experience, disrupting myopic dominant epistemologies and ideologies because it is akin to a lifeline to a 'young me' as I think about what would benefit young scholars personally, educationally and professionally. In evolving a critical 'race' approach for current and new generations I also have in mind the need to disseminate information to practitioners and policymakers for their own professional development. In doing that I am as critical of positions taken by allies, that might include colourblindness (Bonilla-Silva, 2010) or what Sullivan and Tuana (2007) describe as epistemologies of ignorance, as of more obvious adversaries.

My approach to research has become one of advocacy and change which leads to work on diversity, equity and inclusion that emphasises the notion of social transformation underpinned by Critical Race Theory (CRT). Moving from the neutral or solely critical, the political imperative of CRT requires an assessment of 'so what?' in research; a factor not always evident in sport and leisure theorising. However, my first engagement with the politics of 'race', and in particular the heterogeneity of the Black experience, came through my earlier Master's research that explored the experiences of senior Black leisure managers across local authorities. My methodology demonstrated a recognition of 'insiderness' and the strengths of co-culturalness with my sample, yet what my life and educational experience did not prepare me for was a Black manager who rejected any ideas of racial processes affecting her progression, policies or practices. My Master's dissertation observed:

> Discrimination was not a problem for all of the respondents. Jasbir was quite confident that she had never experienced racism of any sort. Compounded by the fact that Jasbir is of Asian origin this was recognised as very surprising and quite an achievement in nineties Britain. The same respondent went on to argue that the problem of racism and discrimination was accentuated by academics who sensationalise it: 'If the problem was not given as much space then it would cease to be a problem'.

Internalised racism and uncritical apolitical viewpoints accompanying institutional hegemony can lead to unexpected claims, but these are lived realities and have their own validity. Research findings would be neater if responses far from the line of best fit were ignored, but reductionist, partial, apolitical, pseudo-objective accounts are unhelpful regardless of the rationale for a study. The important thing for me to recognise as a researcher is that the Black experience is diverse and multifaceted and the background of the researcher cannot justify uncritical or spurious approaches. It is at times like these that reflexivity and the notion of constructed identities and critical 'race' scholarship must coalesce. Any approach to researching 'race' without this critical approach is in itself flawed.

Jonathan's story and reflection

Born in Calcutta where my father worked for ten years after 'Independence'. Parents were members of the social and sports clubs, but I had little awareness of the social significance of these until much later. We left when I was four so have few clear memories. However, it left some trace because for as long as I can remember any political consciousness, and predating any theoretical analysis, I've been uncomfortable with the colonial legacy.... We returned to a very White Norwich. I doubt I saw a Black person in the city the whole time I lived there (much later Norwich City were one of only two clubs initially to refuse to sign the Let's Kick Racism Out of Football Charter – I wrote to the Chairman to protest and was told there wasn't a problem in Norwich because they had no minority ethnic groups living there).

While aware of difference, my appreciation of whiteness was slow to develop. At first this is hardly surprising. Even when we moved to Huddersfield [aged 13 in 1966] where there were Black people from African-Caribbean communities, they played little part in my life. There was both spatial segregation, we lived on the edge of town, and educational segregation, I went to a boys' (state) grammar school. I have no clear recollection of there being African-Caribbeans in the school, and can only remember there being three Asians. Moreover, although we played ordinary rugby rather than 'rugger' I have no memory of playing against school teams with Black players either. My awareness of whiteness only arose while travelling abroad, which is something easily left behind in the quotidian of daily life in the UK.

In comparison with Kevin's account, this reflection points to the asymmetry in racialisation that one of the group referred to between Black awareness of Blackness and White awareness of whiteness; few people in African Caribbean or Asian communities can be so forgetful. Co-researchers observed that my appreciation of difference was an intermingling of class and nation rather than of matters purely of 'race':

You cannot live in Scotland without being aware of a certain antipathy to the English collectively. As an individual though, I was virtually never aware of anything untoward being directed at me. Yet when someone from a minoritised ethnic group suggests to me that they've never experienced racism, I'm openly disbelieving.

I face a dilemma; like Kevin I am surprised by research participants like Jasbir or sport stars who deny that they have ever been treated in a racist manner, yet here was I constructing something akin to that. Rather tongue in cheek one of the others asked whether racist behaviour is just in our imaginations and this is 'why sceptics argue that racism would go away if people like [us] stopped writing about it?' In retrospect there were incidents that may well have been attributable to prejudice against the English. Either I chose to overlook it at the time or attributed some other cause; after all they might have simply not liked me. We often do not know what individual actions may be being taken against our interests, and if we are aware it may be difficult to attribute cause. There is, though, plenty of research evidence to suggest that racism does exist in society in general and in sport in particular.

In my narrative I recounted two incidents separated by some 15 years when my response to racist outbursts was very different. The first involved the casual use of racist language by classmates to put a younger pupil down; I felt ashamed, but did nothing. While that was a stand-out incident for me it was probably quite routine for the Asian youngster. The second was at a Scotland versus England football international at Hampden Park. England had three Black players in that match (Barnes, Blissett and Chamberlain), and part way through someone sitting behind me started some racist chanting. I turned around and not very eloquently told him to shut up – not the smartest thing to do with such an obviously English accent, but the Scottish fan was so clearly taken aback that someone was willing to challenge his behaviour, there was no bother and no more chanting.

Colleagues offered reasoned accounts to explain my different reactions, but I was aware of no conscious calculation; the second response was pure anger. Surviving that foolhardiness, however, gave me the confidence to challenge later incidents. It is also indicative of changing times: a pithy response at Hampden was sufficient because discussions of racism in football meant the perpetrator recognised immediately the nature of my reproach, whereas at school, perhaps 15 years earlier, a lengthy explanation would have been required. The significance of changing times was also evident to me in the interpretations offered by my younger colleagues, whose formative years had been rather later when not only had demographics altered, but debates around racial inequalities had been rehearsed more often. This demonstrated to me how hazardous it can be in applying discourses and understandings developed in one era in analysing another. Contexts can change fast and need to be examined carefully. The observation by Kevin's father about experiencing less racism now than when he moved to the UK may mean no more than there are fewer incidents of overt racism today than in the 1960s/1970s, but there are now more recognised forms of racism and alternative targets of racists.

Some of the group seemed quite clear about moments of racial awakening, but I have no such awareness of a particular moment; for me it was an evolutionary process with no obvious beginning. To attribute it to being born in India would, I believe, be tantamount to false memory syndrome as it is hard to recall life at such a young age. I remember initially taking offence at the Black Power salute by Smith and Carlos at the 200 metre medal ceremony of the Mexico Olympics. As a White middle-class lad in Huddersfield how could I think otherwise in the face of the chorus of disapproval? I lacked the necessary tools, and in the media there was no counter-narrative. Nonetheless, over the next few years I must have found alternative sources because I gradually worked out that their action was both brave and entirely justified. Sadly, for the sake of our narrative project, there had been no Damascene moment, nor devastating critical insight; life is more messy and confused than that.

By whatever route I now recognise a privileged position, though this only happens on reflection rather than in the everyday. For example, I wrote at the time:

> As a member of staff in a university my privileged position allows me to promote anti-racist messages even though I know that Combat 18[5] have threatened some staff doing the same. During the course of our research into racism in sport I have felt that it is easier for me to expose elements of racism than it is for Black researchers in the same field. My critiques cannot so readily be dismissed as special pleading (a Black researcher might be accused of having a chip on their shoulder), but I've still been accused of finding what I want to find, seeing racism where it doesn't really exist. Well, I can take that.

The exercise reinforced how, despite all these experiences and research, my social networks, like those of the vast majority of the White middle class in this country, are still very White. Nonetheless I was still taken aback when, in a recent study of attitudes to sport, few of the White people I presumed to be well connected were able to provide a single referral to someone in black and minoritised ethnic communities.

Connections within the research team and with our research respondents

The asymmetry that we have referred to relates not just to differences in treatment, but to the ability to walk away and take time out from our racialised existence. All those in the project team are acutely aware of the operations of 'race', but we were obliged to recognise that issues of 'race' are ones that the White researchers periodically engaged with, but did not have to live with (in part because of class and spatial factors). It is hardly surprising that someone who has lived with racial prejudice for many years interprets in racialised terms what someone else might see as ambiguous.

Of course, we knew about the asymmetry of racial awareness, but this exercise really brought it home to us. What to Jonathan was just a trite song, to Kevin was another early marker of his increasingly racialised identity. The asymmetry of our stories in terms of their awareness of everyday racialised experiences is indicative of broader patterns in European society. There is more room for White identities to be framed in terms of intersections with other characteristics like class, gender, (dis)ability or sexual orientation, than there is for Black people who are typically obliged to recognise the primacy of racialised distinctions. As Knowles (2003: 73) observes:

> White lives are also raced and ethnicised by different but related means. Race is less transparent in White auto/biographies for a number of reasons. Stories of racial privilege are less dramatic than stories of disadvantage. Privilege imposes less upon its subjects and their consciousness. Privilege is, in the main, taken for granted: it is disadvantage that makes itself felt, and as being felt erupt into narrative and politics.

Whereas most White people in the UK share the privilege of taking their whiteness for granted,[6] the reverse is true with Black people continually having to justify the circumstances of their Blackness. This lies at the core of Critical Race Theory (Hylton, 2009, 2015b), though of course the primacy of 'race' has been challenged by other critical theorists, including Marxists (e.g. Darder and Torres, 2004). At the same time we both need to be wary of taking for granted the 'privileges' of middle-class, non-disabled, heterosexual males and appreciating the burden of constantly being defined in ethnic terms. In such circumstances we should not be surprised when people from minoritised ethnic communities choose to participate in sport with others from the same community to relieve that pressure of justification (Hylton, 2011; Fletcher and Walle, 2015). The privilege of an assumed racialised norm can only be experienced by Black groups when participating in segregated environments, something that, especially in the sports world, is typically denigrated by the organisational establishment and many White players. Because whiteness is the norm, if Black people engaging in sport and leisure object to established practices and language, it is they who are considered to be at fault (Fletcher and Hylton, 2016).

As we had not previously considered some of the insights offered by colleagues it might suggest that we are not always best equipped to interpret our own experiences/behaviours. That might also imply we similarly have to beware the accounts our research participants offer us of their experiences. Equally, there were other observations that the original authors were confident were misplaced, so we need to beware the possibility of researchers not just mis-interpreting but also over-interpreting.

Sharing details of our lives that rarely appear in public was not an easy exercise to engage in. Research methodologists write frequently about empathy and walking in other people's shoes (hooks, 1994; Tuhiwai Smith, 2006; Roberts, 2013). Some of the 'mistaken' responses from people who know us quite well serve to show how easy it is for researchers to fall short of the goals of empathetic research. Our chastened reaction to occasional presumptuous or apparently waspish comments from people we consider friends was a salutary reminder of just what we ask our research participants to sign-up to when we engage them in our research and emphasises our responsibility to them.

In the context of the research that we have engaged in over the years some of the most problematic and uncomfortable moments have been negotiating the process in contract research. The nature of contract research privileges an external client's desire for research to assist them in achieving their own goals. Any clash of ideologies is unequal given the power relations involved. Invariably our starting point has to be the client's even when we would not philosophically choose their original premise. We then try to raise aspirations so that in exploring the liminal spaces of the marginalised communities that our clients may not fully understand, and want to explore, we can work with those 'othered' groups and help to reformulate organisational agendas. For example, in a systematic review of the literature on Black and minoritised ethnic communities in sport and physical recreation that we completed for the race equality body Sporting Equals and the UK sports councils (Long et al., 2009) we sought to: (1) manage expectations regarding the breadth and quality of the literature in the field that would be admitted into the review; and (2) raise aspirations to encourage these key stakeholders to adopt and build upon the recommendations emerging from the study.

Like Lorna Roberts (2013: 342) we are sensitive to the risk of alienating marginalised groups through consultation fatigue (worrying about whether we were taking more than we were giving back), and the risk of reinforcing difference by working with racial and ethnic labels. She goes on to remind us that 'research ... plays a role in framing the very phenomenon it sought to investigate'. For us then it is not enough to be silent on the lived effects of 'race' and racism, to merely espouse ideas of social justice or merely be 'not racist' (Trepagnier, 2010). In looking to identify what constitutes desirable change we need to look beyond the principles of distributive justice outlined in Wetherly et al. (Chapter 2 in this collection) and extend them to redistribution through restorative justice making reparation for previous injustices. Critical research on 'race' needs to move beyond liberal incrementalism and challenge not just existing distributions, but dominant modes of thought. An ahistorical analysis that does not take into account previous distributive injustices accruing through racialised inequalities is unlikely to produce proper understanding or result in fundamental change. This is not just a matter of the distribution of resources, but of competing worldviews.

As Lorde (1979) observed, 'the master's tools cannot dismantle the master's house'. In other words, minor adjustments to promote greater efficiency are unlikely to fulfil the more pressing need for the transformation of racialised relations and the material circumstances accruing from them. A 'redistributive justice' is closer to the social justice agenda that has underpinned our research and subsequent messages over two decades. It also endorses approaches to social justice where inequalities that have favoured already privileged social groups are redressed through a 'bias' toward those previously under-represented in research. Furthermore, Roithmayr (2014) argues that where those previously privileged, which includes both authors, do not challenge their own positions and ability to effect change then they 'lock-in' structural inequalities and the power relations of the status quo.

Conclusions

We do not claim to have all of the epistemological or ontological answers as a result of this exercise, but it certainly casts in stark relief some of the challenges involved in researching 'othered' segments of society. The use of biographical reflections in this chapter has enabled us to:

> look inwards and outwards at the same time. It displays the existential as some of the unique features of lives, at its interface with the social landscape. The story of the self inevitably involves others and hence also inevitably opens onto the social landscape.
>
> (Knowles, 2003: 52)

Through the lens of critical theories like CRT we are reminded that the task when using biographies to analyse 'race' and ethnicity is to move beyond purely individualised experiences to consider the contextual forces of power and ideology (cf. Kivel et al., 2009).

Fundamentally, our research participants have the right to expect that the version of their world that is reported is not one unthinkingly filtered by an asymmetrical relationship. However, we recognise the strengths of critique and subjectivities. We already know about the significance of the understanding of the insider as opposed to the outsider (e.g. Long and Blackshaw, 2000: 240), but given the nature of multiply identified social beings it is questionable when any researcher can truly be an insider (Fletcher 2014). Hence the salience of this kind of work to understand our own standpoints, not as an exercise in self-flagellation over privilege, but to raise awareness that apparently similar stimuli may be very different because they are being experienced in the context of distinct habituses. It is also the responsibility of the researcher to expound those differentiated positions in decision-making environments. Beyond that, though, we can use our very different positionings in a racialised society to argue for the importance of including people from minoritised ethnic communities at decision-making tables.

Our research has always drawn on principles of social justice (see for example, Hylton, 2012, 2015a; Long and Hylton, 2014; Long *et al.*, 2014; Hylton and Long, 2016) yet social justice cannot be taken for granted nor utilised opportunistically or cynically as a principle. We agree with Erickson (2010) who states that, at its best, research should advance human rights and dignity. We have done this by respecting racialised problematics, and by not taking our own subject positions for granted. We write elsewhere that:

> Examining 'Whiteness' more closely should allow researchers to make it visible and open to discussion. Moreover, an understanding of its construction generates the possibility of a clearer understanding of the processes of racism, hence a better chance of disrupting them. The paper demonstrates the complexity of these processes and their interpretation, *which cannot, of course, be achieved independently of the researchers' own Blackness and Whiteness.*
>
> (Long and Hylton, 2002: 100, emphasis added)

We certainly do not presume any essentialised Black or White experience, but if we are to understand issues of sociality we need to appreciate distinctions between our own circumstances and those of the research participants we are working with. Without that we are likely to transpose our reasoning onto their actions. Our ontological propositions are products of our way of knowing which is, in turn, shaped by our own appreciation of the meanings that shape racialised encounters. Black and White experiences are not separate; in processes of meaning-making each interacts with the other. As Stanfield (1993: 4) insisted:

> the study of racial and ethnic issues in the social sciences remained deeply grounded in societal folk belief. Thus conceptualisations of research problems and interpretation of data ... often have been preceded by *a priori* ideological and cultural biases that determine the production of 'objective knowledge'.

Reflective exercises like this one can help to sensitise researchers to the epistemological and policy implications of Stanfield's concerns. In this regard we have been very fortunate to conduct our research as part of a multi-ethnic team with co-researchers prepared to challenge our interpretations. Whereas Reinharz (1983) believed that research is about self-discovery just as much as learning about others, we argue that we can hardly expect to learn about others if we are unable to learn about ourselves.

Notes

1 Though there is debate on the inclusivity of this term, 'Black' is used throughout as an umbrella term to include those who, as a result of colour, physiognomy or culture, suffer from racism and xenophobia.
2 The term 'White' is used throughout as an inclusive term to recognise a socially constructed group recognised through commonly held physiognomic and physical, state and individually determined identifiers of whiteness.
3 Professor Karl Spracklen, Leeds Beckett University, and Dr Ben Carrington, University of Texas at Austin.
4 The term 'Black and minoritised ethnic' reflects the common policy label of 'black and minority ethnic', often reduced to the acronym 'BME'. In this case 'minoritised' also denotes the dynamic processes that might reduce Black women who are part of a majority into a minority. Similarly, as demographics shift and superdiversity becomes commonplace in the UK there are cities where the 'majority' is the 'minority' but still 'minoritised'.
5 Combat 18 was a Far Right neo-Nazi group in the UK. '18' relates to the location of Adolf Hitler's initials in the alphabet.
6 We recognise there may be exceptions – e.g. poor White people living in some parts of Bradford.

References

Arai, S. and Kivel, B. D. (2009) 'Critical race theory and social justice perspectives on whiteness, difference(s), and (anti)racism: a fourth wave of race research', *Journal of Leisure Research* 41(4): 459–470.

Bonilla-Silva, E. (2010) *Racism without Racists: Colorblind Racism and the Persistence of Racial Inequality in the United States*. Lanham, MA: Rowman and Littlefield.

Darder, A. and Torres, R. D. (2004) *After Race: Racism after Multiculturalism*. New York: New York University Press.

Du Bois, W. E. B. (1994) *The Souls of Black Folk*. New York: Dover Publications.

Erickson, F. (2010) 'Affirming human dignity in qualitative inquiry: walking the walk', in Denzin, N. and Giardina, M. D. (eds) *Qualitative Inquiry and Human Rights*. Walnut Creek, CA: Left Coast Press, 112–122.

Fletcher, T. (2014) '"Does he look like a Paki?": an exploration of "whiteness", positionality and reflexivity in inter-racial sports research', *Qualitative Research in Sport, Exercise and Health* 6(12): 244–260.

Fletcher, T. and Hylton, K. (2016) 'Whiteness and race in sport', in Nauright, J. and Wiggins, D. K. (eds) *Routledge Handbook of Sport, Race and Ethnicity*. London: Routledge, 87–106.

Fletcher, T. and Walle, T. (2015) 'Negotiating their right to play: Asian-specific cricket teams and leagues in the UK and Norway', *Identities* 22(2): 230–246.

Gunaratnam, Y. (2003) *Researching 'Race' and Ethnicity: Methods, Knowledge and Power*. London: Sage.

hooks, b. (1994) *Teaching to Transgress*. London: Routledge.

Hylton, K. (2009) *'Race' and Sport: Critical Race Theory*. London: Routledge.

Hylton, K. (2011) 'Too radical? Critical race theory and Sport Against Racism Ireland', in Long, J. and Spracklen, K. (eds) *Sport and Challenges to Racism*. London: Routledge, 229–246.

Hylton, K. (2012) 'Talk the talk, walk the walk: defining critical race theory in research', *Race, Ethnicity and Education* 15(1): 23–41.

Hylton, K. (2015a) ' "Race" talk! Tensions and contradictions in sport and PE', *Physical Education and Sport Pedagogy* 20(5): 503–516.

Hylton, K. (2015b) 'This way … this explains my reality: critical race theory in sport and leisure', in Fink, J., Doherty, A. and Cunningham, G. (eds) *Routledge Handbook of Theory in Sport Management*. New York: Routledge, 321–329.

Hylton, K. and Long, J. (2016) 'Confronting "race" and policy: "How can you research something you say does not exist?" ', *Journal of Policy Research in Tourism, Leisure and Events* 8(2): 202–208.

Kivel, B. D., Johnson, C. and Scraton, S. (2009) '(Re)theorising leisure, experience and race', *Journal of Leisure Research* 41(4): 473–493.

Knowles, C. (2003) *Race and Social Analysis*. London: Sage.

Long, J. and Blackshaw, T. (2000) 'Back to literacy', *Leisure Studies* 19(4): 227–245.

Long, J. and Hylton, K. (2002) 'Shades of white: an examination of whiteness in sport', *Leisure Studies* 21(2): 87–103.

Long, J. and Hylton, K. (2014) 'Reviewing research evidence and the case of participation in sport and physical recreation by black and minority ethnic communities', *Leisure Studies* 33(4): 379–399.

Long, J., Hylton, K. and Spracklen, K. (2014) 'Whiteness, blackness and settlement: leisure and the integration of new migrants', *Journal of Ethnic and Migration Studies* 40(11): 1779–1797.

Long, J., Hylton, K., Spracklen, K., Ratna, A. and Bailey, S. (2009) *Systematic Review of the Literature on Black and Minority Ethnic Communities in Sport and Physical Recreation*. Birmingham: Sporting Equals.

Lorde, A. (1979) 'The master's tools will never dismantle the master's house', in Lemert, C. (ed.) *Social Theory: The Multicultural and Classic Readings*. Boulder, CO: Westview Press, 484–487.

Reinharz, S. (1983) 'Experiential analysis: a contribution to feminist research', in Bowles, G. and Duelli-Klein, R. (eds) *Theories of Women's Studies*. New York: Routledge and Kegan Paul, 162–191.

Roberts, L. (2013) 'Becoming a black researcher: reflections on racialised identity and knowledge production', *International Review of Qualitative Inquiry* 6(3): 337–359.

Roithmayr, D. (2014) *Reproducing Racism: How Everyday Choices Lock in White Advantage*. New York: State University of New York Press.

Stanfield, J. H. (1993) 'Methodological reflections: an introduction', in Stanfield, J. H. and Rutledge, M. D. (eds) *Race and Ethnicity in Research Methods*. Newbury Park: Sage, 3–15.

Sullivan, S. and Tuana, N. (2007) *Race and Epistemologies of Ignorance*. Albany: State University of New York Press.

Trepagnier, B. (2010) *Silent Racism: How Well-Meaning White People Perpetuate the Racial Divide*. Boulder: Paradigm Publishers.

Tuhiwai Smith, L. (2006) 'Choosing the margins: the role of research in indigenous struggles for social justice', in Denzin, N. and Giardina, M. (eds) *Qualitative Inquiry and the Conservative Challenge*. Walnut Creek, CA: Left Coast Press, 175–192.

Chapter 12

Black women, Black voices

The contribution of a Spivakian and Black feminist analysis to studies of sport and leisure

Aarti Ratna[1]

Introduction

Black[2] feminist thought emerged through authors who questioned the epistemological practices of white feminists that universalised the experiences of *all* racial and ethnic 'Others', ignorant to racial power bestowed upon them as white women (Amos and Parmar, 1984; Collins, 2000; Mirza, 1997). Fighting for social justice in/through white feminist sisterhood was deemed impossible, as the values and ethics entrenched in the imperial legacies of postcolonial times rendered invisible (thus unaccountable) the racial and ethnic differences in and between white and Black women (Amos and Parmar, 1984). Gayatri Chakravorty Spivak's (1988) 'Can the Subaltern Speak?' is particularly evocative here. In this chapter, I draw from Spivak in order to make the philosophical principles behind her evocation accessible to a wider sport and leisure audience. While others might arguably lament the differences between Black feminist thought and the theoretical position of Spivak, my purpose here is to draw on their respective, yet different, mutually supportive principles which relate to Black women's 'voices'. It should be acknowledged that the number of scholars who have attempted to adopt Black feminist thinking and/or the theoretical ideas of Spivak beyond a tokenistic way in sport and leisure socio-cultural analysis remains limited (Aitchison, 2001; Burdsey, 2006, 2015; Scraton, 2001; Scraton and Watson, 1998; Scraton *et al.*, 2005; Stride, 2014; Walton, 2012). This chapter aims to provide a more detailed theoretical account of both Black feminist epistemology and Spivak's thesis and its significance and relevance for critical social science work in sport and leisure. Initially, I address the problematic representation of Black women in sport and then examine the epistemological tenets of the work of Spivak and Collins. I provide some consideration of 'who' should and could represent the sporting lives and voices of Black women and I conclude by reflecting on the value of postcolonial thinking (Spivak) and Black feminist thinking (Collins) for social justice projects.

Sporting representations of Black women

In a recent review of sporting literature, I found that while there is a growing body of progressive research about Black women and sport, much of the work rarely queries sport as an economic, political, cultural and ideological arena of control and domination which is deeply unequal and thus contested (Ratna, 2015). Moreover, research about Black women in the sports literature, despite the critical interventions of Birrell (1989), Hargreaves, (2000), Smith (1992) and Scraton (2001), continue to falsify the bodily characteristics and ethnic cultural sensibilities of Black women. For example, Vertinsky and Captain (1998) and Van Ingen (2013) provide compelling her/stories about how controlling discourses objectified and silenced the realities of African American sportswomen as 'natural' athletes and mannish. For South Asian women across the diaspora, their lives continue to be represented in sporting discourses in quite narrow terms, as between two cultures and variously dictated by ethnic cultures, religions and parental wishes (Benn *et al.*, 2010; Hargreaves, 2004; Kay, 2006; Maxwell *et al.*, 2013; Snape and Binks, 2008; Walseth and Strandbu, 2013). Furthermore, little is known about 'other' ethnic groups of women as their sporting preferences are often interpreted through popular representations of both African American and South Asian women (Ratna, 2015). As a result, we know very little about 'who' Black women are and how they see their sporting lives beyond such hegemonic re/presentations. Sport's function as a mechanism for integration, liberation and modernisation is assumed, despite evidence to the contrary (Darnell and Hayhurst, 2011; Samie *et al.*, 2015). Re-asserting the claims of Birrell (1989), Hargreaves (2000), Ismond (2003) and Scraton (2001), there still is an urgent need for researchers to engage in 'other ways of knowing' (Sudbury, 1994) the multifarious, dynamic and sporting experiences of Black women. I contend that the political concerns and everyday realities of Black sportswomen can be illustrated by adopting the postcolonial ideas of Spivak and the Black feminist thinking of Collins.

Can the subaltern speak?

The erasure of Black women's voices in the context of broader social ontologies involves understanding slippage between the two meanings of representation, *vertreten* and *darstellen*, that Spivak draws on (based on the nineteenth-century Marxist text, *The Eighteenth Brumaire of Louis Bonaparte*). Differentiating between the instinct of a class subject and their connected agency, which she (and others) relates to the connected terms of consciousness and conscience, Spivak regards representation (*vertreten*) as a political action taken by someone else who appears to work in another's interest to represent the stories, political consciousness and values important to the subaltern. *Darstellen*, on the other hand, is a form of re/presentation which she describes as drawing a portrait of the subaltern conscience which may be multiple and diverse. The erasure of the subaltern, why she/he cannot speak, is because through both forms of representation her/his voice about how she/he sees their social reality is missing. Spivak suggests that it is not that the subaltern cannot speak, 'as they can speak and know their conditions' (1988: 78), but that their voices are not *heard* or *made audible* through political acts and/or the portraitures of their lives. Spivak claims that this epistemic violence obscures the subjectivities of subaltern figures, their stories become mis-represented and/or ignored. She argues that the task of the intellectual is therefore to deconstruct history to understand why some versions of social reality become the normative frame of reference, and other versions slip from critical analysis. She suggests dominant discourses become legitimated by 'who' is doing the telling; for example, the history of colonialism in India was told by the elite class, 'some of Indian blood and colour but English in taste, in opinions, in morals, and in intellect' (ibid.: 77), who were proxies for white colonials, conveying and perpetuating problematic representations to the masses. These accounts arguably become regarded as authoritative pieces that show little political convergence with the everyday realities of subordinated groups. Much of Spivak's (1988) critique appropriates as well as speaks back to the work of social science philosophers, such as Derrida, critically interrogating the production of the colonial 'Other' as ostensibly linked to the representation of 'Europe' as 'Subject'. Such representations limit the possibility of knowing the investments and power of the 'Other' as separate from, and something other than, the formation and representation of the 'Subject'.

Spivak is influenced by the French philosopher Pierre Macherey (1978) whose arguments about ideology she develops, though according to her he fails to make connections between his key arguments and debates about the representation of the 'Other'. She argues that research analysis must question what literary work 'does not say', which is not the same as what it/people refuse to say (Spivak, 1988: 81). Macherey claims that what a work cannot 'say' is a 'sort of journey to silence', a closing-down of consciousness. Spivak points to the role of the intellectual to cast aside what they think they know about the world and to make possible the *utterance* of different kinds of knowing based on the insurgency of the subaltern subject, and not merely as objects of study seen in the researcher's own reflection. Research about diasporic groups of Black women, whether they constitute a majority or minority population, in and across the global north and south, have arguably been historically erased through such problematic representations (Mohanty, 1992). That is:

It is, rather, that, both as object of colonialist historiography and as subject of insurgency, the ideological construction of gender keeps the male dominant. If, the context of colonial production, the subaltern has no history and cannot speak, the subaltern as female is even more deeply in shadow.

(Spivak, 1988: 82–83)

For women on the other side of this imperial, white 'sisterhood', they cannot know or speak the text of this feminist rhetoric even though the (non)representing white feminist has made space for her to exist within the sphere of the debate (ibid.). Thus, Spivak claims the subaltern woman is 'doubly in shadow' (ibid.: 84). The heterogeneity of the subaltern woman is not known as white feminists have closed off the opportunity to learn about her by constructing a homogenous 'Other', only made knowable to the reader through dominant discourses promulgated through western and Eurocentric accounts. Spivak puts forward the notion of keeping our analytical gaze on the history and socio-cultural dynamics of society, which structure how we read the 'Other', as an important tool for knowing the world and acts of insurgency that arise from this knowledge. Spivak writes:

> In seeking to learn to speak to (rather than listen to or speak for) the historically muted subject of the subaltern woman, the postcolonial intellectual *systematically* 'unlearns' female privilege. This systematic unlearning involves learning to critique postcolonial discourse with the best tools it can provide and not simply substituting the lost figure of the colonized.

In relation to this, criticism of Spivak's work points to how Black men and women continue to be positioned as objects of study through representations that do not acknowledge their subjectivities. Yet Spivak explains that this is a mis-reading of her work. She addresses more directly the 'voice-consciousness' of the subaltern woman through an unpacking of the statement 'white men are saving brown women from brown men' (ibid.: 92). In reference to the story of an Indian woman who took her own life on the pyre of her dead husband as a form of *satee*, she laments that the imperialists banned *satee* (white men saving brown women) while some Indians explained the widow's sacrifice as evidence of the woman wanting to die (connected to the cultural traditions of brown men). The two oppositional re/presentations go a long way to legitimating each other; the imperialists as modern bearers of civilisation and the subaltern 'Others' as backward and uncivilised. But what is lost in both narratives is the 'testimony of the woman's voice-consciousness'. Spivak goes on: '(S)uch a testimony would not be ideology-transcendent or "fully" subjective, of course, but it would have constituted the ingredients for producing a counter sentence' (ibid.: 93). Through an interrogation of other widow sacrifices recorded by the police, not just one voice is audible but a heterogeneity of cases across different caste lines. Critical to examining this public issue, the postcolonial intellectual would ask 'what does this mean? – and begins to plot a history' (ibid.: 93). Spivak unravels the historical practice of satee and how it has been interpreted by a range of authority figures:

> Between patriarchy and imperialism, subject constitution and object formation, the figure of the woman disappears, not into pristine nothingness, but into a violent shuttling which is the displaced figuration of the 'third-world woman' caught between tradition and modernisation.
>
> (Ibid.: 102)

Spivak argues that 'when the subaltern makes an effort to the death to speak, she is not able to be heard, and speaking and hearing complete the speech act' (in interview with Landry and Maclean, 1996: 292). The crucial question is then '(W)ith what voice-consciousness can the subaltern speak?' and how do we ensure we *hear* their voices? (Spivak, 2006: 32). Without voice, and in light of false or problematic representations and re/presentations, the 'subaltern' becomes 'a person without lines of social mobility' (ibid.: 28) to action social change on their own behalf. Furthermore, how do we qualify subaltern women's acts of insurgency and the grounding conditions for that agency with 'evidence' of her conscience-being? If the subaltern female cannot be heard we must pay careful attention to the silences (what is not said about her social realities), acts of insurgency (through ritual, bodily practices/movement/actions as well as speech acts) and tracing the historical and social itineraries of subaltern women as a method of recovering their multiple and different political locations of being. What is being argued here is the importance of coupling representation (a political act) with re/presentation (the material conditions that ground individual and collective acts of differential agency). Arguably, this would enable subaltern women's metaphorical speech acts to be centred, heard, interpreted and connected to better facilitating effective social change.

Within a sporting context Burdsey (2015) captures some of the complexity of how and when the subaltern speaks in his deconstruction of the male cricketer, Moeen Ali. Burdsey states that when Ali does speak it is often within the narrow confines of populist discourses about the visceral threat presented by radical Islam and yet he still has performative power to present counter-narratives, e.g. supporting the civil rights of Muslim people in Palestine. But as Burdsey acknowledges, we still do not know Ali or arguably how he 'feels' about the discourses which position him as 'Other' and/or as celebrated cricket hero (read 'insider'). In her research about the South African male Black runner Sydney Maree, Walton (2012: 127) appropriates Spivak's term 'catachrestic' to explain how one word can be used or mis-used for another enabling the subaltern subject to express alternative ways of being:

> moments of catachresis can allow the 'subaltern' or those suppressed within colonising systems, to use the language and culture structure in which they are subsumed but not explicitly expressed. In doing so, they express themselves using the language and culture of those in power but with alternative meanings. Catachresis used in this way uncovers knowledge of the occult.

Black feminist intellectual Audre Lorde (1984/2007) has attested that 'the Master's tools will never dismantle the Master's house' because the epistemologies and the process of critical interrogation cannot and does not fully capture or express the agitations of the subaltern subject. As bell hooks (1989) asserts, even though the Master's tools are stifling, this language can nevertheless be used to speak back to dominant colonial and cultural hegemonies. Thus, catachresis provides the subaltern with some power of resistance even within the confines of the coloniser's language, and Spivak's insights resonate with Black feminist intellectual thinking which aims to 'talk back' to dominant ideological, socio-cultural, political and economic histories (hooks, 1989).

Black feminist thought and epistemological implications

Representational mis-naming and interpretational slippage has rendered invisible Black women's experiences of social injustice. Crenshaw (1991) suggests that this has occurred as the gender politics of Black women are obscured from anti-racist agendas, while at the same time feminist politics have ignored or universalised white women's being as representative of *all* women's experiences. Black feminist philosophy has been continually ignored in quests for knowledge framed by white, western, male and Eurocentric lenses, erasing how different groups of Black women may construct and understand 'truths' about their own realities, accounting for the multiply-constituted forms of oppressions that they individually and collectively have endured (Collins, 2000). While other Black feminist intellectuals have attempted to define and to seek validation for their ways of knowing the 'truth', I privilege the work of Collins (2000) as she appropriates the political critiques of Black women to articulate more explicitly the contours of a Black feminist epistemology. She provides theoretical insights about *how* critical scholars can uncover the social realities of Black women above and beyond the narrow and problematic re/presentations critiqued by Spivak. The five ways of knowing that Collins puts forward (the focus on lived experience, dialogue as a means of assessing knowledge claims, ethics of caring, personal accountability and recognising Black women as agents of knowing) have the potential to frame and guide other scholars in their quest to recover critical understandings of the multiplicities of Black women's lives.

First, the focus upon lived experience as a criterion of meaning: Collins (2000) suggests that those who have experienced oppression are more credible as narrators of Black women's subjectivities than those who have merely read about those experiences. She further stipulates that related to this are two key sites of knowing: one through the body and the space it occupies and the other passing beyond it, that is, a critical review of both the margin and the centre. She argues this way of knowing privileges the Black women themselves as both knowers (representing their consciousness) and the known (representing their conscious selves) rather than centring abstract theorising *about* Black women and/or reducing their bodies to non-feeling vessels through representations and re/presentations.

Second, building from this, Collins argues that dialogue is significant in assessing knowledge claims. That is, what we know is very rarely developed in isolation but becomes knowable through dialogues with others where we respond and challenge oppressive forces. For Black women, this dialogical potential and resource to talk to one another as well as talk back to oppressive forces of constitution is a key dynamic of their own Black cultural solidarity (hooks, 1989). However, the principles of dialogical capacity have purpose beyond the Black sisterhood, to include others as part of a deeper desire to foster humanistic goals (Collins, 2000). Ratna *et al.* (forthcoming) also argue that dialogue in and between different groups of women as well as between varying manifestations of feminisms (and other disciplinary paradigms) enables knowledge claims to be critically interrogated in order to provide insights that respond to creating research for the 'greater good'. Dialogue also involves power and this requires the researcher to question their ethics and personal responsibilities as part of the research process (e.g. Hargreaves, 2000; Watson and Scraton, 2001, forthcoming).

Third, Collins promotes the ethics of caring that requires the listener to show understanding, care and empathy when lived experiences are being told. She suggests this requires valuing the uniqueness of the individual experience, to 'hear' the emotions and affect of material conditions and to show empathy as a means to validate the stories being shared; Belenky *et al.* (1986) claim these mechanisms may enable Black women to uncover their 'inner voices' (Collins, 2000: 264). While I would be wary of claiming a 'true' authenticity of accounts being shared, in my own work I have attempted to read critically the testimonies of British Asian female footballers in relation to the broader context, so that what the participants said or did not say was critically unpacked in order to reveal underlying tensions and forms of exclusion (Ratna, 2008, 2009, 2011).

Fourth, as part of the ethics of personal accountability, Collins claims that re/interpreting the shared testimonies of Black women may thus involve probing their ethics, examining their personal values and belief systems, in order to gain a better understanding of how they interpret their lived experiences. I would argue further that such accountability also applies to those who are listening and representing those testimonies. An assessment of the researcher's own histories and related belief systems are likely to influence how they re-narrate and make sense of the conscience being and consciousness of Black women (Watson and Scraton, 2001). Finally, Collins advocates the need to recognise Black women as agents of knowledge, as knowers of their own reality and given primacy in the telling of *their* stories, in their own words, and as they see them. Arguably, her framing promotes working towards the 'truth' in terms of respecting Black women's political right for self-definition as well as the process of how we arrive at such 'truth' claims and echoes Spivak in that regard.

Despite calls from Birrell (1989) and Scraton (2001) for Black feminist thought in sport, only a minority of scholars have applied this lens to it (Edwards, 1999; Pelak, 2005; Ratna, 2008; Scraton *et al.*, 2005; Stride, 2014). Stride (2014), for instance, applies Collins' matrix of oppression in order to critically analyse South Asian (Muslim) girls' relationships to sport, across different spaces of home and school, in which the agency, differences and voices of her participants are centralised. She illustrates the intersectional experiences and choices of South Asian girls as they refute, negotiate and accommodate discourses and practices to maintain a positive sense of self. Stride (2014) claims that Collins' framework is too deterministic, though another reading of Collins' book, *Black Feminist Thought*, would suggest that she does indeed create a balanced tension between structure, discipline and ideology and the agencies, inter-personal dynamics and voices of Black women. In my own research I also prioritised a Black feminist lens with the aim of tracing the intersectional contours of British Asian girls and women's racialised and gendered experiences of women's football, specifically connecting structure and agency to make visible the struggles, resistance and strategic negotiations of these different and diverse actors (Ratna, 2008). I argue that the sporting troubles of British Asian girls and women and/or other groups of Black girls and women are rarely connected to wider social forces of inequality and discrimination, more often their experiences are reduced to individual or family matters. There is a political need to move beyond this individualised focus and to interrogate critically the role and function of wider structural determinants, without losing focus on the agentic potential of social actors within these systems. Institutions of sport therefore must consider Black women's involvement in sport as a wider public issue if equalising changes are to be actioned. Referring back to Spivak, this goal can only be achieved when representations of Black women's lives capture the issues significant to their locations of being.

Who does the research?

Black feminist intellectuals have consistently queried 'who' is best placed to re-interpret the lived experiences of Black women. They have questioned the masculinist bias of their racialised male peers, who they have argued ignore gender politics within their research and praxis, and white feminists for universalising their experiences as indicative of the lives of *all* groups of women (Collins, 2000; hooks, 1989; Lorde, 1984). Hargreaves (2004), amongst others, previously made this point in relation to research about sport. She specifically argued that men are unwilling to consider or recognise gender politics within sporting cultures and white women have tended to be blind to racial differences between them. Collins (2000) has also argued that examining gender politics would decentre debates about race relations and thus has not been part of some Black men's political activism. Yet this is not to say Black men have not adopted Black feminist thinking in their scholarship in and beyond the field of sport (Carrington, 2007).

Black feminists have questioned the appropriateness of white people researching Black people, with the claim that they cannot see beyond their own white privileges (Mirza, 1997). Moreover, as stated, Black women 'have long claimed the right to speak for themselves, rather than having others speak for them' (Sudbury, 1994: 27). Arguably, speaking as an 'outsider within' has enabled Black women to use their unique positionality as a basis to express their politics of resistance and, also, as a basis for social critique (Collins, 2000; Okin, 2000; Sudbury, 1994). Thus, Black women's experiences of multiply-constituted forms of oppression are viewed as the basis for justifying their epistemic value. Yet, while the strategic essentialism of adopting an 'outsider within' position was important for the mobilisation of black feminist thinking in the 1960s, at the same time it masked connectivities to other subordinated groups (Collins, 2000). Scholars such as Spivak have also previously argued that in some contexts, 'situation-specific' subject positionality is necessary to exploring a given social problem but she questions why this theorising is not connected to strategy and progressing socio-political goals; possibly because such strategic essentialism flattens and reifies differences between Black women in terms of class, sexuality, disability, age, generation and diaspora. Spivak is more interested in critiquing essentialism in order to explore the ways different identity positions may collide, 'metabolising', in and through specific social conditions and periods of time. In this respect she no longer subscribes to a strategic essentialist viewpoint (and is often mis-quoted) but to a 'differences among these so called essences' approach without regressing into a postmodern melange of endless heterogeneity (Danius and Jonsson, 1993: 36).

The subscription to standpoint theories may, if uncritically applied, also re/produce the notion of an authentic Black positionality that only one who shares that oppression can understand. As Sudbury (1994) articulates, it centres the positions of some groups of Black women while simultaneously marginalising the politics of other Black women. Moreover, it fails to recognise how we may all, regardless of our race, over time and space, experience varying degrees of both power and inequality (Collins, 2000). Sensitive to claims about the epistemic value of 'outsiders within', Collins also acknowledges that the fact of being a Black researcher does not necessarily guarantee the ability to garner deeper insights into Black women's experiences of different oppressions. In my own research (Ratna, 2011, 2012), I have reflected on the moments of dissonance as well as moments of connectivity that I encountered while interviewing women similar to myself in terms of both race and gender about their experiences of playing football which were not smooth or friendly exchanges but involved tensions and uneasy dialogues.

Following from this critique it might be argued that men can research the lives of women and white people can research the lives of black people. Yet, continued discussion about who is best placed to research the lives of Black women is a distraction from the critical research that actually needs to be done in this field. Furthermore, the burden of representation continues to fall on Black scholars and removes white men and women from the responsibility for addressing the lives of people different from themselves. For those scholars, irrespective of their racial and ethnic heritages, who do take up this challenge, they must question the epistemological tools adopted to expose multiply compounded forms of social injustice. Watson and Scraton (2001), in their article about the leisure lives of older South Asian women, respond to such a call in acknowledging the privileges of their whiteness and the responsibilities that arise from this positionality. They enable their reflexivity to 'come alive' by directly exploring in and through detailed examination of their empirical findings. In this case, confronting their whiteness ensured they acknowledged and made accountable their own racial differences and how the racialised scripts of both Others and themselves were read and interpreted in and through the research process. Crucially, as they acknowledge, this process is never fully achieved as identities evolve and take shape across time and space.

Lewis (1996), as a Black woman writing from a Black British feminist perspective two decades ago, offered an insightful solution to the conundrum of who should do the research by asserting the importance of prioritising the politics of location. Indeed, postcolonial feminist scholars such as Spivak and Mohanty concur with Black feminists such as Lewis and Collins, that the politics of location demands the researcher, regardless of their own race, gender and subject positionality, to centre Black women's histories in a way that identifies the geographical, cultural and psychic boundaries which orientate people with others. Thus, while the 'outsider within' position is still significant to centring the experiences of marginalised groups, it requires a narrowing of location which resists essentialising subject positionality (see Spivak above), and facilitates a relational analysis by linking to the position of others. Sudbury (1994) illustrates that this would involve providing more detail about 'who' we are speaking about, for example Black women from Britain, the United States or Nigeria, whether we mean women of African or South Asian heritage who are heterosexual, able-bodied, working-class etc. Locating women's positionality thus requires identifying the structures which locate people in relation to one another at particular moments in time, across spaces and places, and in regards to changing ideological representations. Arguably, the positionality of researchers' insider/outsider status (which can only at best be temporal as identities fluctuate, are hybrid and complex) can be made accountable as part of research designs to capture the voice-consciousness of different Black women.

Conclusion

How Black women's lives are represented through sporting debates and narratives matter as they can either reproduce stereotypical assumptions or facilitate other ways of knowing their lived subjectivities. Thus, 27 years after Birrell (1989) first made her call, I echo her vision of adopting a critical analysis of sport in order to elucidate the multifarious, complex and changing experiences of Black women. Not just to make visible their varied experiences, but to use deeper political insights to fight for concerns relevant to them as individuals and as a collective. In this chapter, I have argued that the intellectual influences of both Spivak and Collins are useful in responding to continuing calls for research in this area. Yet, a more sophisticated use and application of their respective works, to date, have been missing from the socio-cultural analyses of sport and leisure. In relation to this, I would argue that we cannot take for granted that we know all there is to know about postcolonial and/or Black feminism just because some of the terms of the debate (e.g. 'can the subaltern speak?') are popularly bandied around. As demonstrated, the deeper significance of what is meant by such a term lacks detailed consideration and results in an unwillingness to 'hear' the intellectual reasoning of scholars such as Spivak. The de/construction and re/construction of discourses about subaltern subjects is thus a significant aspect of making visible multiple subjectivities, and claims to social justice. Building from Spivak's analysis, in order to support the recovery of Black women's voice consciousness, I advocate the use and application of Black feminist thought. Moreover, paying particular attention to Collins' ways of knowing, being sensitive to how we approach research, for whom, by whom and for what purpose.

In the sports literature, while others have previously emphasised the need to engage with critical theories, including cultural analysis and black feminism (Birrell, 1989; Hargreaves, 2004; Scraton, 2001), research about the sporting experiences of Black girls and women, on the one hand, seems to be growing but, on the other hand, is mixed in terms of academic quality (Ratna, 2015). Thus, by moving from Spivak's arguments about representation and re/presentation to Collins' insights about how to apply Black feminist knowledge, this chapter offers scholars other ways of more adequately recovering the material needs of different groups of Black women. I suggest that the theoretical insights included in this chapter may provide sport and leisure researchers with one way of garnering knowledge that can be used to improve Black women's material realities.

The humanist vision of intellectuals such as Spivak and Collins reflects their political desires to effect change for the good of humankind more broadly, for women and men who need strategies to thrive and survive in relation to conditions of marginality and discrimination. The arguments of sports scholars such as Birrell (1989), Hargreaves (1994, 2000, 2004) and Scraton (1994, 2001) resonate with what Black feminists such as Collins (2000) have always claimed, that 'action' and 'thought' must 'inform one another'. Hence cultural analysis is important to building deeper knowledge about the socio-cultural realities of Black women's lives, but this must be done in addition to community engagement, practice and academic interventions which capture the feelings of their (dis)locations of being. The latter is also necessary in order to challenge problematic re/presentations, making knowable alternative frames of history and culture (Alexander and Arday, 2014) and the dissemination of researcherly[3] work which is grounded in relation to the lived experiences of Black women. I therefore urge scholars to engage in 'other ways of knowing' (Sudbury, 1994), to elucidate the hopes and needs of Black women in and through *both* sporting representations and lived experiences.

Notes

1 Thanks to Dr. Daniel Burdsey and Dr. Beccy Watson for their kind comments, which were useful in the final re-drafting of this chapter.
2 For clarification, I use the marker of 'Black' to refer to the politics of women who may constitute an ethnic minority or majority population within national boundaries (and as a diasporic group) but who may be racially different from one another (Mirza, 1997).
3 I thank Professor Kathy Jamieson for introducing me to this term as a means of prioritising our active reflexivity, as part of our 'researcherly' agendas and practises.

References

Aitchison, C. (2001) 'Theorising Other discourses of tourism, gender and culture: can the subaltern speak (in tourism)?', *Tourist Studies* 1(2): 133–147.
Alexander, C. and Arday, J. (2014) *Aiming Higher: Race, Inequality and Diversity in the Academy*. London: Runnymede Perspectives.

Amos, V. and Parmar, P. (1984) 'Challenging imperial feminism', *Feminist Review* 17: 3–19.

Belenky, M. F., Clinchy, B. M., Goldberger, N. R. and Tarule, J. M. (1986) *Women's Ways of Knowing: The Development of Self, Voice, and Mind.* New York: BasicBooks.

Benn, T., Pfister, G. and Jawad, H. (eds) (2010) *Muslim Women and Sport.* London and New York: Routledge.

Birrell, S. (1989) 'Racial relations theories and sport: suggestions for a more critical analysis', *Sociology of Sport Journal* 6: 211–227.

Burdsey, D. (2006) *British Asians and Football: Culture, Identity and Exclusion.* London: Routledge.

Burdsey, D. (2015) 'Un/making the British Asian male athlete: race, legibility and the state', *Sociological Research Online*, doi:10.5153/sro.3768.

Carrington, B. (2007) 'Merely identity: cultural identity and the politics of sport', *Sociology of Sport Journal* 24(1): 49–66.

Collins, P. H. (2000) *Black Feminist Thought: Knowledge, Consciousness and the Politics of Empowerment*, 2nd edn. New York and London: Routledge.

Crenshaw, K. (1991) 'Mapping the margins: intersectionality, identity politics, and violence against women of color'. *Stanford Law Review*, 43(6), 1241–1299.

Danius, S. and Jonnson, S. (1993) 'An interview with Gayatri Chakravorty Spivak', *Boundary 2* 20(2): 24–50.

Darnell, S. and Hayhurst, L. M. C. (2011) 'Sport for decolonization: exploring a new praxis of sport for development', *Progress in Developmental Studies* 11(3): 183–196.

Edwards, J. (1999) 'The Black female athlete and the politics of invisibility', *New Political Economy* 4(2): 278–282.

Hargreaves, J. (1994) *Sporting Females: Critical Issues in the History and Sociology of Women's Sport.* London: Routledge.

Hargreaves, J. (2000) *Heroines of Sport: The Politics of Difference and Identity.* London: Routledge.

Hargreaves, J. (2004) 'Querying Sport Feminism: Personal or Political?', in: Giulianotti, R. (ed.) *Sport and Modern Social Theorists.* London: Palgrave Macmillan, 187–206.

hooks, b. (1989) *Talking Back: Thinking Feminist, Thinking Black.* Boston: South End Press.

Ismond, P. (2003) *Black and Asian Athletes in British Sport and Society: A Sporting Chance?* Basingstoke: Palgrave Macmillan.

Jamieson, K. M. (2003) 'Occupying a middle space: toward a mestiza sport studies', *Sociology of Sport Journal* 20: 1–6.

Kay, T. (2006) 'Daughters of Islam: family influences on Muslim young women's participation in sport', *International Review for the Sociology of Sport* 41(3–4): 357–373.

Landry, D. and Maclean, G. (1996) *The Spivak Reader.* New York and London: Routledge.

Lewis, G. (1996) 'Situated voices: "Black women's experience" and social work', *Feminist Review* 53: 24–56.

Lorde, A. (1984/2007) *Sister Outsider: Essays and Speeches by Audre Lorde.* Berkeley: Crossing Press.

Macherey, P. (1978) *A Theory of Literary Production*. London: Routledge & Kegan Paul.

Maxwell, H., Foley, C. and Taylor, T. (2013) 'Social inclusion in community sport: a case-study of Muslim women in Australia', *Journal of Sport Management* 27: 467–481.

Mirza, H. S. (1997) *Black British Feminism: A Reader*, New York and London: Routledge.

Mohanty, C. T. (1992) 'Feminist encounters: locating the politics of experience', in: Barratt, M. and Phillips, A. (eds) *Destabilising Theory*. Cambridge: Polity Press, 74–92.

Okin, S. M. (2000) 'Feminism, women's human rights, and cultural differences', in: Narayan, U. and Harding, S. (eds) *Decentering the Center: Philosophy for a Multicultural, Postcolonial, and Feminist World*. Bloomington, IN: Indiana University Press, 26–46.

Pelak, C. F. (2005) 'Negotiating gender/race/class constraints in New South Africa: a case-study of women's soccer', *International Review for the Sociology of Sport* 40(1): 53–70.

Ratna, A. (2008) 'A "fair game?" British Asian females' experiences of racism in women's football', in: Magee, J., Caudwell, J., Liston, K. and Scraton, S. (eds) *Women, Football and Europe: Histories, Equity and Experiences*. Oxford: Meyer and Meyer Sport, 77–96.

Ratna, A. (2009) ' "Off with their headscarves, on with their football kits?" Unveiling myths and exploring the identities of British-Muslim female footballers', in: Wagg, S. and Bramham, P. (eds) *Lucky Leeds: Sport, Leisure and Culture in a Postmodern Northern City*. Aldershot: Ashgate Press, 171–188.

Ratna, A. (2011) ' "Who wants to make aloo gobi when you can bend it like Beckham?" British Asian females and their racialised experiences of gender and identity in women's football', *Soccer and Society* 12(3): 381–400.

Ratna, A. (2012) 'Intersectional plays of identity: the experiences of British Asian female footballers', *Sociological Research Online*. Available from: www. socresonline.org.uk/18/1/13.html.

Ratna, A. (2015) 'Why do we know so little about Black women and sport?', paper presented at the North American Sociology of Sport Association Annual Conference, Sante Fe, 1–4 November.

Ratna, A. and Samie, S. F. (eds) (forthcoming) *Race, Gender and Sport: The Politics of Ethnic Minority Girls and Women*. London: Routledge.

Ratna, A., Samie, S. F., Jamieson, K. and Thangaraj, S. (forthcoming) 'Learning lessons from the feminisms of ethnic "Others" ', in: Mansfield, L., Wheaton, B., Caudwell, J. and Watson, R. (eds) *Handbook of Feminism, Sport, Physical Education and Leisure*. Basingstoke: Palgrave Macmillan.

Samie, S. F. (2013) 'Heterosexy self/body work and basketball: the invisible sporting women of British Pakistani Muslim heritage', *South Asian Popular Culture* 11(3): 257–270.

Samie, S. F., Johnson, A. J., Huffman, A. M. and Hillyer, S. J. (2015) 'Voices of empowerment: women from the Global South re/negotiating empowerment and the global sports mentoring programme', *Sport in Society: Culture, Commerce, Media, Politics* 18(8): 923–937.

Scraton, S. (1994) 'The changing world of women and leisure: feminism, "postfeminism" and leisure', *Leisure Studies* 13(4): 249–261.

Scraton, S. (2001) 'Reconceptualising race, gender and sport: the contribution of black feminism', in: Carrington, B. and McDonald, I. (eds) *Race, Sport and British Society*. London: Routledge, 170–187.

Scraton, S. and Watson, B. (1998) 'Gendered cities: women and public leisure spaces in the "postmodern city"', *Leisure Studies* 17(2): 123–137.

Scraton, S., Caudwell, J. and Holland, S. (2005) '"Bend it like Patel": centring "race", ethnicity and gender in feminist analysis of women's football in England', *International Review for the Sociology of Sport* 40(1): 17–88.

Smith, Y. (1992) 'Women of color in society and sport', *Quest* 44(2): 228–250.

Snape, R. and Binks, P. (2008) 'Re-thinking sport: physical activity and healthy living in British South Asian Muslim communities', *Managing Leisure* 13(1): 23–35.

Spivak, G. C. (1988) 'Can the subaltern speak?', in: Nelson, C. and Grossberg, L. (eds) *Marxism and Interpretations of Culture*. Basingstoke: Macmillan Education, 271–313.

Spivak, G. C. (1996) 'Explanation and culture: marginalia (1979)', in: Landry, D. and Maclean, G. (eds) *The Spivak Reader*. New York and London: Routledge, 29–52.

Spivak, G. C. (2006) 'Can the subaltern speak? (abbreviated by the author)', in: Ashcroft, B., Griffiths, G. and Tiffin, H. (eds) *The Post-Colonial Studies Reader*, 2nd edn. London and New York: Routledge, 28–37.

Stride, A. (2014) 'Centralising space: the physical education and physical activity experiences of South Asian, Muslim girls', *Sport, Education and Society*, 21(5): 677–697.

Sudbury, J. (1994) *'Other Kinds of Dreams': Black Women's Organisations and the Politics of Transformation*. London and New York: Routledge.

Thangaraj, S. (2015) *Desi Hoop Dreams: Pickup Basketball and the Making of Asian American Masculinity*. New York and London: New York University Press.

Van Ingen, C. (2013) '"Seeing what frames our seeing": seeking histories on early black female boxers', *Journal of Sports History* 40(1): 93–110.

Vertinsky, P. and Captain, G. (1998) 'More myth than history: American culture and representations of black females' athletic ability', *Journal of Sports History* 25(3): 532–561.

Walseth, K. and Strandbu, A. (2013) 'Young Norwegian-Pakistani women and sport: how does culture and religiosity matter?', *European Physical Education Review* 20(4): 489–507.

Walton, T. (2012) 'Developing catachrestic sport histories: toward a critical biography of elite distance runner Sydney Maree', *Journal of Sport History* 39(1): 123–138.

Watson, B. and Scraton, S. (2001) 'Confronting whiteness? Researching the leisure lives of South Asian mothers', *Journal of Gender Studies* 10(3): 265–277.

Watson, B. and Scraton, S. (forthcoming) 'Reconfronting whiteness: ongoing challenges in sport and leisure research', in: Ratna, A. and Samie, S. F. (eds) *Sport, Gender and Race: The Politics of Ethnic 'Other' Girls and Women*. London: Routledge.

Chapter 13

Researching the wrong in sport and leisure

Ethical reflections on mapping whiteness, racism and the far-right

Karl Spracklen

Introduction

Understanding the marginal voice and social injustice within sport and leisure means that researchers rightly make critical choices to include marginal voices and accounts of the unjust in their sport and leisure research. In the rest of this book, my colleagues quite rightly focus on how voices from the margins may be heard, and how we as scholars of sport and leisure might focus on exploring the intersectionalities of social justice (Sen, 2009) in the object of our studies. It is a matter of fundamental importance that we as critical social scientists explore the myriad ways in which marginal voices and agents are constrained in sport and leisure, while simultaneously mapping the spaces and the strategies in which such agents may be empowered to create belonging and identity.

Our political commitment to social justice should inform our praxis as critical scholars (Barry, 2005), as well as our ethical choices in the research process. If we choose to be critical social scientists, we have to develop an ethics based on that choice. In many cases, this means the kind of work my colleagues in this book excel at – highlighting the leisure lives and leisure spaces of those marginalised by intersectional inequalities, those whose choices remain constrained even in this new century of globalisation and post-modernity: minority ethnic groups, women and girls, the lower classes, new migrants, people with disabilities and people of non-heteronormative sexualities. But sometimes our political commitment to social justice can take us to methodological spaces and ethical choices that focus on the politics of exclusion, rather than the politics of resistance. In this chapter, I suggest that to understand the mechanics of exclusion and hegemony it is sometimes necessary to explore the voices and spaces of the hegemons in sport and leisure. But there is a danger with writing about the hegemons and their power – without explicitly condemning it, much of this work seems to end up justifying the social injustice and inequality normalised by that power. Much of the work on masculinities in sport, for example, blurs the ethical line between critique and apologism. That is, studies that focus on the leisure of heterosexual, hegemonically masculine men watching soccer or playing rugby, for example, often theorise the activity and the leisure space as masculine but do not then condemn the maintenance of such hegemonic activities (Connell and Messerschmidt, 2005). Social justice, as a moral imperative (Sen, 2009), means that we have to address the structural and cultural inequalities that lie at the heart of sport and leisure, while offering solutions or policies or directions for ourselves or others to take action. And if we cannot effect political change towards social justice we should be strong in our condemnations of the *status quo ante*. It is our role as critical scholars of sport and leisure to reveal the hidden mechanisms through which sport and leisure make the world a world of privilege for some, and of exclusion for others.

In this chapter I will reflect on the methodological and ethical issues involved in mapping whiteness, racism and the far-right in sport and leisure, using my own research on heavy metal as a case study on how to situate oneself as an ethical but critical researcher. I will explore my research on black metal (Lucas *et al.*, 2011; Spracklen, 2006, 2009, 2013a, 2013b; Spracklen *et al.*, 2014), and more recent work on folk metal (Spracklen, 2015). This research, of course, is part of my wider research interest in leisure, identity and exclusion. I am politically and morally committed to social justice. I want to live in a world where inequality and poverty are removed, where the ethics of social justice ensure sexism, racism and other forms of hegemonic power are eliminated. So my research programme explores the potential and the limitations of social justice in and through leisure – my methodological choices are based on this personal ethic. In the 1990s, I explored the forms of community and belonging associated with the two codes of rugby in the north of England, with a strong critique of both codes as leisure spaces that excluded as much as they included (Spracklen, 1995, 1996, 2001). While rugby league at least served as a resistive space for subaltern classes in the north of England, it served the same role as rugby union in normalising hegemonic masculinity and whiteness. I have since spent many years working with others in this book mapping and critiquing the role of sport in essentialising 'race' and normalising racial inequalities, and the challenges to such hegemony sport and leisure may provide (Long *et al.*, 1997, 2005, 2014; Spracklen *et al.*, 2006, 2010, 2015). Since the 2000s I have developed a research programme critically exploring belonging and exclusion in a wider range of leisure activities and spaces than sport (Spracklen, 2009, 2011, 2013b), most significantly for this chapter, research on heavy metal. This has become in one aspect – the critical lens that helps me theorise leisure – an exploration of Habermasian rationalities that compete in leisure spaces for control of the lifeworld: communicative rationality predicated on freedom to think and choose, and instrumental rationality imposed on the lifeworld by the systems of modernity, which restricts such freedom of thought and freedom of action (Habermas, 1984, 1987). After I have discussed the case study on heavy metal, I will suggest that the strong ethical positions I have chosen to take on whiteness, racism and the far-right have ensured that the necessary critique has not led to being an apologist for such ideologies. Rather, by exposing such ideologies I remain committed to exploring the potential for social justice in leisure.

Black metal

Black metal is a sub-genre of extreme metal, related to death metal but constructed in opposition to it. Debates about black metal's origins and the key bands in its establishment can be found elsewhere (see Spracklen, 2009). The focus of my academic interest is the black metal scene that has emerged since the 1990s, when the 'second wave' of black metal – musicians and bands based in Norway – was associated with headlines around the world about black magic, real Church burnings and actual murders. Black metal spread around the world following those headlines and stimulated by the evil sounds and imagery, as well as black metal's anti-Christian, heathen, nationalist and elitist ideologies (Spracklen, 2006). I was a fan of black metal, as I was a fan of heavy metal, but my interest in metal had waned when black metal was becoming notorious, and black metal bands and fans were to be found round the world. My return to heavy metal as a fan came with listening to the progressive death metal band Opeth in 2001, and realising that there was still a place for riffs and technical flair in a period dominated by the poppy sounds of nu-metal. Listening to Opeth led to a search for other extreme metal bands and an appreciation of the sub-genres in extreme metal, so I came to the Norwegian black metal bands of the 1990s – Mayhem, Immortal, Emperor, Darkthrone, Satyricon, Burzum and Enslaved – fascinated by the mythology associated with them, but drawn to their cold sounds. These bands were not all political racists, but all of them wrote lyrics and spoke in interviews of their suspicion of Christianity and modernity, or their pride in the history of Viking Norway. I soon became familiar with the different elitist ideologies in black metal, from the heathenism of Enslaved (which rejected racism altogether in favour of a recreation of 'Vikingness') to the existence of National Socialist Black Metal bands, and the extreme right-wing politics of Varg Vikernes of the band Burzum. Vikernes was established as the most famous of the musicians associated with the Norwegian scene due to his murder of his bandmate and subsequent trial and imprisonment. Vikernes became the hero of neo-Nazis and other far-right ideologists in black metal, writing books and making statements in the press – even while in prison – that outlined his adherence to essentialist theories of racial biology and culture, and his belief in the racial purity of Northern Europeans and the need to stand firm against Jews, Muslims and other minorities.

So when I started to research black metal I was aware of these tensions over what the ideology of black metal was supposed to be, the different elitist ideologies presented by bands, fans and writers on-line: the belief that black metal was somehow Satanic or at least anti-Christian; the belief that black metal was misanthropic; the belief that black metal was a rejection of Christianity in favour of heathenism; and the belief that black metal was a space for the romantic, conservative nationalism espoused by the neo-Nazis. My first attempt to research black metal involved exploring postings on an on-line fan forum (Spracklen, 2006). I wanted to explore what people thought they had to say about black metal in a debate about its borders and its content. I did not seek permission to use the material as I considered it to be in the public domain – and all the people who posted messages had avatars with pseudonyms. In this first piece of research I argued that for black-metal fans it was important to claim black metal as a form of communicative rationality, and to be suspicious of those who tried to 'sell-out' – but at the same time, the fans adopted instrumental rationality when it came to their 'bought' identity, as well as through ideas of gender and sexuality. My second venture into the field involved a combination of reflective ethnography with interviews with fans I knew from the north of England (Spracklen, 2009). In interviewing those fans I was able to assure them that I was a fan, too. I allowed the fans to create black metal pseudonyms, but I was also sure, through knowing the fans, that they were not at the political racist end of the black metal ideological spectrum. This solved the ethical and methodological issue about my safety in interviewing people with extreme racist views (it is important not to shy away from research with such people, but there are ways in which such views can be recorded, which is why I do most of my research on such topics on-line). Some of my respondents made a point not to listen to the sub-genre called National Socialist Black Metal (NSBM), but others did not let the political content stop them from listening.

At this point in my black metal research, and my black metal fandom, I had come up with a rule of my own. I would not listen to or buy anything that was advertised as NSBM with explicit racist lyrics. But I would listen to and buy black metal that was associated on-line or in the press with individuals or organisations known to have sympathies with the far-right – it is probably hypocritical of me, but if the music is available to buy in HMV, then it is tolerable. So I allowed myself the pleasure of listening to the Burzum albums released before Vikernes went to prison and wrote his racist diatribes. I bought music by bands released through Supernal Music, a label owned by an individual who supported far-right politics so much that he eventually moved into being a writer and ideologue in that scene. Only once did I buy an NSBM release – so that I could comment on its content as an academic. My personal politics of not giving a platform for fascism fits uneasily with the libertarian ethics of metal, which states that everybody is free to do and say whatever they wish, and also fits uneasily with the communicative rationality that is at the heart of black metal. My excuse for listening to the music of a band like Burzum is that the aesthetics outweighs my displeasure with its creator, and the early music does not use lyrics reflecting racist ideologies.

My research on black metal fandom on-line was eventually noticed by black metal fans on-line via the same forum and other ones. Many fans seemed to support my account of black metal fandom and its ideologies, and I even ended up meeting one forum user who was a music student at my own institution when he came up to introduce himself. Some fans were upset about the suggestion that the scene had an ideology of elitism that included racism and sexism. I did not receive any personal abuse in my email inbox, though one infamous far-right web-site suggested my Jewishness (presumably a reference to my German-sounding name?) explained why my research was false.

After meeting with two colleagues from the University of Leeds doing PhDs on metal, I developed a third research project on black (and extreme) metal: exploring how four black (and extreme) metal bands in the north of England used their music to construct identity and belonging, and how the musicians in those bands reflected on that identity work in their music-making (Lucas et al., 2011; Spracklen et al., 2014). In this work we used the names of the bands, as we had to discuss their albums, songs and lyrics, but we offered and gave anonymity to the individuals we interviewed. One of the bands – Old Corpse Road – did not write songs that were based on any problematic themes, using instead ghost tales from folklore. The other three bands – Winterfylleth, Wodensthrone and Oakenshield – did write lyrics that played with and legitimised exclusive notions of Englishness, northern identity and hegemonic masculinity. I came to know the musicians of three of these bands personally, so I came to understand their personal politics – and would say that they were classically liberal. They all feel strongly that Christianity, modernity, globalisation and global capitalism have made the north of England less enchanted, and fractured the connection between the people who live there and the land and its history. While I feel sympathy with this view – and the suspicion of big bankers and governments implied in it – I am not so comfortable with claiming some true history of the north or of England as 'mine'. In the papers I wrote with Lucas and Deeks, and in my own paper on whiteness in black metal and English folk music (Spracklen, 2013a) I hover around the authenticity of the performance of exclusive masculinity and identity at work in the 'other three' bands, especially in Winterfylleth (do these musicians truly believe what they are saying in their performances, their lyrics and their interviews, or is it an act to sell records and t-shirts? Do they understand the political implications of what they are saying?), trying to get to the heart of their place in my field, and their place as decent people I know.

Folk metal fantasies

My interest in English folk music and extreme metal bands that used history and folk culture led me logically to an exploration of the sub-genre of heavy metal called folk metal. I had been attending folk metal gigs for some years, as well as watching folk metal bands at festivals such as Wacken (Germany), Warhorns (UK) and Bloodstock (UK). As a fan of folk music I liked the way many folk metal bands combined heavy metal with traditional folk instruments and folk motifs. Folk metal was and is a big part of the wider heavy metal scene, and the big bands such as Finntroll and Turisas count hundreds of thousands of Facebook fans: not nearly as much as mainstream rock and metal bands, but big enough to ensure people listen to their music and buy their merchandise. But my knowledge of the use of folk music – and black metal – to promote exclusive and narrow forms of belonging led me to realise the same kinds of things were at work in folk metal. The bands were not overtly racist or sexist, but the construction of their music, and the reception of that music in the metal scene, ensures that myths of national purity and hegemonic masculinity were legitimised. Many of the bands from northern Europe focus exclusively on pagan Viking warriors as their historical root: their lives as strong fighting men and defenders of national pride and racial purity become the exemplar for the metal scene today. If bands and fans embrace the idea that this mythical past was better because we were all warriors defending our pure, authentic culture, then what does that say about what we think about the present day?

The research began with a contemplation of ethics. I was not interested in what bands might have told me in an interview – I concentrated instead on the content they created: lyrics, album covers and official web-sites. I also explored how fans spoke about folk metal songs and bands. So the research was all in the public domain, and low risk. I had no moral dilemma naming the bands and the authors of comments on-line, so long as those comments were in a public space (Eynon *et al.*, 2009). Combined with my own history as a fan attending gigs I had enough ethnographic data to provide a strong critique of folk metal. I first presented my findings at a conference in York on Metal and Marginalisation. I said there:

> It could be argued, then, that folk metal has become something that serves as a comfortable, communicative leisure space for those who have lost power in the recent decades: the white European, working-class men who have faced challenges to their assumed privileges from women, globalisation, immigration and postmodernity. But folk metal cannot be easily dismissed as a fantasy space for young, white European men left behind by postmodernity, postcolonialism and a rearrangement of the gender order. Rather, folk metal remains central to

the ongoing construction of heavy metal as a form of commodified, instrumental leisure ... that makes the power of western, instrumental whiteness and hegemonic masculinity invisible, while ironically being in plain sight. It is part of the dominant culture – hegemonically masculine, white (northern/western European) – that embraces the narratives and myths of neo-liberal individualism and nationalism.

(Later published in Spracklen, 2015: 373)

Like all academic conferences, I received a range of comments, from the mundane to the critical, but overall people in music studies and gender studies understood what I was saying. This is not anything radical or novel – many people have been saying the same thing for many years, from scholars in Critical Race Theory to radical feminists – that popular culture is a contested space in which various structures and powers operate to impose exclusive notions of identity and culture. This led to submitting my paper for a special issue of *Metal Music Studies*, and it was published in September 2015. In the review process, some of my language was toned down, and some of my bold statements questioned. I made sure through the review process that I made it explicit that there are many female heavy metal fans and musicians, and many folk metal fans and musicians who are women. I also acknowledge that there are folk metal bands and fans who are not white Europeans or white Americans. But the existence of these does not undermine my thesis about the folk metal bands who sell records and headline festivals, and their fans.

I make a habit of letting the media team at the university know about my publications. Sometimes they are interested and I get a news story on the web-site and a press release out to the usual channels. In this case I was sure they would publish something. The stories on my heavy metal research have proved popular, more so than the new stories about real-ale or whisky tourism, for example. I knew the media office would write something and they did. On 1 October 2015 the story was placed on the main page of the university web-site with the headline 'Racism and sexism in heavy metal highlighted in new study' (http://mediacentre.leedsbeckett. ac.uk/press-release/racism-and-sexism-in-heavy-metal-highlighted-in-new-study, accessed 10 February 2016). At the time I thought the headline was fair: I was highlighting racism and sexism in heavy metal, albeit in the subgenre of folk metal. The press release had a long quote from me about the research, which ends as follows:

The warrior myth that folk metal is focused on is normalising this masculine predominance in our modern day world – men still have enormous social, cultural and political power. Folk metal's obsession with warriors and cultural purity, displayed through tales of Vikings and dressing up as Vikings on stage, reduces belonging and identity in a multi-cultural, cosmopolitan society to a few exclusive myths. It is showing white men how to be white men and showing women and ethnic minorities their place in European society.

I stand by every word in that quote. The first paragraph of the press release summarises the conclusion of my paper in non-academic words:

A new study from Leeds Beckett University has revealed how the metal music subgenre of folk metal is not only a fantasy space for young, white European men but also an important example of how heavy metal can be seen to normalise masculinity and 'whiteness' and perpetuate sexism and racism.

Reading that through slowly the only things I am uncomfortable with are the wording that suggests the study has been done by Leeds Beckett University, and the language about a revelation. On the first point, I am employed by the university, of course, but this seems to imply the university owned or led or directly funded the work. On the second point, the research has not revealed anything that was not already known by many people in heavy metal, and many people in metal music studies. But these minor quibbles aside, there is nothing in the sentence that troubles me.

But trouble did follow the story – especially reactions to it on the internet. The press release was picked up by a number of new channels and that led to people on Twitter becoming agitated. I became the subject of a Twitter storm as people posted their anger about my work on the social media site underneath the Leeds Beckett University's newsfeed. People even posted angry comments under the story on the Leeds Beckett University website. The lead musician and front man of Turisas, and the singer of the Irish metal band Primordial, both got involved – questioning my right to say negative things about metal, and folk metal. Initially I was unaware of this social media activity. I only noticed when I started to get emails asking me why I thought metal was racist or sexist. Some emails came from people who wondered whether I was being racist and sexist, because I was supposedly denying the existence of non-white and female fans and musicians in metal, I also got a few more sinister emails that accepted my argument that folk metal was racist and sexist, but did not see a problem with that. This email from someone called JS (9 October 2015) is typical of the type:

Why is it you only criticise the masculinity of european men? Why don't you just come out and say you want to see the annihilation of indigenous europeans?

'Folk metal's obsession with warriors and cultural purity, displayed through tales of Vikings and dressing up as Vikings on stage, reduces belonging and identity in a multi-cultural, cosmopolitan society to a few exclusive myths. It is **showing white men how to be white men** and showing women and ethnic minorities their place in European society.'

Why is what I've highlighted portrayed as negative? European man's masculinity has been devastated by decades of propaganda inspired by the likes of Adorno and other Jewish academics. Take note: we are the counter-culture now. Unlike Fukuyama's wishful thinking, *history never ends*. Our time will come, and with screeds like this it's clear the left are just starting to realise that.

There were overt threats made on the intent, to me and to my family, but I did not even try to engage with the people posting comments on-line, and I won't bother to reference them in this chapter because there are literally hundreds of them. A quick internet search will help you find them. For many on the internet, I was branded as a 'social justice warrior', a figure of hatred and derision. The lead singer of Primordial muttered in a column he writes for the magazine *Zero Tolerance* about 'social justice' types who are trying to stop heavy metal being heavy metal, those people trying to censor or change the ideology or community of heavy metal by condemning sexism and racism (Averill, 2015). This is of course a common reaction by people with power who are faced with research and arguments that question their own position in maintaining social injustice (Sen, 2009).

The paper was downloaded over 1,000 times from the Leeds Beckett University Repository in October 2015 alone, and has become my most downloaded paper ever across the Repository and on journal web-sites. I have clearly made a strong societal impact with this research. The story became seen by some libertarian news channels as proof of the stupidity of the liberal media and social sciences, and they had good fun claiming I was saying anyone who dressed as a Viking or watched a film about Vikings was racist. I did try to respond to every email, as I felt morally obliged to answer comments written by people who had made the effort to get in touch. But I tired of responding to people who use the discourse of the far-right to frame their arguments, and I decided to not respond if their emails turned that way. Most people who emailed me were offended by the fact that I had supposedly betrayed heavy metal and its culture, which they believed to be inclusive; they thought I was an outsider who knew nothing about folk metal, and did not understand the performativity and the escapism of it all. To those people I have responded and engaged in discussion with them, showing them I am a fan and I belong to the metal community, and I am aware of the ways metal is inclusive and promotes social justice. However, all this aside, I stand by the conclusions in my folk metal paper.

Conclusions

On reflection, I feel some ethical concern for my fellow researchers, who may now find it harder than it might have been to gain access to the black metal and folk metal scenes. The rhetoric on-line seems to be that academic studies of heavy metal are to be shunned because 'we' are critical of 'their' leisure activities and spaces. As such, there may well be a backlash for the next researcher who tries to gain access to one or other of these scenes, especially if they want to speak to actors in those scenes about identity. It is always difficult to gain the trust and confidence of any actors in any space, but there is in this space a suspicion of 'liberal academics' and 'social justice warriors' who want to spoil the fun.

I think, however, that is my ethical duty to shine a light on the forms in which whiteness and male privilege is constructed in black metal and folk metal. We all have a duty to be critical researchers, and thinking about the consequences for other researchers in the future should not be at the forefront of our minds when we are writing up our findings. I am a strong advocate of social justice, a defender of liberal views about equality and society – and a strong critiquer of capitalism and hegemonic power – so I am not afraid to be described as such by metal fans. Too many studies of music scenes or sports activities are written by fans who want to remain uncritical fans. This is bad for leisure studies. Sociological leisure studies more generally should not operate in a functionalist or positivist paradigm. We have a moral duty as critical leisure scholars to unpick the tensions and the injustices. At the same time we have to respect our sources as much as we can. For people I have interviewed I provide that respect even if they have said things I am uncomfortable with politically. For things that are posted on-line in a public space, there is no concern about anonymity – but there is an ethical issue over how we use that material in a way that is fair to the people posting it. In this case, I think I managed to balance the line – I have not distorted the viewpoints of the on-line communities I have researched.

I am aware of my own whiteness and masculinity in all of this. I am from the marginalised working-class north of England, but I am privileged. I have easy access to power and to leisure and cultural spaces. Am I merely duplicating that privilege in my work? I do not think so, even though I am morally bound to reflect carefully and fairly on what actors in leisure are saying. There may be some anger among some subaltern groups in metal, and those studying them, that my research has legitimised white male privilege and justified the myths told by white men in metal: that metal has been, is and will be for white men only. I am aware that the racist person who emailed me was quite happy with my conclusion. But I do not believe that metal was, is and will be exclusively for white men. I recognise that there have been non-white musicians, fans and scenes in heavy metal; and that women have been involved in metal's history and culture too (see the extensive literature review in Spracklen, 2015). That is obviously true. But white men have had dominant roles in the scene in Europe and North America historically, and have policed the boundaries of the community and its myth-making to make that dominance into a matter of fact that reduces subalterns to the margins (or whitewashes them out altogether – see Spracklen, 2013a). And despite major challenges to that white male cultural space (from postmodernity, globalisation, from women and from minority ethnic groups and metal fans from the global South), it remains a haven for white male hegemony. This is why I had to say what I said, and why the internet reacted as it did – and why I will do it all again when the research project demands it. Academics have a role in identifying the potential for social justice in the modern world, and the limitations and ideologies the modern world puts in the way of social justice (Sen, 2009). By exposing such ideologies I remain committed to exploring the potential for social justice in leisure.

References

Averill, A. (2015) 'View from the bunker', *Zero Tolerance*, 69: 96.

Barry, B. (2005) *Why social justice matters*. Cambridge: Polity.

Connell, R. W. and Messerschmidt, J. W. (2005) 'Hegemonic masculinity: rethinking the concept', *Gender and Society* 19(6): 829–859.

Eynon, R., Schroeder, R. and Fry, J. (2009) 'New techniques in online research: challenges for research ethics', *21st Century Society* 4(2): 187–199.

Habermas, J. (1984) *The theory of communicative action. Volume one: reason and the rationalization of society*. Cambridge: Polity.

Habermas, J. (1987) *The theory of communicative action. Volume two: the critique of functionalist reason*. Cambridge: Polity.

Long, J., Carrington, B. and Spracklen, K. (1997) ' "Asians cannot wear turbans in the scrum": explorations of racist discourse within professional rugby league', *Leisure Studies* 16(4): 249–260.

Long, J., Hylton, K. and Spracklen, K. (2014) 'Whiteness, blackness and settlement: leisure and the integration of new migrants', *Journal of Ethnic and Migration Studies* 40(11): 1779–1797.

Long, J., Robinson, P. and Spracklen, K. (2005) 'Promoting racial equality within sports organizations', *Journal of Sport and Social Issues* 29(1): 41–59.

Lucas, C., Deeks, M. and Spracklen, K. (2011) 'Grim up north: northern England, northern Europe and black metal', *Journal for Cultural Research* 15(3): 279–296.

Sen, A. (2009) *The idea of social justice*. Harmondsworth: Penguin.

Spracklen, K. (1995) 'Playing the ball, or the uses of league: class, masculinity and rugby', in McFee, G., Murphy, W. and Whannel, G. (eds) *Leisure cultures: values, genders, lifestyles*. Eastbourne: Leisure Studies Association, 105–120.

Spracklen, K. (1996) *Playing the ball: constructing community and masculine identity in rugby*. PhD thesis, Leeds Metropolitan University.

Spracklen, K. (2001) 'Black pearl, black diamonds: exploring racial identities in rugby league', in Carrington, B. and McDonald, I. (eds) 'Race', sport and British society. London: Routledge, 70–82.

Spracklen, K. (2006) 'Leisure, consumption and a blaze in the northern sky: developing an understanding of leisure at the end of modernity through the Habermasian framework of communicative and instrumental rationality', World Leisure Journal 48(3): 33–44.

Spracklen, K. (2009) The meaning and purpose of leisure: Habermas and leisure at the end of modernity. Basingstoke: Palgrave Macmillan.

Spracklen, K. (2011) 'Dreaming of drams: authenticity in Scottish whisky tourism as an expression of unresolved Habermasian rationalities', Leisure Studies 30(1): 99–116.

Spracklen, K. (2013a) ' "Nazi punks folk off": leisure, nationalism, cultural identity and the consumption of metal and folk music', Leisure Studies 32(4): 415–428.

Spracklen, K. (2013b) Whiteness and leisure. Basingstoke: Palgrave Macmillan.

Spracklen, K. (2015) ' "To Holmgard … and beyond": folk metal fantasies and hegemonic white masculinities', Metal Music Studies 1(3): 354–377.

Spracklen, K., Long, J. and Hylton, K. (2006) 'Managing and monitoring equality and diversity in UK sport', Journal of Sport and Social Issues 30(3): 289–305.

Spracklen, K., Long, J. and Hylton, K. (2015) 'Leisure opportunities and new migrant communities: challenging the contribution of sport', Leisure Studies 34(1): 114–129.

Spracklen, K., Lucas, C. and Deeks, M. (2014) 'The construction of heavy metal identity through heritage narratives: a case study of extreme metal bands in the north of England', Popular Music and Society 37(1): 48–64.

Spracklen, K., Timmins, S. and Long, J. (2010) 'Ethnographies of the imagined, the imaginary, and the critically real: blackness, whiteness, the north of England and rugby league', Leisure Studies 29(4): 397–414.

Chapter 14

'Problems at the boundary'?

South Asians, coaching and cricket

*Thomas Fletcher, Dave Piggott and
Julian North*

Introduction

The *Active People Survey* 8 suggests that South Asian participation in sport falls consistently below other social groups (Hylton *et al.*, 2015). Cricket is rather different as South Asian communities have a long association with the game, both in their country of origin and in the UK. Research for the ECB (the 'Eureka!' insight programme) identified that no less than 30 per cent of grassroots cricketers are drawn from minoritised ethnic groups, and the game is particularly popular among those from South Asian Communities (the *Active People Survey* indicates that Asian adults (aged 16+) are more than six times as likely to play cricket as their White counterparts) (ibid.). The England and Wales Cricket Board (ECB) is keen to engage South Asian groups to meet its twin strategic aims of raising participation levels and fostering elite development (Sport England, 2015; also see Ratna *et al.*, 2016). The proportion of South Asians playing cricket far outweighs the overall proportion of South Asians in the UK population and thus, for many, will represent a success story of cricket's inclusivity. However, it should be stressed that representation on the pitch is not evidence of inclusion in all areas of the sport. It is also worth noting that participation statistics remain limited as they are unable to provide insight into playing experiences. Indeed, Hylton and Chakrabarty (2011) argue that positive news stories about on-field representation can often mask social exclusions and problematic recruitment policies, rendering cultures of inequity invisible and unremarkable.

In 2014 researchers at Leeds Beckett University were commissioned by the ECB to explore South Asian male players' and coaches' experiences of coaching and progression through coach education pathways. The ECB is concerned that the apparently high proportion of cricket players from South Asian backgrounds are not extending their engagement into coaching. As cited above, estimates suggest that just under a third of the total adult playing population are from minoritised ethnic communities, many of whom are South Asian, yet South Asians constitute only 6 per cent of all UKCC Level 2 qualified coaches. In almost all sports, Level 2 is the minimum qualification coaches need to work independently and be paid for coaching. To support the wider participation and performance object-ives noted above a diverse coaching workforce is crucial, providing role models and evidence of equitable career development pathways to support, for example, South Asian engagement with and success in the sport.

The aim of this chapter is to understand South Asian men's experiences of playing and coaching cricket. Data for this chapter were collected via in-depth, semi-structured interviews carried out with a sample of 33 male South Asian players and coaches, from two different geographical areas (London and Yorkshire) and from a sample of clubs with different levels of ethnic diversity. We begin by providing a short overview of current liter-ature into minoritised ethnic communities and coaching. In subsequent sec-tions we present our data, which highlights how South Asian male cricketers feel marginalised from a 'coaching system' that they feel is both separate and exclusionary.

Coaching and minoritised ethnic communities

In the UK, recent research documents an over-representation of White participants, coaches and decision-makers within sporting contexts (Fletcher and Hylton, 2016; Rankin-Wright et al., Chapter 15 in this col-lection). In contrast, minoritised ethnic groups are under-represented at all levels of sport – from players and coaches to managers in sport govern-ance. Evidence suggests that 97 per cent of the UK coaching workforce is White, meaning only 3 per cent of individuals who coach in the UK are minoritised ethnic. This latter percentage decreases further within the context of qualified coaches, where only 1 per cent are from minoritised ethnic groups (Sports Coach UK, 2011).

Indeed, this pattern is recreated in cricket where, despite relatively high participation rates among men from South Asian backgrounds, only a small proportion are qualified coaches. Understanding how to enable players to make the transition into coaching, how to facilitate their motiva-tion and remove the constraints or barriers to entry and progression into coaching is hindered further by a lack of research into minoritised ethnic communities' engagement in sport coaching.

Recent research into the experiences of minoritised ethnic men and women in sports coaching found that inclusive sporting environments, including a diverse workforce, are highly motivating for entry into, and progression in sport (Norman et al., 2014). Evidence also suggests that while playing experiences within a sport can be positive as a whole, and entry into coaching fairly smooth, significant and powerful barriers exist that prevent the progression of minoritised ethnic individuals into higher-level coaching qualifications and job roles (Long et al., 2009; Norman *et al.*, 2014). In an attempt to understand this problem, Bradbury (2013) examined the relationship between the continued under-representation of Black and minoritised ethnic groups in leadership positions in football in Europe and the processes and practices of institutional racism (also see Bradbury, 2016). Like Lusted (2009) and Cunningham *et al.* (2012), he argues that practices of institutional racism reproduce whiteness in sport and are underpinned by patterns of hegemonic White privilege embedded within the core structures of decision-making bodies at the highest levels of football, including coaching.

Other research describes how coaching can be a difficult profession for minoritised ethnic groups to progress in due to institutional and individual factors. For example, minoritised ethnic coaches often lack a social or professional network to support their professional development. This is reflected in a lack of mentoring, or opportunities to develop their coaching expertise, as well as inaccessible, infrequent and costly training courses (see Bradbury, 2016 for a discussion of the COACH bursary programme in football). The nature of the coaching appointment process, described by minoritised ethnic coaches as informal, closed and lacking transparency, excludes and marginalises many minoritised ethnic coaches from new opportunities. These networks are described as privileging White men and are therefore described as both raced and gendered (Norman *et al.*, 2014). The conscious or unconscious outcome of such raced and gendered processes means that employment opportunities tend only to be available to coaches with similar characteristics and thus ultimately, preventing the progression of minoritised ethnic candidates. The interplay of these social, cultural, economic and institutional barriers serve to construct what could be described as a 'glass ceiling' for many minoritised ethnic coaches (ibid.).

A statement of value and approach

Before presenting the evidence, we (the authors) would like to state our commitment to social justice which we understand as being about fairness and equity. We are also committed to anti-racism. It is important to stress here that a focus on social justice must be coupled with the belief in the existence and identification of 'injustice', before change can occur (Fletcher and Hylton, 2016). In this sense the tools of analysis are important. Very often racial inequalities are conceived within a 'deficit model', emphasising the collective cultural inadequacies of those it affects. The problem with adopting a target-group approach is that it problematises the target group, while not recognising the cause(s) of estrangement (Carrington *et al.*, 2016). Henderson (2014: 344), for example, warns how a deficit model 'usually results in descriptions that victimise populations, and in so doing, may reaffirm their helplessness'. She advocates an asset model for sport and leisure practitioners, which generally addresses resources to help groups overcome injustices and social inequities, and in so doing, provides solutions to change the status quo. In our analysis we attempt to provide a data structure that allows for explanation of the problems identified at a number of different levels inside and outside South Asian and non-South Asian groups, and where possible at the agential, institutional and wider socio-cultural levels.

Findings

Reasons for low participation in coaching among South Asian communities are complex and multifactorial. In our original report to the ECB we attempted to capture this complexity with the development of four broad interrelated themes:

1   **Coaching is low priority and low value** for many within South Asian communities, with no perceived career pathway and with few experiences of receiving effective (formal) coaching …
     … *combined with South Asian cricketers often playing in …*
2   **Separate systems and pathways,** which are less formal and feel separate from the 'mainstream' White British system, and therefore have little access to governance networks and, hence, knowledge of coaching pathways and qualifications …
     … *and …*
3   **'The cricket system' is currently exclusive,** with very few South Asian coaching role models and a very strong sense that county coaching roles (and therefore level 3 awards) are protected *by* White gatekeepers *for* White coaches …
     … *which perpetuates the feeling that …*
4   **White privilege underpins a system** that reproduces racialised differences and inequalities in cricket.

All of which means that South Asian players participate in an environment and culture where they are unlikely to engage in coaching and, even when they do, will not feel supported in progressing to higher roles of influence and power. Space does not permit a full exploration of all four themes in this chapter, so the following discussion focusses on illustrating just two: separate systems and pathways; and the exclusive cricket system.

Separate systems and pathways

That cricket maintains a culture of whiteness at a variety of levels serves to perpetuate not only the dominance of White people (mainly, though not exclusively, men), but the exclusion of minority ethnic groups. Previous studies have identified how, under these conditions, and when faced with White racisms, minoritised ethnic communities will actively seek out separate spaces of play (see Fletcher and Walle, 2015; Hylton *et al.*, 2015).

Many of the players and coaches felt that they were part of a different system with a distinct style of cricket. The South Asian 'system' (as depicted by participants in this study but not necessarily generalisable beyond it) is typically informal: it is established early in life, both in the UK and the Indian subcontinent, through 'street cricket'. It is in stark contrast to the 'mainstream' system (consistently referred to by our research participants as being 'White') which is highly organised and affiliated to the governing body (Fletcher and Walle, 2015; McDonald and Ugra, 1998; Ratna *et al.*, 2016).

The separate system provided a very distinct experience of coaching. In most cases there was an absence of more formalised coaching forms:

> We played on our own, no coaches there [Pakistan]. In every age group there are very good, qualified coaches, and they pass experience on and when you are 13 and 14 you know everything (in mainstream cricket). But, in Pakistan and Asian countries, you have to work hard and learn things, no coaching, nothing.
>
> (Coach L2)

> I did not have a coach because we start from street cricket. When we have club, you know, local club, we don't have a coaching system.
>
> (Player L5)

Generally, South Asian players were more likely to appreciate the value of coaching others if they had had positive experiences of being coached. Some connected this informal, unmediated introduction to the game with the similarly informal and transient way in which team and club cricket occurs in many South Asian communities. This transience was used to explain some of the challenges faced when trying to create an effective club identity, retain players as committee members and encourage others into coaching after they had finished playing. This was captured best by Player Y3:

> For most the club model doesn't exist, it's a team model whereas in the White communities it's a club model so you will be part of that club. You and your kids will be part of that club for a long time because it's your club, whereas here we don't have that. We have a team, you'll be part of the team but the club doesn't matter.... The guys before I was at this club were predominantly White guys and they had a real sense of belonging, and of club. They'd come in every Tuesday night to the clubhouse and those that were handy with a

hammer and nail would be fixing everything, they'd be doing what needs doing and they'd do that because they'd been there a long time and their father had been there. That was their community; that was their club. And the other thing is the social aspect…. Unfortunately, where we play cricket, there's no social aspect at all so you play cricket, you get here for one o'clock and the game starts at two. As soon as the game finishes, everyone runs off.

As a result of being part of this separate system it was felt South Asians lack access to formal networks and, thus, an understanding of coach education pathways. Also, because they play in clubs and teams that often eschew a traditional club structure and identity, there are simply fewer opportunities and incentives to take up coaching. Indeed, without a tradition of volunteering, and without a strong club identity (linked to, among other things, socialising and a drinking culture), it makes it less likely that South Asian teams and clubs will consistently be able to engage ex-players in coaching roles or develop effective club structures (e.g. junior squads) as vehicles for coach development.

Moreover, South Asian players often lack the social networks and relationships with influential people needed to develop their clubs and access coaching. The significance and influence of this network was believed to be more challenging as coaches tried to progress within the system:

> Has anything hindered my coaching opportunities? I think that the initial early levels I have been fine, but the more elite level, a certain amount of networking is required and this network may not readily exist for the South Asian community.
>
> (Coach Y3)

In addition, there was a sense that because many South Asians experience their cricket from outside the mainstream 'system' they do not get selected for representative teams, or invited onto coaching courses.

For example, the respondents suggested they were not being given equal opportunities as players (especially with regards to county clubs). A number of reasons for this were proposed; namely that scouts are disproportionately targeting mainly White (often private) schools; and alternative spaces for cricket (e.g. Sunday and/or mid-week competitions) are not currently monitored, recognised or scouted:

> It's the players who are going to go on to coaching, so you've got to sort the players out first and then go on to coaching. How many players from our background are selected through the ranks? They don't go to boarding or private schools so they can't go forward.
>
> (Player Y1)

I didn't think they [White coaches] gave enough of a chance to some of the players that didn't come from private schools, what we call the 'blazer boys'. The blazer boys were getting all the chances because the coaches that were coaching were from private schools so they'd get selected.

(Coach Y4)

Many of the respondents had aspirations of progressing in cricket as either players or coaches (or both), however, they did not necessarily think the 'system' was providing them with either the resources or opportunities to do this. Most respondents said this study was the first (and only) time they had heard of the ECB being proactive towards South Asian under-representation:

I know nothing, I'm not aware of anything ... the things I read on the websites, the coaching websites, and the material they send, there's nothing in there about any initiatives or anything special that they're doing, or even if they particularly recognise if there is a problem.

(Coach Y7)

The extent of this lack of communication was evident in the fact that many of the participants did not know anything about the coach education pathway, in particular, how to access information about it. However, there was clearly a latent demand for coaching courses:

At our cricket club there's a number of players, if you say 'Do you want to be a Level 2 coach?' I could guarantee you now nine out of ten of them wouldn't even know where to start. [But] you've got to educate people, and encourage them more. You've got to go down to grassroots.

(Coach Y6)

Many of the coaches said they first became involved with coaching through recommendations from existing coaches. Rarely had they accessed information about coaching directly from the ECB or other information sources. Thus, those who knew people in the system (e.g. other coaches, sport development officers/managers) held a much more positive attitude than those who did not:

I'm lucky because I've got two guys here that I can tap into, but had they not been here, then it's a different question because then it would be difficult for me to do that. But because I've got [name] and [name] here, I'm connected.

(Player Y3)

The importance of this observation is that the majority of respondents believed the ECB should be communicating information about the courses much more effectively, rather than relying on the current 'word of mouth' system. This would inevitably mean reaching out and targeting South Asians specifically with relevant and inclusive strategies.

Targeting these communities is not straightforward however. As Fletcher *et al.* (2014) and Hylton *et al.* (2015) have previously noted, engaging with South Asian communities specifically means being flexible about the forms of cricket being played and the spaces in which play is taking place are recognised as 'proper'. In other words, in order to expand the coaching base, it must be acknowledged that cricket is being played in a variety of forms and spaces in addition to those recognised by the ECB and county boards:

> I think if a county board representative turned up at a park's pitch on a Sunday and said 'Hi, I'm from Yorkshire County Board, do you have any of your guys here who would like to become coaches? We would love to see you at this venue, at this day, and this is how much it will cost you.' Now I don't think that approach or that conversation has ever happened.... Make them aware that these opportunities are there.... They don't get literature, they don't get mailshots from the ECB. These are park cricketers.
>
> (Coach L4)

Respondents in this research suggested that the ECB needs to be more proactive in their attempts to communicate with, and actively recruit, potential South Asian coaches. The most common way of encouraging communication identified by the respondents was for representatives of the ECB and county boards to go physically into South Asian communities where cricket is being played and share information about what opportunities are available and how these can be accessed. This raised further questions about the 'system' and its inclusivity.

'The exclusive cricket system'

There was a deeper and more pervasive feeling that playing and coaching opportunities were being denied on the basis of 'race'. Some felt their voices were being ignored by county boards, whereas others felt that attempts to reach out and listen to South Asian views were little more than tokenistic 'box ticking' exercises on the governing body's behalf:

> There's still a big divide. If you had to interview most Asians, their immediate reaction to lack of privilege and disadvantage is 'It's racism. It's because we're Muslims, it's because we're Pakistani.'
>
> (Coach Y7)

That's an issue for me, my colour of skin – I don't want to go down that route, I've had a good time here growing up with English friends, neighbours, lovely, brilliant, wouldn't change it – but when it comes to that hierarchy, pushing up, I really feel that you[1] [*sic*] want us involved in the game, just for that box ticking.

(Coach L1)

There is an increasing array of research questioning the commitment of sporting institutions to make positive and meaningful changes in how they tackle racial inequalities (see Hylton and Long, 2016). When applied specifically to coaching, respondents felt that their chances of progression into county roles would be denied (or heavily restricted) on the basis of their skin colour:

All the clubs prefer White coaches. They don't prefer South Asian coaches for the county. I mean they have a different value for White coaches.

(Player L6)

Whilst it was acknowledged that more South Asians are accessing entry-level coaching qualifications there was a perception that the higher up the system they go, the more exclusionary it becomes. What the respondents meant by this was that as individuals move from Level 1 to Level 2 to Club Coach and so on, there is a marked reduction in the proportion of South Asian attendees and, also, coach educators:

In terms of attendees, level one was a healthy mix.... Level two, there were a few Asians, but not to the same level as Whites. Club Coach was predominantly 'White White', much higher than level two. I don't think there are many, if any, Asians on the level three. [What about the coach educators?] There was one Asian.... He was on the level two. The others were White.

(Coach Y3)

The lack of South Asian coach educators was highlighted as an issue on the basis that the players and coaches believed that other South Asians would be 'put off' from courses where they did not feel represented. This was coupled with a perception that access to higher-level coaching qualifications and jobs were restricted to, and 'guarded' by, White people:

I've asked the ECB, I've asked, 'Can I volunteer?' I've applied for a job with the English deaf cricket team. Now, okay, they said, 'Thank you very much, we're not interested'. Then I replied back to human resources, 'Can I, at my expense, so I can learn, can I shadow the selected or appointed official, the coach?' Didn't hear anything. It's a closed door.

(Coach L1)

A number of respondents were suspicious of how open and fair the selection and recruitment processes for higher-level courses are. Coach L7 in particular highlighted how the nomination/endorsement process is largely self-perpetuating, in that, to gain an endorsement, one would likely need to be part of an established network which, frequently, they are not:

> I'm not exactly sure how it works, but it seems to me it's not easy to break into. My perception is that there's some sort of little network where you need some sort of nomination. It goes to some sort of board meeting and they say 'yea' or 'nay'. It's a bit exclusive.
>
> (Coach L7)

Coach Y3, who has ambitions of gaining his Level 3 qualification noted that he was finding it difficult to get on a course. He was reluctant to identify the existence of racism, but it was evident from his interview that he had doubts about whether his application was treated fairly compared with White applicants. There were repeated references to Yorkshire County Cricket Club's (YCCC) historical exclusion of minoritised ethnic communities (see Fletcher and Swain, 2016). And while it was acknowledged that YCCC has made a great deal of progress with regard to this and that its image within South Asian communities is considerably better than it was perhaps even a generation ago, a number of respondents continued to question the Club's inclusivity. Therefore, while the Club may feel as if it has done enough to overcome historical associations of racism, evidence from this research suggests that further transparency may be required.

Respondents were also asked their views on coach education resources. There was general agreement that, in terms of the depth and clarity of information, examples, visual support etc., they were fit for purpose. However, given some of the communication and English language difficulties experienced by some South Asians there was some debate over whether resources could be made more accessible by, for example, being translated into different languages. It was believed that lack of English language skills was a barrier. This was identified as an issue lying principally with first- and some second-generation South Asians who have not been educated in the UK. However, given that many South Asians may opt to become coaches after they finish their playing careers, this is an issue that will likely affect the current generation of older players:

> With some of the South Asian community … work that I've done … there are many, many players' parents who say actually we would love

to become a coach but the language is a barrier; understanding is a barrier.

(Coach L4)

There was also evidence that some South Asians do not feel comfortable on the courses because they do not fully understand what the coach educator is saying. Moreover, some said they would be uncomfortable questioning/ challenging a White coach educator due to language or communication issues. Similarly, language could also be a barrier when South Asians are expected to perform skill demonstrations as part of the course.

In addition to language issues, the technical content of resources (the 'what' of coaching) was also perceived to be a potential barrier insofar as they promoted a traditional 'English' style of play, very different to the more fluid, attacking and expressive style associated with cricket on the Indian subcontinent. Many respondents spoke about 'the ECB manual'[2] and the influence this has on their motivation to become a coach and their subsequent progression:

> I strongly believe that a lot of South Asian people don't necessarily like coaching qualifications: 'Why should I play like that? If I can hit a ball from outside off through mid-wicket for six, why should I then be playing that through the offside?' Because the coach and manual says that's what you're meant to do!

(Coach L3)

Such perceived barriers are important to address – even if they may be mistaken in some senses – as they clearly have an influence on South Asian players' perceptions of their place in the 'system' and the value they attach to cricket coaching in general.

Conclusion

We have tried to outline and illustrate some of the nuanced mechanisms and processes that contribute to the marginalisation of South Asian communities from cricket coaching (especially higher coaching) roles.

Our research participants spoke of a separate South Asian cricket system, composed of clubs and teams with transient membership and a lack of identity. The perception that cricket is run by White people for White people therefore leaves many South Asian cricketers feeling outside the (White) 'system'. This separation of systems and lack of access to the 'right' networks means that the ability of the ECB to communicate with these communities is impaired.

Identifying and documenting mechanisms of marginalisation and exclusion is a relatively straightforward task. The more important challenge is

Table 14.1 Recommendation chain 3: making coach education and coaching more accessible

No.	Recommendation
9	Increase the visibility of South Asian coaches, in the county system where possible, to act as inspirational role models to aspiring coaches. This may encompass a degree of positive action in recruitment practices. Where candidates have similar experiences and expertise choose the South Asian candidate especially for county-level or more senior positions.
10	Establish a strategy aimed at engaging with a potential 'missed generation' (i.e. players in the 35–45 age bracket coming to the end of their careers, likely to have experienced overt and covert racism and may be disillusioned with the system).
11	Undertake a review of coaching resources and course material in terms of: (a) their form, language and accessibility; and (b) the technical scope and flexibility.
12	Increase funding available for coaching qualifications and increase local delivery of courses.

to scrutinise what sport and leisure research might do to mitigate (or, ideally, eradicate altogether) these mechanisms and subsequent injustices. It requires more than simply identifying injustices or, indeed, suggesting potential solutions. Academic research is a necessary first step, but change will only occur if this research is translated into practice.

In our report to the ECB, we made 12 recommendations, formulated as three 'chains', wherein a *series* of actions were argued to be necessary, and only collectively sufficient, to bring about meaningful change. The example of our final recommendation chain is reproduced above. This example was chosen as it is most closely associated to the two themes addressed in this chapter.

To take a single example from the 'chain', point 9 suggests that 'positive action' will be necessary if the ECB are to meet their target of achieving 'a workforce that reflects participation demographics' (ECB, 2014). And, while 'positive action' is permitted under the Equality Act 2010 (and recognised by the ECB in their policy documents) in cases where 'participation is disproportionately low compared to other users' (e.g. coaching), the extent to which the organisation engages with such practices – among many others noted in our report – will be the true test of their commitment to social justice.

Notes

1 It was not unusual for respondents to incorrectly identify members of the research team as being representatives/employees of the ECB. In this example, the reference to 'you' was a conflation of the research team and the ECB.
2 It is important to point out that the ECB no longer has a single technical manual for coaches, but the perception of a White English 'hidden curriculum' of old-fashioned techniques – forward defensive, high elbow, line and length – was nevertheless a pervasive perception among our respondents.

References

Bradbury, S. (2013) 'Institutional racism, whiteness and the underrepresentation of minorities in leadership positions in football in Europe', *Soccer and Society* 14(3): 296–314.

Bradbury, S. (2016) 'The progression of Black and minority ethnic footballers into coaching in professional football: a case study analysis of the COACH bursary programme', in Allison, W., Abraham A. and Cale A. (eds) *Advances in coach education and development*. London: Routledge, 137–148.

Carrington, B., Fletcher, T. and McDonald, I. (2016) The politics of 'race' and sports policy in the United Kingdom. In: Houlihan, B. (ed.) *Sport in Society 3rd Edition*. London: Sage, 222–249.

Cunningham, G., Miner, K. and McDonald, J. (2012) 'Being different and suffering the consequences: the influence of head coach–player racial dissimilarity on experienced incivility', *International review for the Sociology of Sport* 48(6): 689–705.

ECB (England and Wales Cricket Board) (2013) 'Participation', www.ecb.co.uk/development/get-into-cricket/participation, accessed 21 April 2016.

ECB (England and Wales Cricket Board) (2014) *One game – inclusion and diversity strategy 2014–2020*. Lords Cricket Ground, London.

Fletcher, T. (2011) ' "Aye, but it were wasted on thee": "Yorkshireness", cricket, ethnic identities, and the "magical recovery of community" ', *Sociological Research Online* 16(4).

Fletcher, T. and Hylton, K. (2016) 'Whiteness and race in sport', in Nauright, J. and Wiggins, D. K. (eds) *Routledge Handbook of Sport, Race and Ethnicity*. Abingdon: Routledge, 87–106.

Fletcher, T. and Swain, S. (2016) 'Strangers of the north: South Asians, cricket and the culture of "Yorkshireness" '. *Journal for Cultural Research* 20(1): 86–100.

Fletcher, T. and Walle, T. (2015) 'Negotiating their right to play: Asian-identified cricket teams and leagues in Britain and Norway', *Identities: Global Studies in Culture and Power* 22(2): 230–246.

Fletcher, T., Piggott, D., North, J., Hylton, K., Gilbert, S. and Norman, L. (2014) *Exploring the barriers to South Asian cricket players' entry and progression in coaching*. Leeds: ISPAL.

Henderson, K. (2014) 'The imperative of leisure justice research', *Leisure Sciences* 36(4): 340–348.

Hylton, K. and Chakrabarty, N. (2011) ' "Race" and culture in tourism, leisure and events', *Journal of Policy Research into Tourism Leisure and Events* 3(2): 105–108.

Hylton, K. and Long, J. (2016) 'Confronting "race" and policy: "how can you research something you say does not exist?"', *Journal of Policy Research in Tourism, Leisure and Events*, 8(2): 202–208.

Hylton, K., Long, J., Fletcher, T. and Ormerod, N. (2015) *Cricket and South Asian Communities*. Leeds: ISPAL.

Long, J., Hylton, K., Spracklen, K., Ratna, A. and Bailey, S. (2009) *Systematic Review of the Literature on Black and Minority Ethnic Communities in sport and physical recreation*. Report to Sporting Equals and the Sports Councils by the Carnegie Research Institute, Leeds Metropolitan University.

Lusted, J. (2009) 'Playing games with "race": understanding resistance to "race" equality initiatives in English local football governance', *Soccer and Society* 10(6): 722–739.

McDonald, I. and Ugra, S. (1998) *Anyone for cricket? Equal Opportunities and Changing Cricket Cultures in Essex and East London*. London: Roehampton Institute for New Ethnicities Research.

Norman, L., North, J., Hylton, K., Flintoff, A. and Rankin, A. (2014) *Sporting experiences and coaching aspirations among Black and Minority Ethnic (BME) groups*. Leeds: sports coach UK.

Ratna, A., Lawrence, S. and Partington, J. (2016) ' "Getting inside the wicket": strategies for the social inclusion of British Pakistani Muslim cricketers', *Journal of Policy Research in Tourism, Leisure and Events* 8(1): 1–17.

sports coach UK (2011) *Sports coaching in the UK III: a statistical analysis of coaches and coaching in the UK*. Leeds.

Sport England (2015) 'Involvement in organised sport for Sport England NGB 13–17 funded sports', www.sportengland.org/research/who-plays-sport/national-picture, accessed 5 May 2016.

Chapter 15

The policy and provision landscape for racial and gender equality in sport coaching

Alexandra J. Rankin-Wright, Kevin Hylton and Leanne Norman

Introduction

In United Kingdom (UK) sport organisations and national governing bodies (NGBs), research suggests that diversity in the workforce remains poor. Specifically, research has evidenced a disproportionate under-representation of Black and minoritised ethnic (BME)[1] sport coaches. Notwithstanding intensifying calls for parity from the media and wider politics regarding the under-representation of Black[2] coaches, Hylton and Morpeth (2012) note that a trend towards the silencing of 'race' and racism is a typical institutional response to such issues. Therefore, the dominant values that reinforce these inequalities and disparities such as meritocracy, 'sport for all' and colourblindness remain 'locked in' (Roithmayr, 2014).

This chapter explores the social justice issues of racial and gender equality and diversity in sport coaching. Specifically, it focuses on organisational perspectives on racial and gender equality(ies) and addresses the often unacknowledged and unproblematised question of institutional accountability. The chapter is divided into five sections. First, we provide a brief overview of the UK sport coaching landscape through the lens of equality. We then outline our Critical Race Theory (CRT) and Black feminism approach, employed together as the framework for this research, and detail the methodology. In the fourth section, our findings illustrate that racial and gender equality are compromised in sport coaching due to the pursuit of elite performance and the ways that key stakeholders dissociate responsibility and accountability. We conclude that social justice issues and values are poorly conceived within sport coaching and that more informed leadership is required at all levels within organisations to ensure that these issues are centralised and mainstreamed. This would ultimately help organisations to recognise and challenge racial and gender discrimination.

The sport coaching landscape

The UK Coaching Framework was published in 2012 by sports coach UK (scUK), the central UK coaching agency that works principally with NGBs in the recruitment and development of sport coaches. This framework provided a common vision and practical reference point to guide the development of UK coaching practice and stated that a more diverse, inclusive and equitable coaching workforce were among the central strategic objectives (sports coach UK, 2012). Sport coaching organisations were also cited as having a responsibility to provide 'inclusive coaching guidance' that cover the equality strands, including women and girls, and 'race' and ethnicity (sports coach UK, 2012: 26). Additionally, following the government report *Equality and Diversity: Making it Happen* (Equality Institutions Review, 2002) and aligned with the wider societal shift to a more generic equity strategy, *The Equality Standard: A Framework for Sport* (Sport England, 2004) was launched in 2004 and updated in 2012 by UK Sport and the four Sport Councils[3] (Sports Council Equality Group, 2012). The Standard aimed to provide direction to UK sports organisations and NGBs to develop processes and structures to become more equitable in organisational and service development. This standard, along with the equality statutory legislation documented in the Equality Act (2006, then re-written in 2010), had a major impact in terms of updating policies and documents to ensure that they were compliant within the new legal framework. Success was recorded against four levels: foundation, preliminary, intermediate and advanced, to which funding was previously linked (Shaw, 2007; Sport England, 2004). Shaw (2007) expressed concern with this audit-based approach of *The Equality Standard*, arguing that focusing on equality *outcomes* rather than *processes* may result in sport organisations and NGBs paying lip service to required objectives without regard for the structures, cultures and processes by which outcomes can be achieved. As Spracklen *et al.* (2006: 20) state:

> The failure is built into the discourse of the Equality Standard, which demands evidence of action but not evidence of change, and which positions itself as a framework to help British sport work with 'them': groups defined in opposition to the mainstream of sport.

Without this critical reflection of actions and a consideration of the diverse communities to which sports organisations deliver services, Shaw (2007) argues that, while sports continue to serve traditionally privileged groups, they will reinforce long-held stereotypes. Furthermore, conceptualising a social justice aim such as equality as achievable and measureable 'ignores the complex power and political relations that are inherent in considering the intersectionality' of both privileged and marginalised groups in sport (Shaw, 2007: 426). The following section outlines the CRT and Black feminism approach for this research.

Critical Race Theory, Black feminism and social justice

Critical Race Theory (CRT) is a theoretical framework that facilitates a politics of social justice that begins with centring 'race' and racism in society. Its starting point is that racism is embedded in broader society and that it structures our everyday relations. Where CRT has emerged in disciplines, geographic locations or in relation to specific issues, it has been as a response to social arrangements that reflect the subordinating experiences of disenfranchised or oppressed groups and individuals. As a result, the emergence of CRT in critical debates has stimulated alternative agendas that force more established positions to be re-evaluated in light of previously absent or marginalised perspectives and include alternative ideas to enhance established epistemologies. On this note, CRT is not a 'single issue' framework but unashamedly argues for 'race' to be central where in many disciplines, professions and issues, 'race' is conspicuous by its marginal or absent status.

A CRT framework incorporates a plethora of perspectives, from a multitude of realities, yet it is identifiable by consistent underpinning tenets. Hylton (2005) outlined five key elements: (1) the centring of 'race' and racism; (2) resisting narrow dominant ideologies that draw on notions of colour-blindness, race neutrality and objectivity, and meritocracy; (3) a commitment to social justice that incorporates elements of an agenda for liberation and transformation; (4) an emphasis on the Black experience that speaks lived 'truths' to power; and (5) transdisciplinary, that is embracing philosophies that eschew dogma and pedantry, and encouraging a search for constructive approaches to transformation and social justice. Hylton went on to justify how a CRT framework could contribute to an informed social justice agenda that would not ignore broader racialised implications for sport when he argued that:

> The resultant outcome of using a CRT perspective is likely to lead towards a resistance to a passive reproduction of the established practices, knowledge and resources, that make up the social conditions that marginalise 'race' as a core factor in the way we manage and experience our sport and leisure.
>
> (Hylton, 2005: 81)

This sharpening of the intellectual tools available to sport coaching is only part of the story. CRT is a theoretical framework that has many activist scholars, with a multitude of agendas and ideas, drawing on important organising principles that have become central in mainstream sociological thought. Just as interest convergence and the rules of racial standing (Bell, 1992), the racial contract (Mills, 1997), front and backstage racism

(Hylton and Lawrence, 2016; Picca and Feagin, 2007) and whiteness studies (Fletcher, 2014; Fletcher and Hylton, 2016; Gillborn, 2011; Long et al., 2014) enable a different focus or approach to CRT, the anti-essentialism of CRT ensures that intersectionality is maintained as one of those key concepts (Delgado and Stenfancic, 2012).

Kimberle Crenshaw is commonly attributed with coining the term 'intersectionality' to emphasise the salience of other identities in complex 'raced' lives (Crenshaw et al., 1995; Matsuda et al., 1993). As a Critical Race Theorist she engages a Black feminist standpoint that employs a politics of 'race' and gender, recognising that in many academic and policy circles, all women are White and all Blacks are men. Black feminism and CRT more generally are concerned with ideologies and practices that Mirza (1997) would describe as having 'blind spots'. For Black feminists, the suggestion that social justice agendas benefit all women equally can oversimplify the nature of oppression (Davis, 1984; hooks, 2000). Black feminists are first concerned with the intersection and salience of 'race' and gender as they intersect with related identities and forms of oppression. Davis (1984) cautions that abstract notions of womanhood suffering sexism that excludes an intersection with related oppressions such as 'race' is likely to perpetuate the separate narratives of 'race' and gender, and the invisibility of Black women (Mirza, 1997).

In sum, this CRT and Black feminism framework focuses on the multiplicity of identity privileging through the grounding of the lived experiences of marginalised groups (Collins, 2000; Crenshaw, 1989; hooks, 2000). In sport coaching, the necessity for such critical voices becomes apparent in any concerted critique of the dominant epistemologies and inconsistent approaches to inclusive practice in the academy and related professions. This empowerment of lived realities challenges dominant cultures and discourses within society to work towards social justice (Carter and Hawkins, 2011; Collins, 2000; Hylton, 2005). Thus, social theory can enable activist scholars to teach to transgress, talk back (hooks, 1989, 2000), empower (Collins, 2000) or speak from places unknown, unimagined and perhaps never asked (Delgado and Stenfancic, 2012; Gillborn et al., 2012; Mirza, 1997).

Methodology

This qualitative study involved fifteen semi-structured interviews with seventeen staff leading on equality policy and strategy or coaching recruitment, education and performance from three national sport organisations (scUK, Sport Northern Ireland and UK Sport), two equality organisations (see Table 15.1) and six NGBs[4] (see Table 15.2), all based in the UK. The sport organisations were purposively selected due to their influence on, and as funders of, sport policy and practice, and coach recruitment and

Table 15.1 The sport organisations, equality organisations and participants

Sport/equality organisation	Participant's title	Ethnicity	Gender
UK Sport	Equality Officer	White	Male
	Coaching Development Manager	White	Male
sports coach UK	Development Lead Officer (equality)	White	Female
	Coach Education Advisor	White	Female
Sport Northern Ireland	Policy Planning and Research Manager (equality)	White	Male
	Performance Systems Manager (coaching)	White	Male
Sporting Equals	Head of Consultancy	British Indian	Male
Women's Sport and Fitness Foundation (WSFF) (now Women In Sport, WIS)	Sports Partnership Manager	White	Female

development in NGBs. The two equality organisations, Women In Sport and Sporting Equals, advise and support policymakers and sport deliverers on issues of gender and racial equality in sport, respectively. The six NGBs included a mixture of team and individual sports, sports traditionally associated with men, sports traditionally associated with women and gender-balanced sports. All six NGBs were working towards achieving *The Equality Standard*.

All interviews, except two, which took place over the phone, were conducted face-to-face by Rankin-Wright using a pre-planned interview guide. These interviews provided insight into each organisation's or NGB's equality policies and practice, engagement with coaches, and coach development pathways. Rankin-Wright, as a White, female researcher was arguably in a privileged position, due to her whiteness, working within and researching predominantly White dominated institutions. Thus, it is conceded that if an interviewer with different identity characteristics had carried out, and analysed, the interviews, some differences in knowledge may have been shared and (re)produced. The key themes identified, using a thematic analysis approach, were: (1) equality takes a backseat: policy implementation tensions; and (2) the dissociation of accountability and responsibility. The remainder of the chapter is devoted to analysing each of these.

Table 15.2 National Governing Bodies (NGBs) and participants

NGB (pseudonym)	Details of NGB	Level achieved of The Equality Standard for Sport	Participants interviewed	Ethnicity	Gender
Team Sport (TS)	Team sport, men and women's teams	Intermediate	Equality Lead Coaching Lead	White White	Female Female
Grouped Individual Events (GIE)	Team and individual events, men and women	Preliminary	Equality Lead Coaching Lead	White White	Male Female
Popular Women's Sport (PWS)	Team sport, mainly women	Preliminary	Equality Lead Coaching Lead	White White	Female Female
Individual Disciplines Sport (IDS)	Team and individual events, men and women	Preliminary	Equality Lead	White	Male
Individual Water Disciplines (IWD)	Team and individual events, men and women	Intermediate	Equality Lead	White	Female
Campaigning Sport Organisation (CSO)	Team sport, men and women's teams	Intermediate	Equality lead	White	Female

Findings: policy tensions and dissociating responsibility

Equality takes a backseat: policy implementation tensions

Despite the symbolic commitment to *The Equality Standard* from sport organisations and NGBs the findings illustrate that racial and gender equality were secondary to the pursuit of sporting excellence. Specifically, equality issues, and the recruitment and retention of a more diverse coaching workforce, were either non-existent or very low on their long-term agendas. The Equality Lead for PWS, a NGB that had achieved the preliminary level of *The Equality Standard*, explained how equality issues took a 'backseat' to other organisational priorities:

> I think, the impression I have is.... Performance are all focused on winning the World Cup.... Development are all focused on increasing participation figures and hitting those targets and my department is desperately trying – well my directorate – is providing all the support to that. Little old me coming along and saying 'Oi, what about equalities?' They just go 'What, I haven't got time for that'. They don't know why they should and they don't have time for it, it doesn't feel like a priority.
>
> (Equality Lead, PWS)

In addition, following the announcement by Sport England that funded targets would no longer be linked to equalities work, there were also fewer resources for NGBs to support an equalities agenda. Concern and frustration were voiced that equality agendas were therefore unsustainable:

> That for me is the hardest thing ... that the drive for the equalities agenda may have to take a bit of a backseat at the moment particularly given our funding limitations and the cuts that we're facing.... If you have got your funding requirements and if part of your funding is that you have to demonstrate equality targets that is a really important driver but that's going, you know, that's gone ... and my worry is now for sport in general that it [equality] will start to disappear off the agenda.
>
> (Equality Lead, TS)

Another Equality Lead who worked for one of the largest NGBs that governed a team sport for men and women expressed similar frustrations:

> Resources, resources, resources! ... For me, to do that [equality and diversity work] I'd need to triple my budget and I'd need to triple my staff. That's the bottom line.
>
> (Equality Lead, CSO)

As the Equality Lead for TS, a NGB that had achieved the intermediate level of *The Equality Standard*, explained:

> The difficulty is you have to have a long term strategy; a long term commitment and generally finances. Funding is all around short term KPIs [key performance indicators]. The pressure is on!

These findings resonate with the work of Carrington and McDonald (2003: 138) who suggest that NGBs are reluctant to pursue inclusive policies 'that require significant investment of resources or that threaten entrenched interests of influential people'. The everyday realities and frustrating organisational complexities for those attempting to progress equality work was referred to by many of the Equality Leads as an 'uphill battle'. Therefore, despite an expressed willingness to engage in an equalities agenda from all six of the NGB Equality Leads, the lack of financial investment, and systematic development for equality work and the constant negotiation of priorities was a significant and prohibitive challenge.

In addition to the difficulties in implementing an equality agenda within NGBs, a prominent finding was that 'race' and ethnicity were marginalised within this work. When talking about the inclusion of 'race' and racial equality within NGB sport plans, the Head of Consultancy at Sporting Equals stated:

> I would say you get them [NGB sport plans] across the board, the worst case scenario is ['race' and racial equality are] just absent and you get a statement in the whole sport plan that says 'we'll make sure this reaches all' and that's it, there's no detail or there's no meat in the substance behind the plan, … you'll often find the governing body Equality Officer will not even know that the business plan for their sport has been written, so you can go through the plans and say 'oh this one hasn't consulted the Equality Officer, this one has, this one hasn't'.

Evidently, there was a distinct divide between equality work and sport coaching work, and a stark disengagement with 'race' and ethnicity issues within the broader landscape of sport coaching. The Equality Officer at UK Sport explained:

> Because our focus is performance, I think one of the dangers or one of the pitfalls we have in terms of equality is that we think of it in terms of disability, because we've got Olympics and Paralympics, and also in terms of gender because, again, it's easy, you know, you have separate events for women so I think the natural position is to think of equality in those two areas purely because that's how we can measure success. I guess that's publicly how we can report on being equitable.

In particular, this disengagement illustrated Mirza's (1997) 'blind spots' in mainstream sport coaching policy and practice, which enacted 'race' and gender as separate, stand-alone categories of difference. The precedence of gender and disability in the above quote represents a common theme across the interviews and supports the assertion that NGBs are more proactive around the inclusion of women and disability groups, viewed as separate categories to racial equality. Therefore, racial equality was further down a hierarchy of disadvantage, based on the prioritisation of high performance success in sport and the resulting targets set to achieve this.

Dissociation of accountability and responsibility

The assumed incompatibility between the equality agenda and sport coaching, and the dissociation of key stakeholders in sport coaching from the accountability and responsibility for social justice was evident in the testimonies from those working in high performance sport coaching. These participants believed that addressing equality work was the responsibility of those individuals and organisations whose work targeted mass participation. The following testimony exemplifies this:

> There's a degree of how far our remit goes so essentially, our remit is about winning medals, ... overall our targets are total number of medals as opposed to medals within any particular gender ... there's a certain point in the performance pathway where people come under our sphere of influence ... and below that we can't actually do anything about it apart from try and encourage governing bodies through things like the Equality Standard to put in place more positive action programmes themselves.
>
> (Equality Officer, UK Sport)

These Coaching Leads also placed responsibility on those working with mass participation and ignored notions of 'glass ceilings':

> We can only work with the people that are employed by the NGB and clearly they have to be of an appropriate level to come on to our [high performance] programme in the first place, so to a degree there's only so much control we have over the diversity.
>
> (Coach Educator, Sports Coach UK)

> Until we see the effect of how we've addressed equality and diversity at a lower level through school sport and the experiences that people have at a much younger age we won't see the knock-on effect until that actually converts I suppose.
>
> (Leadership and Coaching Development Manager, UK Sport)

As Long *et al.* (2005) found, despite the production of equality policies and promises of implementation, those within coaching departments did not recognise their collective or individual responsibilities for ensuring equality within sport coaching and for effecting change. Instead, there was criticism of the grassroots sporting environment for not preparing under-represented groups well enough to compete for performance roles:

> I don't think it's a deliberate act on our part, I just think it's not positive enough to bring them into the system in the first place.
> (Coach Educator, Sports Coach UK)

Furthermore, there was an ingrained belief within this 'high performance' discourse that notions of equality, diversity and inclusion were neither compatible, nor relevant, for sport coaching and excellence. As the Leadership and Coaching Development Manager at UK Sport explained:

> Internally there was a barrier around 'well, we can't be equal because there's nothing about being in high performance sport which is equal because it's about being the very best at what we do', which principally that makes sense but it's not about that ... it's more about making sure the opportunities are present and people are given those opportunities to achieve their very best, whether or not you come from whatever background.

This 'internal barrier', that is, excellence means being prepared to be 'unequal', was exemplified by a number of the Coaching Leads. These practitioners maintained that high performance sport *would* discriminate against individuals, but against their ability, as opposed to their background or identity. As the following testimonies illustrate:

> If there's indirect discrimination there then there is. But elite sport in its very nature is discriminatory because it discriminates you against your ability to do stuff. If you're not good enough you are not going to get there and that's it.
> (Performance Systems Manager, Sport Northern Ireland)

> The performance pathway isn't equitable in that it's, you know, there's a selection process that you go through to get onto it ... mass participation is about getting everybody involved and everybody can try it and you know, whereas the [performance] pathway isn't really about that – it's about a real sort of discrete group of athletes that want to go on and play for England one day.
> (Coaching Lead, PWS)

Therefore, a number of the Coaching Leads were unsure how equality and, in particular, how the implications of 'race' and ethnicity linked to sport coaching and their job role. These Coaching Leads were rarely encouraged to think about equality, diversity and inclusion in relation to coach recruitment, development and retention. As the Equality Officer for UK Sport stated:

> I think I would probably go as far as to say it [equality and diversity] isn't practically delivered enough so I don't envisage, for example, a question coming down from the Director's team to even ask the question 'We've run this coaching programme, what do we know about that programme in terms of the equality profile of those that were attending?' They might ask the question 'In terms of coaching performance and ability, etc. …' but I wouldn't envisage anyone asking that question [about equality].

The Coaching Development Manager at UK Sport continued:

> It's [our work] very performance orientated but that's very externally focused … it's [equality and diversity] not something that's referenced explicitly within our work on a regular basis or through dialogue, through our senior management leadership team…. So I think there's an element around visibility … in terms of coaches at a high performance level, I would suggest [equality and diversity is] not even close to being on their radar.

The lack of knowledge and awareness of equality issues exemplifies the gender-blindness and colour-blindness within sport coaching discourse because the active recruitment and development of a diverse coaching workforce is not a major consideration for high performance sport (Norman *et al.*, 2014). The lack of prominence of equality was further illustrated when the Coaching Leads were unable to provide accurate equalities data of their coaching workforce regarding ethnicity and gender. Some Leads failed to recognise the existence or significance of the lack of diversity in the representation of their coaches and were in fact satisfied with the current, but unequal, profile of their coaching workforce. As Norman *et al.* (2014) also reported, their focus is on the performance and ability of those already in the system rather than on challenging the discriminations and inequalities that currently exist within it.

Conclusion and future directions

This chapter has examined the racial and gender equalities policy and practice landscape in relation to sport coaching. Specifically, we have addressed the matter of institutional accountability and responsibility for social justice issues of racial and gender equality, diversity and inclusion. Whilst sport organisations and NGBs had some awareness of equality issues, there was a clear disconnection between those driving an equality agenda, and those working in high performance coaching. Crucially, the prioritising of sporting excellence over inclusive practice(s) was not just a question about the allocation of resources, but more about the mind-set of those favouring a high performance discourse, disengaged from issues of social justice. The assumed incompatibility between equality values and sport coaching meant that equality had not been mainstreamed throughout departments, systems and policies. This is partly because equality is seen to be an issue for those individuals who are excluded from sport coaching, thus concerned with disadvantage and 'otherness', rather than an issue for organisations to address. The concern with this dissociation from equality issues is not only that the context of high performance sport becomes elitist and achievement orientated, but also that it rests upon the sovereignty of merit (Ingham *et al.*, 1999). This neo-liberal ideology ignores the structural and distributional impediments to achieving sporting excellence (Goldberg, 2015; Ingham *et al.*, 1999). Therefore, the focus on 'fitting' individuals within the existing system allows the racialised and gendered structures and processes that sustain discrimination to remain unchallenged (Ingham *et al.*, 1999). In failing to acknowledge and implement values of equality and diversity, the high performance discourse in coaching fails to provide opportunities to all aspiring coaches and, as a result, reinforces these exclusionary racialised and gendered processes.

In regards to 'race' and gender, a CRT and Black feminism approach to this research ensured that 'race', racial equality and the intersections with gender, were centralised and made visible within sport coaching. In making 'race' and gender equality visible we uncover resistance to what Wetherley *et al.* (Chapter 2 in this collection) describe as 'social justice concerns'. We have revealed the extent to which the approach to such agendas can be arbitrary and perfunctorily performed where institutional values do not synchronise with them. Part of this mismatch points to the historical lack of diversity across the sport coaching landscape where 'race' has no place and where those with privilege do little to 'unlock' the racial inequalities embedded in the culture of their organisations (Roithmayr, 2014). In structures where 'race' is absent and whiteness is invisible, the 'race' neutrality of the key players becomes transparent. As an illustration, all but one of the respondents in this study were White. Therefore, the maintenance of a colour-blind ideology is effortlessly maintained and, in this study, worsened in the context of a racist patriarchy through what Jean and Feagin (1998) would describe as the *double burden* that Black women face. The blind spots in mainstream sport coaching policy and practice were illustrated through the categorisation of 'race' and gender as separate, stand-alone categories.

The dominant high performance discourse is persuasive and powerful as it underpins the allocation of funding, the organisation of sporting programmes and drives organisations towards the production of performance outcomes for a few rather than providing opportunities for all. Such a discourse is shown to be embedded in organisational priorities and therefore resistant to a direct challenge. We concur with Shaw and Slack (2002) who argue that, through mainstreaming equality issues and the willingness of organisations (through taking greater responsibility), it is possible to re-conceptualise this philosophy. In order to work towards having an equitable coaching profession that is diverse in its workforce, such philosophies and values need to be prioritised in performance level sport coaching. Organisations as a whole need to reflect upon how their policies, procedures and processes play a role in creating the racialised and gendered patterns that are evident within sport (Rankin-Wright, 2015). It is crucial to shed more light on the raced and gendered processes that result in inequalities to help sport coaching institutions to recognise and disrupt discrimination.

Notes

1 BME (Black and Minoritised Ethnic) is a popular acronym used in policy circles in the UK, used to denote the diverse positions and identities of racialised ethnic groups not included under the label of ethnic majority in the UK.
2 There has been some agreement by critical 'race' researchers and black feminists in the UK that the term 'Black', as a political term, is a meaningful act of identification for individuals that marks a collective presence against challenges of racism and marginalisation. We use the term 'Black' as an inclusive and political term.
3 Sport England, Sport Scotland, the Sports Council for Wales and the Sports Council for Northern Ireland.
4 The NGBs, and those participants working within NGBs, have been assigned pseudonyms to ensure that the analysis and interpretation focuses on the key messages across the sport coaching landscape, rather than on specific sports.

References

Bell, D. (1992) *Faces at the Bottom of the Well: The Permanence of Racism.* New York: Basic Books.
Carrington, B. and McDonald, I. (2003) 'The politics of "race" and sports policy', in Houlihan, B. (ed.) *Sport and Society: A Student Introduction.* London: SAGE, 125–142.
Carter, A. R. and Hawkins, B. (2011) 'Coping and the African American female collegiate athlete', in Hylton, K., Picklington, A., Warmington, P. and Housee, S. (eds) *Atlantic Crossings: International Dialogues on Critical Race Theory.* Birmingham: The Higher Education Academy Network, 61–92.
Collins, P. (2000) *Black Feminist Thought.* New York: Routledge.
Crenshaw, K. (1989) 'Demarginalizing the intersection of race and sex: a Black feminist critique of antidiscrimination doctrine, feminist theory and antiracist politics', *University of Chicago Legal Forum*, 1989: 139–168.

Crenshaw, K., Gotanda, N., Peller, G. and Thomas, K. (1995) *Critical Race Theory: The Key Writings that Formed the Movement*. New York: The New Press.

Davis, A. (1984) *Women, Culture and Politics*. New York: Random House.

Delgado, R. and Stefancic, J. (2012) *Critical Race Theory: An Introduction*. New York: New York University Press.

Equality Act 2006, c.3. London: The Stationery Office.

Equality Act 2010, c.15. London: The Stationery Office.

Equality Institutions Review (2002) *Equality and Diversity: Making It Happen*. Norwich: The Stationary Office.

Fletcher, T. (2014) 'Cricket, migration and diasporic communities', *Identities: Global Studies in Culture and Power* 22(2): 141–153.

Fletcher, T. and Hylton, K. (2016) 'Whiteness and race in sport', in Nauright, J. and Wiggins, D. K. (eds) *Routledge Handbook of Sport, Race and Ethnicity*. London: Routledge, 87–106.

Gillborn, D. (2011) 'Once upon a time in the UK: race, class, hope and Whiteness in the Academy (personal reflections on the birth of "britcrit")', in Hylton, K., Pilkington, A., Warmington, P. and Housee, S. (eds) *Atlantic Crossings: International Dialogues on Critical Race Theory*. Birmingham: CSAP/Higher Education Academy, 21–38.

Gillborn, D., Rollock, N., Vincent, C. and Ball, S. J. (2012) ' "You got a pass, so what more do you want?" Race, class and gender intersections in the educational experiences of the Black middle class', *Race, Ethnicity and Education* 15: 121–139.

Goldberg, D. T. (2015) *Are We All Post-Racial Yet? Debating Race*. Cambridge: Polity Press.

hooks, b. (1989) *Talking Back: Thinking Feminist, Thinking Black*. Boston: South End Press.

hooks, b. (2000) *Feminist Theory: From Margin to Center*. London: Pluto Press.

Hylton, K. (2005) ' "Race", sport and leisure: lessons from critical race theory', *Leisure Studies* 24: 81–98.

Hylton, K. and Lawrence, S. (2016) ' "For your ears only!" Donald Sterling and backstage racism in sport', *Ethnic and Racial Studies*, 39(15): 2740–2757.

Hylton, K. and Morpeth, N. D. (2012) 'London 2012: "race" matters and the East End', *International Journal of Sport Policy and Politics* 4: 379–396.

Ingham, A. G., Blissmer, B. J. and Davidson, K. W. (1999) 'The expendable prolympic self: going beyond the boundaries of the sociology and psychology of sport', *Sociology of Sport Journal* 16: 236–268.

Jean, Y. and Feagin, J. (1998) *Double Burden: Black Women and Everyday Racism*. New York: Routledge.

Long, J., Hylton, K. and Spracklen, K. (2014) 'Whiteness, Blackness and settlement: leisure and the integration of new migrants', *Leisure Studies* 40: 1779–1797.

Long, J., Hylton, K., Spracklen, K., Ratna, A. and Bailey, S. (2009) *Systematic review of the literature on Black and minority ethnic communities in sport and physical recreation*, Carnegie Research Institute, Leeds Metropolitan University.

Long, J., Robinson, P. and Spracklen, K. (2005) 'Promoting racial equality within sports organizations', *Journal of Sport and Social Issues* 29: 41–59.

Matsuda, M. J., Lawrence, C. R., Delgado, R. and Crenshaw, K. W. (1993) *Words that wound: critical race theory, assaultive speech, and the First Amendment.* Boulder, CO: Westview Press.

Mills, C. (1997) *The Racial Contract.* Ithaca: Cornell University.

Mirza, H. S. (ed.) (1997) *Black British Feminism: A Reader.* London: Routledge.

Norman, L., North, J., Hylton, K., Flintoff, A. and Rankin, A. (2014) *Sporting Experiences and Coaching Aspirations among Black and Minority Ethnic (BME) Groups.* Leeds: sports coach UK.

Picca, L. H. and Feagin, J. R. (2007) *Two-Faced Racism: Whites in the Backstage and Frontstage.* New York: Routledge.

Rankin-Wright, A. J. (2015) *Racial and Gender Equality and Diversity in Sport Coaching in the United Kingdom.* Unpublished PhD thesis, Leeds: Leeds Beckett University.

Roithmayr, D. (2014) *Reproducing Racism: How Everyday Choices Lock in White Advantage.* New York: New York University Press.

Shaw, S. (2007) 'Touching the intangible? An analysis of The Equality Standard: A Framework for Sport', *Equal Opportunities International* 26: 420–434.

Shaw, S. and Allen, J. B. (2009) 'The experiences of high performance women coaches: a case study of two Regional Sport Organisations', *Sport Management Review* 12: 217–228.

Shaw, S. and Slack, T. (2002) '"It's been like that for donkey's years": the construction of gender relations and the cultures of sports organizations', *Sport in Society* 5: 86–106.

Sport England (2004) *The Equality Standard: A Framework for Sport.* London: Sport England.

Sporting Equals (2011) *Insight: BME Coaching in Sport.* Birmingham: Sporting Equals.

sports coach UK (2011) *Sports Coaching in the UK III: A Statistical Analysis of Coaches and Coaching in the UK.* Leeds: Coachwise Business Solutions.

sports coach UK (2012) *The UK Coaching Framework: Embedding Excellent Coaching Practice.* Leeds: Coachwise Business Solutions.

Sports Council Equality Group (2012) 'Equality in sport', www.equalitystandard.org, accessed 3 September 2012.

Spracklen, K., Hylton, K. and Long, J. (2006) 'Managing and monitoring equality and diversity in UK sport', *Journal of Sport and Social Issues* 30: 289–305.

Chapter 16

Moving forward

Critical reflections on doing social justice research

Gabby Riches, Alexandra J. Rankin-Wright,
Spencer Swain and Viji Kuppan

Introduction

Much of the postgraduate research that takes place within the Centre for Diversity, Equity and Inclusion (DEI) reflects and is informed by ideas of social justice and equality. These concepts are explored and examined through a range of practices such as qualitative fieldwork, postgraduate seminars and academic events, as well as everyday encounters and experiences of being a doctoral student. The kinds of research projects conducted by postgraduate students within the Centre are diverse, critical and often influenced by personal experiences of marginalisation, adversity and resistance. This chapter outlines how the research of postgraduate students working within the Centre reflects the many 'calls for action' put forward by the authors in this collection, responds to current social justice debates within leisure studies and aligns with and seeks to extend the boundaries of the social justice frameworks informing many of the discussions in this volume. By centralising the voices and experiences of postgraduate researchers, the aim of this chapter is to establish new ways of conceptualising what it means to do social justice leisure research and discuss the potential for its future applications.

It is important to emphasise that the postgraduate voices within this chapter are not meant to define or generalise all doctoral work that takes place within the DEI research centre, rather, it highlights the diversity of approaches and frameworks used in doing social justice research. Although our disciplinary backgrounds differ, it is our mutual commitment to challenging discourses and practices that work to reinforce inequalities that helps to illustrate how academic research, especially at doctoral level, continues to be an important tool for furthering and enhancing social justice policies, initiatives and activism.

In the next section, we review how social justice has been taken up within the leisure studies literature and consider how these debates inform recurring issues in this book. We then reflect upon our own doctoral research experiences demonstrating how social justice can be explored through various approaches and analytical frameworks. We emphasise how researcher responsibility, lived experience, embodied practice and context play crucial roles in advancing social justice initiatives and policies for equity within sport and leisure scholarship. We conclude this chapter by outlining the ways in which we can move social justice strategies forward within the fields of leisure and sport by shifting the focus away from acknowledging and identifying differences to *making* a difference through reflexive research practices.

Exploring the role(s) of social justice in leisure and sport studies

Social justice is a concept that broadly connotes fairness, equality and recognition. Parry (2014: 352) states that although the concept of social justice is dynamic and continually evolving, it tends to accentuate 'fairness, societal transformation, and a critique of institutions, resource allocation, and the opportunity/power to exercise rights'. Scholars have also pointed to how social justice is not only concerned with structural inequalities and injustices but also individual empowerment, and the possibilities for social change that can be achieved once we acknowledge how particular positions are significant factors in the construction of knowledge (Griffiths, 1998). This is important when considering how leisure and sport, which are taken-for-granted, everyday practices, have been conceptualised and defined by particular discourses and structures which work to promote and privilege the interests of dominant groups. The discussions in this collection draw attention to the tenuous relationship leisure and sport can have with social justice in that they are 'actively involved in producing, reproducing, sustaining and sometimes resisting, various manifestations of, and discourses around, oppression and inequality' (Long *et al.*, Chapter 1 in this volume). As products of our social realities, leisure and sport practices are important and productive sites to think through the ways in which equality and social change can be realised within a world that is alive with contradictions, complexities and nuances.

Over the past decade, the concept of social justice and its related principles has received greater visibility in leisure studies research and has gained a more dominant, influential voice within the literature (Bocarro and Stodolska, 2013; Stewart, 2014). The amplified interest in social justice issues is evidenced by a substantial amount of leisure publications and postgraduate dissertations that focus on how different subject positions such as gender, sexuality, disability, race and ethnicity, age and their intersections, shape people's engagement with and experiences of sport and leisure. Stewart (2014: 326) argues that social justice has received more critical attention by leisure scholars because it 'functions as a point of convergence for otherwise isolated pockets of literature'. It has transformed from being a singular, narrowly defined concept to becoming an over-arching framework in which to discuss issues that once were considered distinct to leisure studies research. One could argue that the relevance of leisure scholarship has, to some degree, been enhanced by social justice initiatives.

Yet for some critical leisure scholars the emphasis on 'experiences of difference' is considered a descriptive approach to social justice and there-fore not effective in problematising notions of privilege, the interconnect-ing forces of oppression and the essentialisation of identity categories. More recently, the approaches and methodologies used to examine the relationship between leisure and social justice have been informed by Crit-ical Race Theories and theories of intersectionality (Arai and Kivel, 2009; Henderson, 2014; Johnson, 2014; Parry, 2014; Trussell, 2014). Applying an intersectional lens to concerns of social justice attends to the ways in which differences come to matter through patterns of consumption and how leisure and sport have become key markers of 'economic, social and cultural capital formation shaping identities of class, nation, ethnicity, reli-gion, race, gender, disability, age and all of the myriad intersections between these identities' (Aitchison, 2007: 78). As will be discussed in the next section, doctoral students working within DEI have implemented these frameworks in their analyses, allowing for a more nuanced, contex-tual and reflexive account of what it means to do social justice research. Furthermore, Johnson (2014) argues that in order to address and integrate social justice agendas into our research necessitates the unpacking of con-structed dichotomies between theory/practice, personal/professional and scholar/activist which continue to create divisions and isolate scholars not only from one another but also from the empowering potential of reflexive inquiry.

Voices from the field: postgraduate stories of doing social justice research

The ways in which social justice has been incorporated into the everyday research practices within DEI and discussed throughout this book speaks to how social justice has moved away from being solely defined in relation to income and wealth inequalities to being an indicator for broader, struc-tural concerns related to "fairness, equality, exclusion, discrimination, power differentials and privilege" (Long *et al.*, Chapter 1 in this volume). In the introductory chapter, the editors emphasise how engaging with social justice is not just about having 'the right answers' but about con-ducting research that, through its transformative potential, encourages and enables social change, thereby responding to ontological shifts within the social sciences which place 'becoming' ahead of 'being' (Blackshaw, 2014). According to Allison (2000: 5), in order for social change to occur it is essential to 'understand the institutional conditions, properties, and processes that foster exclusion'. Henderson (2014: 344) expands on this stating that many of the methods used in conducting social justice research differ from 'traditional methods of leisure research and come with a discrete set of outcomes' that go beyond making contributions to theory and knowledge towards enacting social change through community collaboration and empowerment. For many postgraduate students, the ability to effect *real* change through our research practices is mitigated by institutional conditions, pressures and expectations related to completion deadlines, research outputs and time spent in the field. On the other hand, we are also in a unique position as doctoral students to confront openly the emotional vulnerabilities and risks that are involved in doing social justice research through processes of self-reflexivity and sharing our personal stories with others. Johnson (2014: 391) notes that in order to be good social justice researchers we must grapple with 'the complexities and risks involved when research is representational of both participants and the people doing the research' and acknowledge that we are 'both a part of the problem and a part of the solution'. Our critical reflections presented here both reflect and respond to these ongoing concerns of doing social justice research. Our personal research stories speak to the multifaceted aspects of social justice research and to the importance of seeking out new conceptual and methodological pathways that help strengthen leisure's potential for collective action, social change and creating a more just society.

Social justice and the role of the researcher: Alexandra's story

My doctoral research was shaped, foremost, by a motivation for social justice and a desire to challenge and change the current discriminatory practices and inequalities within sport coaching. In this short section, I briefly discuss the Critical Race Theory (CRT) and Black feminism approach chosen for my research before deliberating the responsibility of a researcher in social justice research.

CRT and Black feminism facilitate a politics of social justice by challenging dominant cultures and discourses within society and sport that marginalise and oppress certain individuals and groups (Carter and Hawkins, 2011; Collins, 2000; Hylton, 2005). The principles centred in the framework for this research were drawn out of the main ideas of CRT writers such as Solórzano and Yosso (2002), Hylton (2009) and Rollock and Gillborn (2011), and Black feminist writers including Collins (1986, 2000), hooks (2000), and Essed (1991). They included: the centrality of 'race' and racism(s) and their interconnection with gender, challenging dominant ideologies of colour-blindness, objectivity, meritocracy, 'race-neutrality' and equal opportunity, a commitment to social justice and transformation, and centralising experiential knowledge. Crucially, to ensure that sport equality and anti-racist politics move forwards in the fight for social justice, researchers, policymakers and practitioners have been urged to push an intersectional agenda (Parker and Lynn, 2002). This agenda provides the opportunity to reveal and help understand the power structures embedded within racial and gender inequalities in sport coaching that privilege and promote the interests of dominant groups. It further ensures that these discriminatory structures are not only highlighted but are challenged and resisted.

I argue that sport organisations and national governing bodies have a responsibility and are institutionally accountable for social justice issues, such as challenging inequalities. Researchers too have such a responsibility, and through a CRT and Black feminism approach, are encouraged to take an active part in challenging discrimination themselves, rather than waiting for others to change agendas and behaviours (Blaisdell, 2009; Hylton, 2012; Ladson-Billings and Donnor, 2008). Reflecting on my own doctoral research journey, there were times when I was unsure whether, and how, to act on this responsibility. For example, during interviews, I failed to disrupt racial discrimination and prejudice by not acting at the time to directly challenge participants who expressed racially stereotypical views. Consequently, and like other anti-racist scholars, I have questioned whether I unintentionally contributed to the process of racism through reaffirming and perpetuating the adherence to problematic racialised views (Blaisdell, 2009; Gallagher, 2000; King, 2004). As King (2004: 127) argues 'the anti-racist investigator cannot simply sit back and observe [...] silence represents collusion, and failure to act does not represent protection'.

I was under no illusion that dismantling the multifaceted, embedded racial and gendered ideologies and structures within the sport coaching culture would be easy and two key questions emerged during my research journey. Although Hargreaves (2000) has written that providing research and knowledge is one way to empower marginalised groups, I question if this is enough and ask: how do we go that step further? How do we truly become activist researchers in the struggle for social justice? I hope that this short reflection piece will prompt more researchers to question, debate and act on, their responsibility as researchers working towards social justice.

Hidden voices made visible: Viji's story

The editors of this book argue that social justice is fundamentally concerned with the basic structure(s) of society. I would agree, but contend that there is an over-emphasis on the 'duties' and 'responsibilities' of the individual within their discussion. Social justice is, at heart, a project about transforming the social order, to render it more fair, equal and inclusive. My research investigates the experiences of a range of disabled football fans that are differently 'raced', gendered and impaired. It is a study that privileges black disabled fans; 'black' is used here as a political term, to engender a sense of solidarity between citizens from multiple ethnic backgrounds and communities; where their shared experiences of settlement in Britain have been set against a backdrop of an 'entangled racialised colonial history' (Brah, 1996: 11). A creative and analytical intent of this project is to bring together a theoretical framework, Critical Race Theory (CRT) and the Social Model of Disability (SMD), that can be argued to have been on similar but parallel paths in their quest for social justice; the convergence of these lenses works to deepen, expand and challenge what it means to be human (Garland-Thompson, 2002). This intersectional perspective draws heavily on Black feminist thought, which has persuasively argued that oppression is structured by a 'matrix of domination' (Collins, 2000).

Social justice is a concept woven into the theories and practice of my research; CRT and the SMD dismiss the crude biological determinisms of 'race' gender and disability, understanding that they are socially constructed categories that change over time and place but nonetheless have material, discursive and affective consequences (Ferri, 2010). CRT and the SMD are frameworks that have a shared vision of social transformation, seeking to change the world through praxis, politics and policies (Connor *et al.*, 2016; Hylton *et al.*, 2011; Oliver, 2009; Oliver and Barnes, 2012). As sociologists of sport and leisure, part of our warrant is to listen carefully, making visible the *hidden voices* inside the predominantly white, gendered and ableist culture of football fandom; in addition it is about becoming intimate with the 'concealed operations of power' (Ebert, 1996: 7) in order to illustrate the injustices, inequalities and exclusions that prevail. However, it also involves noticing and illuminating the moments and situations where simultaneously disabled football fans *resist* the oppressive forces of racism, sexism and disablism and are able to participate in the transcendental joys of fandom as fleeting as they often are. Therefore, our work is also about being attentive to what Raymond Williams (1977: 132) called the 'structures of feeling ... that are concerned with meanings and values as they are actively lived and felt'. Such an analysis refuses to reduce the experience of racialized and gendered disablement to one of only social barriers, and instead to produce connected, multiple and layered description and analysis, that may signal optimism and progressive social change even against football's increasingly entrenched neoliberal political economy (Back, 2015).

Leisure, social justice and modernity: Spencer's story

Social justice is a concept that should interest leisure scholars greatly. Particularly when analysing how access to leisure is affected by the distribution of wealth and social opportunity. In order to understand fully the place of leisure within contemporary society, it is important to explore the topic through the philosophical teachings of those scholars who have dedicated their writings to investigating the socio-political environment that characterises the second stage of modernity (Bauman, 2000; Beck, 1992; Giddens, 1991; Maffesoli, 1996). It is widely accepted within such philosophical thinking that society has entered an interregnum, a term used by Antonio Gramsci (Hoare and Nowell Smith, 1971) to exemplify a social environment where the old has died and the new cannot yet be born. This prism of thinking articulates how Western societies have now moved into an epoch of existence, where the old principles of welfarism developed in the late 1940s and 1950s and which championed the values of universal healthcare, civil rights and planned economies, have now died. They have been replaced by the fluid and ephemeral conditions of a world characterised by increasing globalisation, which has set in motion the unleashing of financial markets through policies of deregulation and the dramatic undermining of the welfare state by the neoliberal philosophy of privatisation (Bauman, 2007). This situation has come about through the decline of industrial economies in the West and the replacement of such solidity by rampant, fluid, consumer-based societies. The effects of such a metamorphis can be seen in the way mass society has become fragmented into a variety of different social groups (Maffesoli, 1996) each of which is struggling to condense into a unified image. As a consequence, increased individualisation and uncertainty become the staples of contemporary society, as people turn to the consumer market to solve their personal anxieties and plot their own individualised life projects (Giddens, 1991).

Such a change in the make-up of society has had a pronounced effect upon both leisure and social justice agendas. This can be seen in the way that leisure has become a key site in shaping identities and reflexively organising life projects. A major issue affecting such a drastic change in the social role of leisure is the way that those members of the population who do not have enough financial acumen to engage in such life ventures find themselves blocked from the reflexive projects espoused by individualised society and subsequently barred from entering certain leisure sites. Bauman (1998) refers to these social groups as the new poor, in essence the flawed consumers of modern-day society, those the 'seduced' consumer classes see as being utterly beyond the pale of political redemption via the use of the welfare state. These groups consist of a range of different social groups: the needy, the homeless, new migrant communities and the remnants of the old working classes, all of whom struggle to access certain forms of leisure due to the fact that they are priced, and kept, out of the market. Given the demeaning effects of such a social environment, it is important for critical scholars in leisure studies to expose such inequality through providing detailed research that emphasises how such social injustices are manifest and maintained. This can inform efforts to influence policymakers to champion social policies around the post-war consensus of one-nation politics, based on a very simple but effective premise, that of ensuring equal opportunity within leisure and other areas of social life, through emphasising how the wealthy have a moral responsibility to those in need (Hall, 2010; Heywood, 2002).

Evoking social justice and disruption through bodily praxis: Gabby's story

Notions of progressive politics, activism and social justice inhabit an ambiguous, arguably even a limited, place within metal music studies and research on women's involvement in male-dominated leisure practices. These concepts, to varying degrees, occupied a peripheral position in my research on women's participation in extreme metal music practices because I was unsure how my research could challenge the dominant gendered structures, power relations and discourses that demarcate extreme metal scenes. Metal scholars, such as Kahn-Harris (2007) and Phillipov (2012), have argued that the potential for significant social and political transformations within extreme metal music scenes are hindered by their apparent lack of commitment to progressive political values and an unwillingness to challenge prevailing social and gender inequalities. Furthermore, the idea of extreme metal being a rather antagonistic space for feminist expression and social change is reproduced by the ways in which masculinity has been closely aligned with extreme metal music, its fans and practices. Weinstein (1991) asserts that the subculture of heavy metal is more than just male-dominated, it is *masculinist* in that has shared values, norms and behaviours that highly privilege masculinity. This form of heavy metal masculinity, she goes on to say, operates in opposition to femininity; thus, 'women who want to become members of the subculture must do so on male terms' (ibid.: 134). This discursive rendering of metal music has detached extreme metal from discussions of feminist practice and social justice – a fissure that continues to be overlooked in metal music scholarship. By disrupting these normative discourses, both theoretically and ethnographically, within a localised extreme metal scene, my research revealed how extreme metal does indeed offer spaces for new modes of embodiment and feminist practice.

My approach to (re)thinking women's participation in extreme metal was informed by theories of performativity (Butler, 1990), intersectionality (Watson and Scraton, 2013) and non-representational theory (Thrift,

2007). These three theoretical frameworks aim to de-centre the subject, which in turn draws attention to the ways in which social positions are fluid, relational and are constituted through and by forms of difference. Additionally, these analytical lenses highlight how subjects always exceed their categorisation. This is echoed by Villa (2011: 171) when she explains that '[E]mbodiment as part of any social practice shows that "doing" is *necessarily* more and thus other than the *incorporation* of theoretically and analytically defined central social categories – however many categories there might be'. Compared to the existing discourses around female metal fandom that position women as passive, marginalised, inauthentic scene members, the majority of my female participants spoke about how extreme metal enabled them to experience their bodies differently and it was through their transgressive bodily movements that they were able to enact social change by disrupting hegemonic understandings of female metal fandom and the capacities of the female body.

Bringing corporeality and embodiment into social justice discussions, particularly within a subcultural context, attends to the ways in which leisure can be a form of empowerment and political practice and how it opens up spaces for alternative cultures which challenge unequal gender relations (Scraton, 1994). Referring to Grosz's (2010) discussion on the future of feminist theory, I want to argue that in order for social justice research to develop into a body of scholarship and a movement that is able to address adequately the complexities of everyday life we need to return to and take seriously the significance the fleshy, visceral body plays in actively challenging and breaking down the very structures and discourses that have damaging effects on marginalised groups within alternative leisure communities.

Moving forward: changing the leisure landscape through a politics of hope

Our views illustrate how social justice continues to occupy an important 'voice' within leisure and sport research. The kinds of research schema that doctoral students are engaging with reflect the diversity, multiplicity and complexity of not only the concept of social justice itself but the 'doings' of social justice research. Doing social justice research entails some degree of risk (emotional, physical, academic) and discomfort because these aspects ensure that our 'research agendas, methodologies, and practices are responsive to the ongoing changes to our social landscape, while enhancing the quality of community and social life' (Trussell, 2014: 350). As demonstrated here, issues of social justice and equity can be addressed more effectively when they are examined through lenses of CRT and intersectionality. Even though our doctoral research projects are centred on discriminatory practices and the ways in which differences come to matter in everyday sport and leisure experiences, we want to encourage postgraduates, scholars and practitioners working within the fields of leisure and sport to shift their attention from *marking* differences to *making* a difference through inclusive and participatory research practices (Aitchison, 2007). This shift is partly influenced by Denzin's (2000) politics of hope that has been influential in shaping feminist leisure scholarship and provides a significant contribution in re-conceptualising our role as researchers in challenging normative conceptions of leisure and sport whilst ensuring that social justice continues to be embedded within our research objectives.

Trussell (2014) proposes that social justice research goes beyond descriptive accounts of how power, marginalisation and inequalities are experienced; it is about looking out towards the world through the lens of

> a politics of hope and believing that empowerment and social change can occur through understanding and making that which was once invisible, visible through our research practices. A politics of hope criticizes the status quo and imagines how things *could* be different.
>
> (Trussell, 2014: 350, emphasis added)

Furthermore, a politics of hope alters the ways in which we engage with the world in that leisure research is not solely about focusing on *understanding* how people live and negotiate their leisure experiences within a society defined by differences and inequality, but instead activates social justice concerns by *challenging and breaking down* hegemonic social structures and power relations. In other words, 'it is not enough to *interpret* the world – one must *change it* as well' (Parry, 2014: 353; also Denzin, 2000).

Researchers, scholars and postgraduate students working within DEI exhibit a strong commitment to enhancing social justice and addressing structures of inequality, and this commitment is further evidenced by the amount of publications, academic forums and lecturing materials that concentrate on these matters. The discussions within this book offer multiple visions for how social justice research can be translated into practice and policy which points to the ways in which leisure and sport practices can be transformative avenues for social and political action.

References

Aitchison, C. C. (2007) 'Marking difference or making a difference: constructing places, policies and knowledge of inclusion, exclusion and social justice in leisure, sport and tourism', in: Ateljevic, I., Pritchard, A. and Morgan, N. (eds) *The Critical Turn in Tourism Studies: Innovative Research Methodologies*. Oxford: Elsevier, 77–90.

Allison, M. T. (2000) 'Leisure, diversity and social justice', *Journal of Leisure Research* 32(1): 2–6.

Arai, S. and Kivel, B. D. (2009) 'Critical race theory and social justice perspectives on whiteness, difference(s) and (anti)racism: a fourth wave of race research in leisure studies', *Journal of Leisure Research* 41(4): 459–472.

Back, L. (2015) 'Why everyday life matters: class, community and making life livable', *Sociology* 49(5): 820–836.

Bauman, Z. (1998) *Work, Consumerism and the New Poor*. Philadelphia, PA: Open University Press.

Bauman, Z. (2000) *Liquid Modernity*. Cambridge: Polity.

Bauman, Z. (2007) *Liquid Times: Living in an Age of Uncertainty*. Cambridge: Polity.

Beck, U. (1992) *Risk Society: Towards a New Modernity*. London: Sage.

Blackshaw, T. (2014) 'The crisis in sociological leisure studies and what to do about it', *Annals of Leisure Research* 17(2): 127–144.

Blaisdell, B. (2009) *Seeing with Poetic Eyes: Critical Race Theory and Moving from Liberal to Critical Forms of Race Research in Sociology of Education*. Rotterdam: Sense Publishers.

Bocarro, J. and Stodolska, M. (2013) 'Researcher and advocate: using research to promote social justice change', *Journal of Leisure Research* 42: 2–6.

Brah, A. (1996) *Cartographies of Diaspora: Contesting Identities*. London: Routledge.

Butler, J. (1990) *Gender Trouble: Feminism and the Subversion of Identity*. London: Routledge.

Carter, A. R. and Hawkins, B. (2011) 'Coping and the African American female collegiate athlete', in: Hylton, K., Picklington, A., Warmington, P. and Housee, S. (eds) *Atlantic Crossings: International Dialogues on Critical Race Theory*. Birmingham: The Higher Education Academy Network, 61–92.

Collins, P. (1986) 'Learning from the outsider within: the sociological significance of Black feminist thought', *Social Problems* 33: 14–32.

Collins, P. (2000) *Black Feminist Thought: Knowledge, Consciousness and the Politics of Empowerment*. London, Routledge.

Connor, D., Ferri, B. and Annamma, S. (eds) (2016) *DisCrit: Disability Studies and Critical Race Theory in Education*. New York: Teachers College Press.

Denzin, N. K. (2000) 'Aesthetics and the practices of qualitative inquiry', *Qualitative Inquiry* 6(2): 256–265.

Ebert, T. L. (1996) *Ludic Feminism and After: Postmodernism, Desire and Labour in Late Capitalism*. Michigan, MI: University of Michigan Press.

Essed, P. (1991) *Understanding Everyday Racism: An Interdisciplinary Theory*. London: Sage Publications.

Ferri, B. A. (2010) 'A Dialogue We've yet to Have: Race and Disability Studies', in: Dudley-Marling, C. and Gurn, A. (eds) *The Myth of the Normal Curve*. New York: Peter Lang, 139–150.

Gallagher, C. (2000) 'White like me? Methods, meaning, and manipulation in the field of white studies', in: Twine, F. W. and Warren, J. W. (eds) *Racing Research, Researching Race: Methodological Dilemmas in Critical Race Studies*. London: New York University Press, 67–99.

Garland-Thompson, R. (2002) 'Integrating disability, transforming feminist theory', *National Women's Studies Association Journal* 14(3): 1–32.

Giddens, A. (1991) *Modernity and Self-Identity: Self and Society in the Late Modern Age*. Stanford, CA: Stanford University Press.

Griffiths, M. (1998) *Educational Research for Social Justice: Getting off the Fence*. Buckingham: Open University Press.

Grosz, E. A. (2010) 'The untimeliness of feminist theory', *NORA: Nordic Journal of Feminist and Gender Research* 18(1): 48–51.

Hall, S. (2011) 'The neo-liberal revolution', *Cultural Studies* 25(6): 705–728.

Hargreaves, J. (2000) *Heroines of Sport: The Politics of Difference and Identity*. London: Routledge.

Henderson, K. A. (2014) 'The imperative of leisure justice research', *Leisure Sciences* 36: 340–348.

Heywood, A. (2002) *Political Ideologies: An Introduction*. Basingstoke: Palgrave Macmillan.

Hoare, Q. and Nowell Smith, G. (eds) (1971) *Selections from the Prison Notebooks of Antonio Gramsci*. London: Lawrence & Wishart.

hooks, b. (2000) *Feminist Theory: From Margin to Center*. London: Pluto Press.

Hylton, K. (2005) ' "Race", sport and leisure: lessons from critical race theory', *Leisure Studies* 24: 81–98.

Hylton, K. (2009) *'Race' and Sport: Critical Race Theory*. London: Routledge.

Hylton, K. (2012) 'Talk the talk, walk the walk: defining Critical Race Theory in research', *Race Ethnicity and Education* 15: 23–41.

Hylton, K., Pilkington, A., Warmington, P. and Housee, S. (eds) (2011) *Atlantic Crossings International Dialogues on Critical Race Theory*. Birmingham: The Higher Education Network.

Johnson, C. W. (2014) ' "All you need is love": considerations for a social justice inquiry in leisure studies', *Leisure Sciences* 36: 388–399.

Kahn-Harris, K. (2007) *Extreme Metal: Music and Culture on the Edge*. Oxford: Berg.

King, C. (2004) *Offside Racism: Playing the White Man*. Oxford: Berg.

Ladson-Billings, G. and Donnor, J. K. (2008) 'Waiting for the call: the moral activist role of critical race theory scholarship', in: Denzin, N. K., Lincoln, Y. S. and Tuhiwai Smith, L. (eds) *Handbook of Critical and Indigenous Methodologies*. London: Sage, 61–83.

Maffesoli, M. (1996) *The Time of the Tribes: The Decline of Individualism in Mass Society*. London: Sage.

Oliver, M. (2009) *Understanding Disability: from Theory to Practice*, 2nd edn. Basingstoke: Palgrave Macmillan.

Oliver, M. and Barnes, C. (2012) *The New Politics of Disablement*. Basingstoke: Palgrave Macmillan.

Parker, L. and Lynn, M. (2002) 'What's race got to do with it? Critical race theory's conflicts with and connections to qualitative research methodology and epistemology', *Qualitative Inquiry* 8: 7–22.

Parry, D. C. (2014) 'My transformative desires: enacting feminist social justice leisure research', *Leisure Sciences* 36: 349–364.

Phillipov, M. (2012) *Death Metal and Music Criticism: Analysis at the Limits*. Lanham: Lexington Books.

Rollock, N. and Gillborn, D. (2011) *Critical Race Theory (CRT)*. British Educational Research Association online resource. Available from: www.bera.ac.uk/files/2011/10/Critical-Race-Theory.pdf (accessed 20 May 2015).

Scraton, S. (1994) 'The changing world of women and leisure: feminism, "postfeminism" and leisure', *Leisure Studies* 13(4): 249–261.

Solórzano, D. G. and Yosso, T. J. (2002) 'Critical race methodology: counter-storytelling as an analytical framework for education research', *Qualitative Inquiry* 8: 23–44.

Stewart, W. (2014) 'Leisure research to enhance social justice', *Leisure Sciences* 36: 325–339.

Thrift, N. (2007) *Non-Representational Theory: Space, Politics, Affect*. London and New York: Routledge.

Trussell, D. E. (2014) 'Dancing in the margins: reflections on social justice and researcher identities', *Journal of Leisure Research* 46(3): 342–352.

Villa, P. I. (2011) 'Embodiment is always more: intersectionality, subjection and the body', in: Lutz, H., Vivar, M. T. H. and Supik, L. (eds) *Framing Intersectionality: Debates on a Multi-Faceted Concept in Gender Studies*. Farnham: Ashgate, 171–186.

Watson, B. and Scraton, S. J. (2013) 'Leisure studies and intersectionality', *Leisure Studies* 32(1): 35–47.

Weinstein, D. (1991) *Heavy Metal: The Music and Its Culture*. New York: Da Capo Press.

Williams, R. (1977) *Marxism and Literature*. New York: Oxford University Press.

Index

ability 1, 4, 19, 60, 66, 78–9, 81, 127, 130, 132, 143, 190, 203–4, 218
aboriginal 113–23
access 2, 5, 7, 18, 21–6, 31, 33, 45–6, 52, 58, 60, 66, 72–3, 75–6, 79–81, 108, 126, 128–9, 132, 135, 177, 182–3, 185–91, 215
accountability 160, 194, 198, 202, 204
Active People Survey 2, 9, 126, 180
Activism 32, 45, 54, 113, 161, 209, 216
African American 154
African Caribbean 140, 143
anti-Christianity 170–2
appropriate (quality) 25, 46, 52, 73, 75, 80, 87–8, 93, 134, 161, 202
arts 2–4, 7, 23–5, 30–2, 35, 39, 111, 118–19, 121, 129
Asian/South Asian 3, 24, 76, 118, 142–4, 154, 159–63, 180–91; British Asian 7, 75, 159–60; English/Pakistani/Bangladeshi Asian 71, 73
asset model 182
asymmetry 143, 145–6

barrier 2–3, 24, 59, 66, 75–7, 88, 119–20, 128–9, 132, 136, 181–2, 189–90, 203, 214
Beveridge 30
binaries see binary
binary 51, 54, 85–6, 92, 126, 128
biographical see biography
biography 139–40, 146, 148
bisexual 84–6
Black 24, 85, 122–5, 139–47, 150n1, 150n5, 153–64, 182, 194–7, 214; blackness 140–1, 143, 146, 149

Black and minoritised ethnic groups 3, 24–5, 70, 73, 84–5, 141, 143, 146–7, 149, 150n4, 182, 194, 206n1
Black feminism 153–4, 158, 160–1, 194–7, 205, 206n2, 212–14
Black feminist see Black feminism
black metal 170–3, 177
Black Power 117, 122n5, 145
black women 150n4, 153–5, 157–64, 197, 205
bodies 52, 54, 76, 84, 93, 117, 159, 217
Brah, Avtar 49, 52, 73, 214
British 1, 29, 35, 37, 49–51, 70–1, 73, 183, 195
British Social Attitudes Survey 45
bullying 84, 89, 92–4, 102

Canada 113–15, 117
capital: cultural 9, 25, 58, 211; social 4, 9, 58, 211; sporting 46
capitalism 33, 114, 172, 177
career 46, 181, 183, 189, 191
catachresis 157
CEMA 30
Centre for Contemporary Cultural Studies (CCCS) 34
Christianity 170, 172; see also anti-Christianity
cisgender 86, 95n3
citizen xiii, 4, 18–19, 22–3, 32, 35–6, 38, 70, 80, 98–9, 214
citizenship see citizen
civil rights 18–19, 117, 157, 215
class (social) xi–xiv, 2, 4, 19, 28, 30–1, 33–5, 37, 40, 52, 66, 71–3, 84, 100, 117, 121, 128, 140–3, 145–6, 154–5, 161, 168–9, 171, 177, 215

classification 10, 130–2
Clause Four 29, 34, 39n1
co-conceptualising 101, 103
co-researchers 104, 139
coaches xiv, 11, 13, 50, 91, 129, 131,
    180–92, 194–206, 212–13
coaching see coaches
collective reflection 101–2
Collins, Patricia Hill 153–4, 158–64,
    197
colonial 44, 76, 113–17, 121, 143,
    155–6, 158, 214
colonialism see colonial
colourblind(ness) 141–2, 194
communication 100, 120, 129, 132,
    134, 186–7, 189–90
communicative rationality 169, 171–2
communitarian 101
Conservatives 30–1, 34
construction 5, 26, 87, 128, 135, 149,
    155, 168, 173, 210; construction of
    sport 47, 137
consumer culture 36
cricket 77, 157, 180–1, 183–90
critical research 2–3, 5, 9, 12, 15, 37,
    52–4, 94, 98, 102, 108–9, 120, 128,
    139, 141, 146–7, 153, 158–63,
    168–9, 177, 195, 211–12, 216
critical race theory (CRT) 141–3, 146,
    148, 174, 194, 196–7, 206n2,
    211–12, 214
cross-generational 58, 62
cultural recognition 72, 81
culturalism 49, 52
curriculum 87, 92–4, 102, 105, 135,
    192n2
cycling 38, 44, 48–51, 129
cypher 111–13, 117, 119–21

darstellen 154–5
de-centre 217
Deadmonton 16, 119
deaf 64, 132–3, 188
Deaflympics 130, 132
decision-making xiv, 99, 128, 136, 149,
    181–2
deficit model 5, 182
democracy 25, 32, 52
dePauw 128–30, 136
development pathways 181, 198
diaries 98, 101, 106–9
diaspora 71, 154, 161
dichotomies 211

difference 1, 18–22, 26, 43–4, 48–9,
    52–3, 59, 67, 76, 85, 100, 107, 128,
    130, 132–3, 135–6, 143, 145, 147,
    153, 160–2, 183, 202, 210–11,
    217–18
disability see disabled
disabled 24, 53, 84, 100, 103, 126–37,
    201–2, 214
disabling environments 128
disadvantage xi, 1, 5–10, 17, 22, 25,
    117, 146, 187, 202, 205
disciplines 5, 37–8, 196, 199
discourse 3, 6, 9, 12, 37, 43–54, 58, 70,
    75, 86–7, 94, 114, 116–17, 120, 127,
    141, 144, 154–7, 160, 163, 176, 195,
    197, 203–6, 209–10, 216–17
discourses see discourse
discrimination xi, xv, 1, 19, 23, 38, 51,
    85–6, 88, 92, 142, 160, 164, 194,
    203–6, 213
distribution xi, 3, 15–26, 29, 47, 71–5,
    79–81, 120, 147–8, 205, 215
distributive see distribution
diverse xiv–xv, 4, 26, 34, 43, 45, 47,
    71, 73, 85, 113, 126, 128, 136, 142,
    150n4, 155, 160, 181, 194–5, 200,
    202–4, 209, 217
diversity see diverse
domination 87, 154, 214
due 15–17, 23, 47
dyspraxia 132

ECB 180, 183, 186–8, 190–8
Edmonton 111, 113–14, 116–19, 121
education xi, 18, 20–3, 31, 33–4, 37–9,
    88, 94, 99, 101, 105–6, 113–14,
    116–17, 122, 131, 141–3, 180, 185,
    194, 203, 205; educators 120, 188,
    190, 202–3
EFDS (English Federation of Disability
    Sport) 134
elite xi, 1–2, 4, 24–5, 31–2, 37, 39, 48,
    129, 132, 155, 170–2, 180, 185, 194,
    203, 205
elitist see elite
embodiment 6, 47–8, 59–60, 75, 118,
    216–17; embodied practice 210
empowerment 46–9, 62, 99, 121, 134,
    168, 197, 210–13, 217–18
English 114, 143–4, 155, 172–3,
    188–90, 192n2
Englishness see English
epistemology 153, 158

equal opportunities 6, 9, 18–21, 24–5, 72, 185, 212, 216
equality xii, xv, 35, 44, 46–7, 100, 113, 120, 147, 177, 194–5, 197–206, 209–11, 213; racial equality 173; see also inequality
Equality Act 191, 195
Equality Standard 195, 198, 200–2
essentialism 51, 73, 139–40, 149, 163, 169–70, 211; strategic essentialism 161
ethics 62, 153, 158–60, 168–9, 171; see also research ethics
ethnic(ity) 3, 6, 8, 18–19, 60, 71–4, 76, 80, 139–40, 146–50, 153–4, 162, 164n2, 181, 195, 198–201, 204, 206n1, 211, 214; see also Black and minoritised ethnic groups
everyday, the 4, 7, 52, 54, 141, 145
everyday lives 75, 94, 117, 136, 154–5, 201, 209–10, 217
excellence 2, 31, 200, 203, 205
exclusion xii, 1, 4, 92–3, 129, 131–3, 141, 159, 168–9, 180–1, 183, 188–90, 205, 214
expert ix, 99, 133–4, 182, 191
expertise see expert

fair xv, 1, 3–4, 7, 15, 17–22, 24, 26, 47, 71, 98–102, 107–8, 120, 132, 177, 182, 189, 210, 214
fair distribution 23, 26, 30
fair play 23
fairness see fair
family xi–xii, xv, 20–1, 46, 58–67, 74, 77, 81, 119, 121, 140, 160
fans xv, 24, 170–8, 214, 216
far right 150n5, 169–72, 176
fascism 171
femininity see feminism
feminism 33, 43–54, 58–9, 86–7, 156, 158–9, 164, 174, 216–7; see also Black feminism, Western feminism
feminist leisure research 44, 54, 59, 218
feminist scholars 47, 49, 52, 218
first nations 113–15
folk metal 169, 173–7
football xii–xv, 24, 76–7, 89–93, 143–4, 160, 162, 182, 214
Fordism 33–4, 36; see also post-Fordism
Fordist see Fordism
Fraser, Nancy 48–9, 52, 71–6, 80–1

freedom 16–17, 19, 23, 28, 47, 60, 82, 121, 169–70
Freire 113
fun xv, 119, 135, 176–7
functionalist 177
funds xi–xii, xiv, 31–2, 35, 37, 191, 195, 197, 200–1, 206
funding see funds

Gateway Clubs 130
gay 51, 59, 84–92
gender xii, 2, 4–5, 8, 18–20, 24, 28, 33, 43–54, 58–60, 65–7, 72–3, 75–6, 79–80, 85–8, 92–5, 128, 155, 158, 160–2, 171, 173–4, 182, 194, 197–202, 204–6, 212–14, 216–17
gender justice 24, 43–54, 72, 76
gendered PE curriculum 92
generation 20, 28, 33–4, 45, 58, 60–2, 65–7, 115, 121, 142, 189, 191
genocide 115
glass ceiling 182, 202
globalisation 37, 168, 172–3, 178, 215
good life 16
grassroots 25, 48, 113, 180, 186, 203

Habermas, Jurgen 169–70
heavy metal 169–70, 173–7, 216; see also black metal; folk metal
hegemony 43–5, 49, 51–3, 142, 154, 158, 168–9, 177–8, 182, 217–18; hegemonic masculinity 86–8, 92, 169, 172–4
helplessness 182
heteronormativity 46, 52, 86–7, 92, 94, 168
heterosexuality 2, 33, 46, 51, 52, 59, 62, 67, 86–7, 146, 169
hierarchy 72, 85, 188, 202
hijab xv, 78–80
hip-hop 111, 113, 116–22
homonormative 46
homonormativity see homonormative
homophobia 24, 84, 86–8, 92–4
homophobic see homophobia
humanist 45, 159, 164

identity 1, 5–6, 24, 32, 54, 60, 70, 84–9, 92–3, 100, 106, 115, 128, 143, 161–3, 168–9, 171–2, 174, 176–7, 184–5, 190, 197–8, 203, 211, 215; ethnic/racial 74, 76, 128, 141, 146;

gender 47, 84–7; national 37;
    religious 73, 76; social 5, 120
identity politics 121
impairment 127–8, 131, 134, 214
imperial 72, 153, 156–7
imperialist *see* imperial
inclusive 6, 33, 35, 85–6, 88, 94,
    130–1, 133, 135–6, 176, 181, 187,
    195, 197, 201, 205, 214, 218; *see
    also* exclusive
indentities *see* indentity
India 73, 145, 155–6, 190
indigenous 33, 114, 116–17, 119–20,
    175
inequality 43, 49, 53, 72, 86, 160, 162,
    168–9, 210, 216, 218
insider 142, 148, 157, 163
institutional racism 182
instrumental rationality 169–71
integration 4, 76, 126, 130–1, 133–7,
    154
intergenerational 66
intersectionality 5–6, 8, 12, 25, 53, 87,
    128, 146, 160, 168, 195, 187, 205,
    211, 213–14, 216
invisibility 88, 129, 135, 197
Islam xiii, 70–1, 74–81, 157
izzat 74

KPIs 201

labour 20, 29, 33, 45–6, 59, 72
labour market 21, 33, 46, 71
Labour Party 28–38
ladder of participation 100, 102
laissez-faire 2, 17
learning disabilities 100, 116, 132, 134
Lee, Jennie 30, 35, 39
Leeds 4, 13, 31, 71, 80, 140–1, 172,
    175–6; *see also* northern England
left 20, 30, 34–5; left-liberal 20–2
Leisure Studies Association 3, 5
lesbian 51, 84–7, 91
LGBT xiv, 24, 84–6, 87–91, 93–4
liberty 17–19, 23
liquid modernity 38

marginal 1–2, 4, 6–7, 11–12, 26, 45,
    51, 60, 72, 79, 81, 86–7, 111, 117,
    119, 128, 135, 147, 195–7, 217
marginalised *see* marginal
market 21–2, 24, 35–6, 39, 52, 215–16;
    see also labour market

Marx 5, 8, 28, 33, 146, 154
Marxism *see* Marx
masculinity 46, 51, 86, 92–3, 172,
    175–7, 216; *see also* hegemonic
    masculinity
media xii, xiv, 33–7, 48–51, 70, 114,
    129, 141, 174, 176, 194
medical model 126–7, 129, 133
member xii, 30, 46, 143, 145, 184,
    190, 216–17
membership *see* member
men xii, 2, 24, 51, 79, 86–7, 116,
    156, 162, 169, 173–6, 181–2,
    197–200
merit 2–3, 17, 19, 23–4, 43, 46, 50, 52,
    141, 194, 196, 205
meritocracy *see* merit
metal music 174–5, 216
micro-aggressions 141
Miller, David 15, 18–22, 98
modernity 29, 32–3, 37–8, 169–70,
    172, 215
multiculturalism 141, 175–6
Muslim xv, 70–1, 73–7, 79–81, 157,
    160, 170, 187

narrative 29–34, 44, 48–50, 53–4, 62,
    84, 89, 91–4, 139–40, 144–6, 156–7,
    163, 174, 197
narritivisation *see* narrative
National Front 140
national governing body (NGB) 25, 76,
    130, 194, 199, 202, 213
nationalism xiii, 170–1, 174
need 3, 17–18, 32, 79–81, 85, 94, 100,
    117, 129, 132, 132, 134, 136, 164,
    215–16
neo-Nazi 150n5, 170–1
neoliberal(ism) 17, 32–3, 35, 38, 45–6,
    48, 50, 52, 54, 174, 205, 214–15
New Labour 32, 34–5, 37–8
new right 35
new urban left 34
non-authoritarian 106
normality 127, 132
normative 2, 54, 72, 85–6, 88, 92, 94,
    133, 139, 155, 216, 218
norms 16, 20, 22, 70, 87, 93, 114, 139,
    216
Northern Ireland xiii–xiv, 129, 135,
    197–8, 203
northernness 140, 170, 172–4; *see also*
    northern England

objectification 50, 154
OECD 1
Olympic xi–xii, 37–8, 50, 145, 201
One Nation 38, 216
oppression xiii, 1–4, 28, 75–6, 85, 116, 128, 139, 158–62, 196–7, 210–12, 214
oppressive *see* oppression
'other' 5–6, 11, 25, 72, 74, 86, 141, 147–8, 153–7, 162, 205
outcomes 22, 25, 103, 120, 195, 206, 212
outsider within 161–2

paradigm 4, 26, 32, 159, 177
Paralympic xi, 37, 129–30, 132, 201
participation xi, 2–3, 11, 16, 23–5, 32, 38–9, 45–6, 48, 72–7, 80–2, 84, 88, 99–102, 108, 126–39, 190–1, 183, 191, 200, 202–3, 216
participatory politics 117
participatory research 98, 100–4, 106, 113, 218
parity of participation 51–2, 72, 74–6, 79–81
PE (physical education) 46, 84–90, 107, 133, 135
pedagogies 87, 93–4, 135
performance xii, 22, 47, 51, 78–9, 84, 93, 111, 113, 116, 119, 133, 172, 181, 194, 200–6, 216
performative 157, 176, 216
photograph 61, 101
physical prowess 126
policy 3, 5–7, 11–12, 19, 21, 24–5, 28–38, 99, 115, 126, 130, 136, 149, 191, 197–8, 200, 202, 204–5
positive action 191, 202
post-colonial 8, 34, 113–14, 153–4, 156, 162–3, 173
post-feminist 8, 48
Post-Fordism/Post-Fordist 34, 36
postmodernism *see* postmodernity
postmodernist *see* postmodernity
postmodernity 38, 168, 173
power xiv–xv, 1–3, 5–6, 35, 48–9, 53, 59–60, 72–3, 87, 89, 92, 106, 108, 111, 113, 141, 147–8, 153, 155, 158–9, 162, 173–4, 176, 183, 195–6, 210–11, 213–14, 216, 218
privilege 1–2, 6, 51, 53, 86, 100, 142, 145–9, 156–62, 169, 173, 177, 182–3, 195, 198, 205, 210–11, 213–14, 216

problematise 6, 73, 100, 139–40, 182, 194
PSCHE 105

queer theory 36

'race' 8, 13, 73, 118, 139–50, 161–2, 169, 182, 187, 194–7, 201–2, 204–6, 211–14
racism 3, 34, 70, 113, 116, 122, 140–9, 169–77, 182, 184, 187, 189, 191, 194, 196, 205, 212; antiracism 24, 145, 158, 182, 213–14
racist *see* racism
Rawls, John 16–23
recognition 8, 37, 49, 53, 71–81, 121, 210
recruitment 189, 191, 195, 200, 204
redistribution 22, 30, 35, 49, 53, 71–2, 74, 147–8
redistributive *see* redistribution
reflect 85, 92, 98, 101–2, 108, 140–5, 148, 155, 177, 195, 212–13
reflection *see* reflect
reflexivity 5, 37, 139, 141–2, 162, 211–12, 215
relative freedom 47
religion xiii, 73–8, 81
representation 9–10, 19, 46, 50–1, 114, 117, 129, 153–64, 180–2, 186, 194, 204, 216
research ethics 173
resist 3, 11–12, 28, 32–3, 44, 48, 59, 62, 65, 113, 116–17, 121, 153, 161, 168–9, 196, 205, 214
resistance *see* resist
resources xiv–xv, 2, 5, 9, 16, 18–19, 21–3, 26, 30, 33, 38, 48, 50, 53, 71–3, 81, 92, 94, 120, 128, 148, 183, 186, 189–91, 200–1, 205
responsible xv, 7, 15, 22–4, 46–7, 74, 99, 120, 128, 132, 136, 147, 149, 159, 162, 194–5, 202–4, 206, 210, 213, 216
responsibility *see* responsible
restorative justice 147
reverse integration 134–7
rights 16–19, 22, 32, 99, 115, 120, 210 (*see also* civil rights); equal rights xiii; human rights 44, 99, 121, 149
Rio 2016 49, 51, 74
risk 73, 147, 173, 212
RNIB Clubs 130

role 19, 21, 51, 87–8, 94, 104, 155, 169, 178, 183, 185, 188, 203–4, 210, 212, 218
role model 181, 183, 191
rugby xiii, 84, 88–92, 143–4, 160, 169

Sandel, Michael 16–17
satanic 171
satee 156–7
section 28, 88
segregation 143; sex-segregation 51, 75, 79, 94
self-advocacy 99
self-confidence 133
self-esteem 133–4
Sen, Amartya 17–18, 168–9, 176, 178
separate(ness) 72, 126–7, 130–3, 136, 149, 155, 181, 183–5, 190, 197, 201–2
sexism 34, 49–51, 102, 107, 173–6, 197, 214
sexuality 54, 75, 85–7, 92–4
silence 6, 36, 154–5, 157, 213
silenced *see* silence
sisterhood 153, 156, 159
snatched leisure 58, 63, 66
social contract 23
social inclusion 19, 23–6, 38
social media xv, 118, 175
social minimum 18–19, 21–3
social model 126–8, 131, 214
social networks 145, 185
socialist 22, 30, 32, 34, 36, 48
solidarity xiii, 159, 214
South Asian *see* Asian
Special Olympics 130
Spirit Level 1
Spivak, Gayatri Chakravorty 5, 6, 34, 153–64
Sport England xii, xiv, 126, 195, 200
sport for all 6, 126, 136–7, 194
Sports Coach UK 195, 198
stereotypes xii, 20, 62, 87–8, 92, 114, 117, 119, 129, 195
subaltern 5, 34, 153–8, 163, 169, 177–8, 5
Sutton Trust 1

Taking Part Survey 2, 9
talent 19–20, 22–4, 122n3
targets 38, 200, 202

therapeutic 62; therapeutic recreation 127
time 16, 23, 25, 36, 46, 58–67, 72, 104–7, 162–3, 184–5, 200; free/spare time 30, 33, 36, 59–60
tokenism xiv, 85, 100, 102, 153, 187
Trades Union Congress 30
transdisciplinary 96
transformation *see* transformative
transformational *see* transformative
transformative 2, 9, 45, 113, 118, 130, 142, 148, 196, 210–18
transgender 84–7, 89, 92–3
transgressive 51, 116, 197, 217
truth and reconciliation 115, 121

UK coaching framework 195, 208
United Nations 29, 99
United States xiii, 121n2

values 8, 35, 70, 114–15, 153–4, 160, 194, 205–6, 214–16
Varnish, Jess 50–1
veil 73, 75–7, 81n3
vertreten 154
Vikerness, Varg 170–1
voice 4–5, 34, 36, 53, 71–2, 83, 89, 99, 114, 118, 153–7, 159–60, 163, 168, 187, 197, 211, 214, 217
volunteer 129, 185, 188
volunteering *see* volunteer

welfare 17, 19, 21–2, 33; welfare state 30, 32–3, 215
Western feminism 77
White privilege 161, 182–3
White feminism 153, 156, 161
White feminist *see* White feminism
whiteness 53, 143, 146, 149, 162, 169–70, 174–5, 177, 182–3, 197–8, 205
womanhood 197
women's leisure 47, 54, 58–67
workforce xv, 30, 181, 191, 194–5, 200, 204, 206

Yorkshire 32, 61, 181, 187, 189
young people 84–94, 98–109, 111, 113, 116–21
youth 8, 31, 35, 84–5, 89, 94, 99, 113, 117–21

 Taylor & Francis eBooks

Helping you to choose the right eBooks for your Library

Add Routledge titles to your library's digital collection today. Taylor and Francis ebooks contains over 50,000 titles in the Humanities, Social Sciences, Behavioural Sciences, Built Environment and Law.

Choose from a range of subject packages or create your own!

Benefits for you

>> Free MARC records
>> COUNTER-compliant usage statistics
>> Flexible purchase and pricing options
>> All titles DRM-free.

Benefits for your user

>> Off-site, anytime access via Athens or referring URL
>> Print or copy pages or chapters
>> Full content search
>> Bookmark, highlight and annotate text
>> Access to thousands of pages of quality research at the click of a button.

REQUEST YOUR **FREE** INSTITUTIONAL TRIAL TODAY

Free Trials Available
We offer free trials to qualifying academic, corporate and government customers.

eCollections – Choose from over 30 subject eCollections, including:

Archaeology	Language Learning
Architecture	Law
Asian Studies	Literature
Business & Management	Media & Communication
Classical Studies	Middle East Studies
Construction	Music
Creative & Media Arts	Philosophy
Criminology & Criminal Justice	Planning
Economics	Politics
Education	Psychology & Mental Health
Energy	Religion
Engineering	Security
English Language & Linguistics	Social Work
Environment & Sustainability	Sociology
Geography	Sport
Health Studies	Theatre & Performance
History	Tourism, Hospitality & Events

For more information, pricing enquiries or to order a free trial, please contact your local sales team:
www.tandfebooks.com/page/sales